ALL OR NOTHING

FRAMING *film*

The History & Art of Cinema

Frank Beaver, *General Editor*

Vol. 7

PETER LANG
New York • Washington, D.C./Baltimore • Bern
Frankfurt am Main • Berlin • Brussels • Vienna • Oxford

EDWARD TROSTLE JONES

ALL OR NOTHING

THE CINEMA OF MIKE LEIGH

PETER LANG
New York • Washington, D.C./Baltimore • Bern
Frankfurt am Main • Berlin • Brussels • Vienna • Oxford

Library of Congress Cataloging-in-Publication Data

Jones, Edward Trostle.
All or nothing: the cinema of Mike Leigh / Edward Trostle Jones.
p. cm. — (Framing film; vol. 7)
"A Mike Leigh filmography:" p.
Includes bibliographical references and index.
1. Leigh, Mike, 1943– —Criticism
and interpretation. I. Title. II. Series.
PN1998.3.L445J66 791.43'0233'092—dc22 2003019417
ISBN 0-8204-6745-6
ISSN 1524-7821

Bibliographic information published by **Die Deutsche Bibliothek**.
Die Deutsche Bibliothek lists this publication in the "Deutsche Nationalbibliografie"; detailed bibliographic data is available on the Internet at http://dnb.ddb.de/.

Cover photo by Simon Mein
Cover design by Lisa Barfield

275 Seventh Avenue, 28th Floor, New York, NY 10001
www.peterlangusa.com

Frontispiece: Mike Leigh directing *Secrets & Lies*
(Courtesy of Simon Mein, photographer, and Mike Leigh)

CONTENTS

CONTENTS

ILLUSTRATIONS

PREFACE

This study of Mike Leigh's cinema began at least in a nascent way with a visit to the headquarters of Thin Man Films just off Soho Square in the heart of London in February of 1997. I felt privileged to have an interview scheduled with the filmmaker. Deborah Reade, then Leigh's assistant (as well as post-production supervisor on many of his films and a versatile collaborator), welcomed my wife and me to the offices as Leigh was next door completing an interview for Polish television. Ms. Reade's office is spacious, with framed posters of Mike Leigh films on the walls and neatly arranged boxes with notations like "Budget" and other related matters, sometimes with specific titles of past Leigh films on them. It all suggested a cottage industry crafted by an intimate group of associates; however, in the afterglow of the success of *Secrets & Lies*, with some trepidation, I anticipated meeting the wizard.

Much of my previous scholarship in film had been with cinematic adaptations of literature, and my interest in Leigh represented an alternative to that area. On the other hand, I conceived of Leigh's canon partly as a literary achievement akin to an ongoing serial novel.

Mike Leigh arrived shortly and recommended we go next door to his own offices. In the hallway next to this office was a small hand-lettered piece of paper indicating "French Models One Flight Up." Ms. Reade had already informed us that these women who share the building with the director are truly French. She remarked that she occasionally had lunch or tea with them. Such "models" are often advertised, albeit without a specific reference to Gallic nationality, on other buildings in Soho. The furniture in his office was comfortable, a trifle oversized perhaps; I recall thinking it had something of the effect of *Pee-Wee's Playhouse* about it, and I noticed that I was closer to the ground on the sofa than Leigh, who sat on a higher chair opposite us. My tape recorder appeared unusually diminutive and fragile to me.

Leigh was generous and forthcoming in his responses, but upon returning stateside, I discovered that much of the conversation had been somehow erased. I was unable to publish the truncated dialogue, although some fragments appear in this book. Retrospectively, I have come to view the whole episode as bearing a rueful and hapless resemblance to a Mike Leigh sequence. My role in it assumes a Timothy Spall–like turn at an abortive endeavor roughly comparable to Aubrey's at the ill-fated "Regret Rien" Restaurant in *Life Is Sweet.* I suspect I am not the first nor will be the last to find that at least one episode in his or her life imitates Leigh's art.

The object of this study is the body of cinema written and directed by Mike Leigh over more than a thirty-year period, a rich terrain, to be sure, particularly in quality, but not one with a dramatic beginning, middle, turning point, or, fortunately, terminus. Indeed, Leigh's career mirrors that of most of his films, which tend in their construction to be more episodic than climactic. He is an artist of relationships which acknowledges not only the completed film but also the means he uses in its creation. A satisfactory appreciation of Leigh's cinema involves understanding the somewhat unconventional relationship between what the filmmaker has done and the value audiences assign to it.

Leigh's approach is highly personal, and his work has been received as such. He defies easy categorization. An encompassing pattern or design in his work is not altogether clear. Like Falstaff, Leigh embodies "Give me life," which is quite different from that of reality television as well as that of a philosophical thesis. One thing for certain, however, many Leigh films are not only profoundly immediate and visceral but also persistent and enduring experiences. They remain in the memory of the viewer long after the initial encounter. Mike Leigh has been written about with increasing frequency and growing respect in recent years. In that extensive literature there is general agreement about his importance and contribution to the English-language cinema at the beginning of the twenty-first century.

This study attempts to be both descriptive and critical as a work of assembly, interpretation, and evaluation of Leigh's film career. It is not a synthesis of all previous commentary (as if that were possible), but it does collect, incorporate, and, I hope, concentrate, however selectively and subjectively, a great deal of received opinion. I have tried to include extensive first-person observations of Mike Leigh in his numerous published interviews. My interpretation of Leigh is indebted to earlier researchers, especially the four previous book-length studies: the pioneering Paul Clements' *The Improvised Play: The Work of Mike Leigh*; Michael Coveney's biographical study, *The World According to Mike Leigh*; the critical analysis of *The Films of Mike Leigh: Embracing the World,* by Ray Carney with additional chapters by Leonard Quart; and *Mike Leigh: Interviews*, edited by Howie Movshovitz. In addition, I have been impressed by the quantity and quality of address to Leigh's films by American reviewers in the popular press and magazines, and I have included a number of these remarks throughout. I think Leigh should not be confined to art-house cinema; he is a demotic *auteur*, and journalistic reviewers have, in my opinion, captured this dimension of him especially well.

In this book I have considered only the full-length films, at least 60 minutes long, arbitrary though that might seem. I have omitted from discussion television studio recordings of the 30-minute long *The Permissive Society* (1975) and *Knock for Knock* (1976) and also left out, not without regret, the 25-minute *The Five Minute Films* (1975), the 18-minute *The Short and Curlies,* (1987) and the only film Leigh directed but neither "devised" nor wrote, Jim Broadbent's hilarious 28-minute *A Sense of History* (1992). Leigh screened this film for me in Soho that February day. Broadbent's satirical script and brilliant performance as the tell-all murderous twenty-third earl of Leete guiding viewers over his estate is a devastating send-up of the British heritage film. It is also a homage to writers in the tradition of English literature as diverse as Shakespeare to Ishiguro or *Boewulf* to Virginia Woolf. Broadbent's role is a precursor of both his W. S. Gilbert in Leigh's *Topsy-Turvy* and his Peter Duffley, the inept banker, in the BBC–l production, *The Peter Principle,* as well as perhaps even his recent Academy Award-winning performance as John Bayley in *Iris* (2002).

ACKNOWLEDGMENTS

To many I owe a debt of gratitude for helping me to complete this study of Mike Leigh. I thank President George W. Waldner; the former Dean of Academic Affairs, Dr. Jean A. Wyld, now of Springfield College; and the Board of Trustees of York College of Pennsylvania for awarding me sabbaticals. John and Molly Nicholls and June Baker, friends in England, extended generous help and hospitality. Friends who are librarians have been most kind. I appreciate efforts on my behalf by University Librarian at Syracuse University, Peter S. Graham; Arizona State University West's Media Librarian, deg farrelly; and from York College, Pat Poet, AV Librarian, and Sue McMillan, Reference Librarian, as well as Sue Uhler and Louise Pierce of the Schmidt Library. In addition, I am grateful to York College's excellent projectionist, Gary Keeney, who gave me a copy of *Meantime* and shared periodicals and insights with me. I am pleased to acknowledge the contribution of my York College students enrolled in "Three Movie Directors: Hitchcock, Leigh, and Tarantino" during the fall semester of 1999, especially Frank Cordy, David Rahn, Michelle Shipley, and Derek Sherwood. From my fall 2001 class, I express gratitude to Kerin Ogg, Eric Hayes, Matt Lau, and Dana Morella. It was gratifying to discover that American students, even males in their late teens, could respond favorably to something other than action movies and intelligently to well-developed characters whose foreignness they see and hear as bizarrely British. Other former students, the Rev. Daniel R. Miller, and the talented photographer, James Sheen, have graciously sustained interest and support over the long haul for which I am grateful. I thank Deborah Reade, Claire Broughton, and Mike Leigh for the photograph of the filmmaker and in addition to them, photographer Simon Mein for permission to use his examples from *Naked* and *Secrets & Lies*. Other photographs are courtesy of the Jerry Ohlinger Archive. Quotations from the published screenplays and Graham Fuller's interview with Mike Leigh included in *Naked and Other Screenplays* by Mike Leigh have been licensed to me by Faber and Faber Ltd.

Family members have been supportive, patient, and helpful: thanks to Ruth, my wife; Vanessa, our daughter, and son-in-law, Jesse Rutledge; and especially Miranda, our other daughter, whose computer literacy and talent were invaluable preparing a final copy. I thank Eric Levy of Greenwood Publishing Group; Professor Frank E. Beaver, editor of this cinema series; Dr. Phyllis Korper, Acquisitions Editor; and Bernadette Shade, Production Supervisor at Peter Lang, for their encouragement.

INTRODUCTION

Getting Real

The deceptively easy explanation for the success of Mike Leigh as a sophisticated filmmaker who treasures simplicity and directness is that he has never lost his interest in people nor abandoned his commitment to honesty in his portrayal of them in almost Chekhovian simplicity. He fulfills Leonardo da Vinci's claim that simplicity is the ultimate sophistication. As he explained to Judy Bloch in 1991 in an exchange in *Mike Leigh: Interviews*, edited by Howie Movshovitz, "...what we're dealing with is making people like people really are, behaviorally" (20). Hence Leigh and his actors create characters with persuasively real personalities, nuanced and familiar with one another in ways that many other films barely simulate.

His films, perforce, are exultantly character driven, mindful of human limitations and modest in their ambition, giving shape and form primarily to feeling. In conversation with me, the filmmaker disavowed the appropriateness to his own work of Horace Walpole's famous eighteenth-century dictum that the world is a comedy to those who think and a tragedy to those who feel in favor of a conception of tragicomedy enshrined in much twentieth-century dramatic literature. To that extent, Leigh disengages himself from the theorizing on comedy by authorities like Henri Bergson, who argued that the experience of the comic requires separation of intellect from emotion. Leigh would seem closer to Paul H. Grawe's position that "most comedy engages our emotions as much or more than our intellects, and most audiences are far more willing to have their emotions titillated by comedy than their minds" (52).

Leigh is an intuitive rather than a conceptual filmmaker. He uses physical, material details and telling gestures to carry emotional values and to challenge the reifying abstractions of words. Over the years many of these attributes have been associated with English films in general, described by A. O. Scott in a Sunday *New York Times* "Arts and Leisure" piece as "small, intimate movies, attuned to details of character and location. Their intelligence is manifest above all in their efficiency, in the precise calibration of visual effect and moral resonances" (AR 9). Leigh's comment to David Sterritt from *The Christian Science Monitor* (reprinted in the Movshovitz volume) serves to define his work: "I don't make films to be decoded by intellectuals. I am not a manufacturer of esoteric formulas. I am an emotional and intuitive filmmaker" (44). He has not succumbed to making a virtue of ironic detachment. Leigh echoed similar sentiments about his credo in a *Washington Post* interview with Desson Howe in 1994 (also reprinted in the same volume):

> My ongoing preoccupation is with families, relationships, parents, children, sex, work, surviving, being born and dying. I'm totally intuitive, emotional, subjective, empirical, instinctive. I'm not an intellectual filmmaker. Primarily my films are a response to the way people are, the way things are as I experience them. In a way they are acts of taking the temperature. (46)

As accurate as this self-assessment may be, Leigh also demonstrates in a number of his films a large complement of intellectual curiosity and energy, exemplifying an inherent intelligence without compromising his unique emotional center. His films are surely not devoid of ideas, but their ideas are inseparable from the materials of which they are composed. The characters, actions, setting, and language are the films' meaning rather than mere illustrations of themes neatly realized at the conclusions of the film. Leigh recognizes that an audience does not experience considerable emotional impact without some principle of organization in the presentation. He demonstrates an astonishing ability to observe what is going on in the world he puts on film, absorb it, internalize it, and re-express the quandaries of daily experience in both local and universal terms. We might say that Leigh practices a less extreme English version of what Robert Stam in *Film Theory: An Introduction* calls, after Bakhtin, the Carnival's "grotesque realism" (18) with various degrees of verisimilitude.

Leigh grounds much of his understanding of people in their appetites, which define human life and the fulfillment of human needs. He is perceptive in displaying how much of the quality of life is encoded in, and possibly determined by, the tiny, repetitive, trivial choices about what people will or won't eat. In addition, food can be seen metaphorically in a variety of ways, not least for the offering or withholding of emotion, because meals are intimate. Leigh uses food as an entree into the way his characters live, the manner in which they treat others, and how they perceive pleasure. It is but one factor in the way Leigh asserts his comic faith in the forces of life, which serves as the dominant element in his own undidactic but nonetheless compelling moral attitude that film's style, form, and content should be close to life.

To survey Leigh's impressive output for the cinema, including the full-length television films and the theatrical releases, is to discover how much of his work is thematically and structurally interconnected and to recognize his humane understanding of life's essentials. Leigh has distinguished himself as an anthropologist of work and daily life, yet he evokes more than the banalities of his society, however much he incorporates into his storytelling the merchandise, mental and physical impairments, food, and cooking that are all part of everyday existence. He largely avoids simplified and exaggerated notions of working-class consciousness, but he preserves a sense of the vividness of the actual world and respect for the people in it who demonstrate flexibility of mind and heart. His attention to the family reflects his appreciation of the continuity of life itself apart from any "family values" predicated upon specific religious or moral doctrine but surely not indifference to family power and the strength it provides. Leigh views the family in his films as a complex structure often divided against itself, as something of a trap but also a source of nurture.

As a filmmaker and storyteller, Leigh has always acknowledged that what viewers see, feel, and think about are so inextricably connected that thoughts and feelings cannot easily be separated. To a degree Leigh with his remarkable empathic intelligence enters into a relationship with his viewers, as he does with his actors, that amounts to an ongoing conversation, inviting them not to solve plot puzzles but to look within themselves. Leigh creates emotional impact within his actors and audience rather than only simulating it in film action. The director expressed his position especially well in a *Cineaste* interview with Lee Ellickson and Richard Porton in the Movshovitz volume: "For me, the whole experience of making films is one of discovery. What is important, it seems to me, is that you share questions with the audience, and they have to go away with things to work on" (63). Ellickson and Porton further connect Leigh's perspective with a distinctly British literary and film tradition:

> By the standards of Hollywood narrative cinema, very little happens in a Mike Leigh film. Although Leigh resolutely refuses to engage in sloganeering, his films are acutely political, since they consistently articulate an often hilarious critique of everyday life. This critique is always rooted in the idiosyncrasies of individual characters. To call the films character-driven would almost be an understatement, since Leigh's work is constantly fueled by the sometimes endearing and frequently infuriating eccentricities of quintessentially English individuals. (60)

As in any profound conversation, he provides hints in his films of how to continue thinking about them after they end. Leigh's films often seem organized to provoke thought rather than urge conclusions. Consequently, his films abide long after the initial acquaintance in viewers' minds, partly because, unlike postmodernists, Leigh does not undermine references to reality in the images he presents.

Largely ignoring the British historical stiff-upper-lip tradition and its accompanying culture of deference, Leigh appears, if not actually radical in the political sense, at least strongly individualistic in respect to an art informed by Anglo-Saxon pragmatism. He wants his films to manifest that they owe their existence to the attention paid to the current moment in all its tangled, painful, and perplexing details, both private and public, and the way his characters hold to preferred but often deluded images of themselves and others. The practical Leigh has always believed he could make films his way, and his impressive oeuvre demonstrates that he has been able to do so without the compromise, as he put it, of "'having to reduce everything to a formula even before you start being creative'" (Brunette, C1). Leigh does not discuss his films beforehand with producers because they interfere too much and might force him into such compromise. Of course, securing funding without such preliminaries has been an abiding concern for Leigh throughout his career, but it is a price he has been willing to pay for the freedom and independence he has always enjoyed in the development and production of his films. He has never been the victim of the too-many-cooks and second-guessers syndromes or the rewrites by committee that plague so many American movies.

Decorous restraint has not been characteristic of Leigh's portrayal of British society except when he draws attention precisely to it by exaggerating such restraint for satirical purposes. Indeed raw emotions and even indecorous behavior constitute Leigh's view of British manners, seen less as self-consciousness than simply the lived texture of social life. The plots of his films appear to be formed instant by instant through his characters' impulsive responses and full disclosure. Vincent Canby contrasted Leigh with the social realists who preceded him in the history of the British film in "Down from Hopeless, to Hilarious." This *New York Times* article was published on the occasion of a major two-week retrospective of Leigh's films, including those done for television with the wonderful title "Life Could Be Better: The Films of Mike Leigh" at the Museum of Modern Art in 1992. Leigh, as Canby observed, "radically changed the socially conscious English cinema from the tradition established by the shapely, poetic working-class films made in the 1950's and 60's by Tony Richardson, Karel Reisz and Lindsay Anderson" (C1). Canby brilliantly described the effect Leigh achieves:

> Mr. Leigh's films appear to be shapeless, devoid of poetry. They are unforgiving in their portrayal of squalor. They shuffle along on tired feet, seemingly as aimless and inarticulate as their characters. Yet at some point in each of his films there comes a transforming moment when the unbearable and the hopeless fuse to create an explosion of recognition, sometimes of high, incredible hilarity. (C1)

These scenes, in which Leigh has few rivals, are rendered with real depth and power. His type of verisimilitude and eye for the actual seem particularly appropriate to comedy. To quote Canby yet again: "Leigh has found some kind of meta-working class idiom, one that need not be solemn to be serious, nor frivolous to be funny" (C1). Leigh presents ordinary existence with such assurance and palpable authenticity that it becomes revelatory. He works in his films much the way Alice Munro does in her short stories to achieve, as she describes in "An Ounce of Cure," illumination of the shameless, marvelous, shattering absurdity of life. Versimilitude as he practices it, where even the obvious holds ambiguity and indeterminacy, reveals what lies behind the commonplace and daily trivia, all without prettifying people's mean and petty terms.

Others, like John Hill in *British Cinema in the 1980's*, have argued that histrionic elements in Leigh's performances, derived perhaps from the filmmaker's theatrical work, subvert "verisimilar" codes of acting because, as Hill sees it, "'behavioural' traits are magnified and the 'actorliness' of the performance is apparent" (195). Hill further describes an effect upon the spectator that he thinks results from this "overt 'performativity' of the acting," which, in turn, "tends not only to inhibit the spectator's emotional identification with characters but also to encourage a degree of critical distance from, and superiority, to them" (195). Variations on this assumption of Leigh's patronizing attitude toward his characters reappear among Leigh's critics, early and late. Hill submits that "so much of the comedy—or, indeed, satire—of Leigh's work rests upon an implicit distance from the behaviour and tastes of the characters whom we see" (195).

Leigh cuts through false dignity to a frank recognition of what is abject or debased in his characters' personalities and social positions, yet he eschews self-pity. John Lahr in his *New Yorker* essay, "This Other England," noted that "Leigh's camera seeks out and dissects those sensitive moments of humiliation and antagonism which are the by-products of a class-ridden society and give a defining defensive energy to English life" (52). Remarkably, Leigh achieves this representation of social reality in films that are neither nihilistic nor labored and dreary but, most often, comic. Brigid Brophy observed in "The British Sense of Humour" that the "only consistent success British education has had is in teaching us not to weep when we naturally want to, and to laugh when we naturally don't. Classroom and playground alike constitute an academy of dramatic art where the pupils learn to turn on laughter on demand and in defiance of the physiological fact that the natural response to a comic stimulus is at most a giggle and often no outward sign at all" (33). Leigh's representation of British life invites a more patent audience response in smiles and frequent laughter.

Leigh's often gritty portrayal of British civilization for what it is and has been during his career opposes the longings of Americans and others who wax nostalgic for what they suppose England used to be, well mannered and tasteful. Tim Parks in a review of Ian Buruma's *Voltaire's Coconuts* in *London Review of Books* observed that "most Anglophiles are snobs. They see the English social world as offering a recognition which elsewhere neither money nor celebrity can buy. He [Buruma] points out convincingly to the many foreigners who become English lords and gentlemen that England offers this odd opportunity" (30). Leigh's films appear diametrically opposed to the refined Merchant-Ivory and *Masterpiece Theatre* mode of representation of people in glittering period decor behaving in a refined manner. Leigh explores rather what it takes to cross the borders of taste and transcend the numerous attitudes, labels, and prejudices that separate people one from another.

Ismail Merchant and James Ivory, in particular, are associated indelibly with cinematic adaptations of novels by E. M. Forster. Nevertheless, maybe surprisingly, as Michael Coveney reveals in *The World According to Mike Leigh*, Leigh greatly admires the novels of E. M. Forster. This early twentieth-century novelist, Leigh says, as quoted by Coveney, "'deals with characters, both passively and dispassionately; the character is always at the centre, but there's always a high degree of objectivity, too'" (62–3). Leigh exhibits this near-Brechtian attribute, but his detachment is less indebted to Brecht's "alienation effect" than an impersonalty that is part of a long tradition of British literature extending at least as far back as Chaucer and forward to a twentieth-century practitioner like Forster. He does not try to define and refine his audience's response; he simply presents the stimulus.

Paul Clements in *The Improvised Play* explained that Leigh asks his actors to demonstrate a measure of objectivity in developing characters with him through improvisations by referring to their characters in the third person (35). Like Forster, Leigh aims much of his satire at those people who suffer from underdeveloped hearts and juxtaposes classes in order to enlarge perspective and liberate his audience from rigid social distinctions. Indeed, given his attention to social relationships and the importance of human connectedness in so many of his films, Leigh may well have internalized the famous epigraph to Forster's *Howard's End* (1910) in his own films. However his sense of "only connect" is informed by broader and deeper comic humor than Forster delivers.

Leigh, unlike Forster, does not show "people relating to people as if free of external determinants" (68), to appropriate what Jim Reilly in "The Novel as Art Form" decribes as D. H. Lawrence's objection to Forster's abundance of people *ad nauseum* and their personal relationships. Indeed, Leigh would seem closer to Lawrence than to Forster in his understanding and portrayal of socio-economic realities as they impact on the possibility of making choices on the part of his characters.

In the context of the British film in the last quarter of the twentieth century, another pairing of often assumed similarity actually is a matter of difference, that is, Mike Leigh and the other contemporary social realist with whom he is often compared, Ken Loach. This difference primarily lies in their cultural and political representation of society. While Leigh demonstrates an underlying moral and moderately left-wing, even socialist, humanism, he does not adopt Loach's propagandist socialist agenda. In a November 11, 1999, *Guardian* interview at the National Film Theatre, Leigh responded to Michael Billington's question, "How do you feel when people bracket you with Ken Loach?" in the following way:

> Well apart from the fact that for me would qualify as a compliment, obviously Ken Loach and I are bemused by it. When you look at it, we make very different kinds of films, and Ken Loach, although a great humanitarian filmmaker, still is a man [who] makes films motivated by a very clear political agenda, in the way that my films certainly are not. I defy anybody to walk away from any film of mine with a very clear-cut sense of what I'm saying politically; it's always, I hope, ambivalent and leaves you things to go away and ponder and argue about.

Loach's "socialist realism" contrasts with what we might call Leigh's "intimist realism," which is frequently both hilarious and affecting. Certainly Leigh has not demonstrated disappointment with the limitations of realism as many other writers and filmmakers of the late twentieth century have; neither has he appropriated the position of postmodernists who have shown the "real" to be only a discursive effect. Besides, Leigh fits far more comfortably than Loach into a comic tradition long venerated in British fiction and film, including the post–World War II and 1950's "little" Ealing comedies that Leigh has acknowledged enjoying. He might possibly have been influenced by their narrative structure, and he may have borrowed from even lesser monuments of British cinema. For example, John Hill observed in *Sex, Class, and Realism: British Cinema, 1956 - 1963* that unlike the narratives of the new wave which "are conventionally organised around one central character, the plots of the Carry On [popular farcical '50s British film series] favour a multiplication of leading characters. As a result, the causal logic of classic narrativity is replaced by a more loosely motivated plot, less developmental than episodic" (142). As already noted, that British delight in the eccentric and idiosyncratic is rarely absent in Leigh films, but Leigh can be funny without being facetious or insensitive to the point of being cruel. Terrence Rafferty, referring to Leigh's *Life Is Sweet*, admires the filmmaker's "naturalistic examination of one of the primary sources of British humor: the insouciance with which people accept the incongruous, and proceed as if nothing unusual were going on" (102). Bert Cardullo contrasts Leigh's work with that of both Loach and Terence Davies, contemporaries with whom he has been compared:

> He has managed to conduct his cinematic investigations without the political tendentiousness bordering on religious affirmation of Ken Loach (at his worst), or the passionate self-regard approaching masochistic exaltation of Terence Davies (at his best), the two countrymen of Mike Leigh's who are best known for treating the same central subject on film. (113–4)

Few novelists, playwrights, painters, or directors, on stage or in film, have come close to Leigh's democratic embrace and fundamental sympathy with British life, especially the happiest tradition of English resilience and the capacity for survival in the past thirty or so years. As a classical realist, through the truthful representation of social experience, he lets his audience understand what it is like for ordinary people to live in contemporary England. He shows, usually with humor artfully mingled with an underlying sense of sadness, how the material of daily existence molds, enriches, and/or defeats both the individual soul and the collective spirit. No one now is more adept than Leigh at delineating social relationships and how their import dawns only gradually on both the characters in his films and the audience. He understands also that truth—to whatever extent any of us grasps it—is usually somewhat elusive and ambiguous. Moviegoers cannot expect a standard rising action-climax-falling action scenario in a Leigh film. He trusts that his audience is capable of extending patience to the characters on the screen, as people often do in life, and then will reward them immeasurably. In exchange for quick, obvious, and predictable plot development, Leigh gives us the texture and ambiguity of life itself that does not exclude energy, zest, and even fun.

Mike Leigh was born in 1943, the son of a Jewish doctor named Abraham, whose father, Mayer Liebermann, had emigrated from Russia to escape tsarist conscription (the family name was subsequently shortened and anglicized before Mike was born). Leigh grew up in Salford, Lancashire, just outside Manchester. These minimal biographical facts may provide a clue to his appreciation of detail, material and otherwise. The significance of this portion of England has been forcefully described in Martin Green's *A Mirror for Anglo-Saxons* several years before Leigh took up filmmaking; and because of its potential applicability to Leigh, it justifies extended quotation:

> The reasons why the North is different are no doubt complex, but one may point out that the people of the North live among the really dramatic ruins of England. The castles and abbeys are not more alive to the imagination than Hollywood imitations, but those Northern industrial towns are smoking, blackened ruins of the great thrust of energy that swung the world on its pivot, flung us into the momentum and direction we are trying to control today. These are the ruins, still alive, and yet are soaked in local and national memories; that is living tradition. The charm of the English countryside is irredeemably "olde worlde," the towns are too pretty and trivial, the history is hopelessly in the hands of Olivier, but Wigan, Preston, Salford keep their intensity and freshness of impact, which is by no means simply, or even dominantly, ugliness. To live and move among those buildings is to be sharply challenged every day, to be held to a highly charged battery and tested, to suffer a strongly cauterizing touch on your purposes and passions. (64)

Gritty Salford is also the setting for Harold Brighouse's perennially popular stage comedy, *Hobson's Choice* (1916), which amused audiences throughout most of the twentieth century with its Lancastrian playwright's attention to local detail and forthright Northern speech that seem like a precursor of Mike Leigh's cinema.

The reference to cauterization in Green's quotation links an appropriate medical metaphor to Leigh, himself the son of a physician and a self-declared admirer of that remarkable Russian practitioner, Chekhov. I found particularly regrettable erasure of Leigh's extremely cogent remarks on Chekhovian tragicomedy as a possible lens into his own films in my interview with him. On the other hand, as antecedent for his tragicomedy, in "The Case for Mike Leigh," also part of the Movshovitz collection, Kenneth Turan offers Leigh's acknowledgment that "on another, more sophisticated level it would be quite dishonest if I were to deny my films are Jewish in their way. The tragicomic view of life, the melancholy, if you know what you're talking about, there is a Jewish flavor to it, a Jewishness in the spirit of it. I could deny it, but it would be stupid" (90). Coveney quotes David Thomson's description of Leigh's camera work as "a detached, medical watchfulness" (12). It is within the sub-

tached, medical watchfulness" (12). It is within the substantial everyday world that Leigh experienced in Salford that his art took root. From there he found the cinematic means to involve viewers almost physically and materially in the reality to heighten their awareness of the everyday and reward them with an ache of recognition together with a renewed sense of what matters.

Henry James may have sought the figure in the carpet, but Mike Leigh projects his own cultural insight from what is found in the cupboard, on the walls, or atop the telly. John Lahr's description of Leigh's favored milieu explains the distinctiveness of the filmmaker's content:

> His films have a particular density of details, an almost ruthless focus on that drab intersection of working-class and middle-class life: a zone of impoverishment, resignation, and aggression where a large part of the English population lives—and generally a cinematic no go area. (50)

That "drab intersection," as Lahr terms it, is the lower middle class, which is beginning to receive some scholarly attention, and Leigh merits recognition for his contribution to advancing our understanding of it. Rita Felski in "Nothing to Declare: Identity, Shame, and the Lower Middle Class," her introduction to a *PMLA* selection of essays on "Rereading Class" discusses her impressions of how this class is perceived:

> ...I am interested in the lower middle class, my social origin. Being lower middle class is a singularly boring identity, possessing none of the radical chic that is sometimes ascribed to working-class roots. In fact, the lower middle class has typically been the object of scorn among intellectuals, blamed for everything from exceedingly bad taste to the rise of Hitler. Yet as older forms of class polarization and class identification begin to dissolve, the lives of ever more individuals in the industrialized West are defined by occupations, lifestyles, and attitudes traditionally associated with the lower middle class. (34)

Mike Leigh, by his avoidance of facetious and puerile superficiality in the presentation of his characters, exhibits advocacy and respect for this neglected social class, not voyeuristic appropriation of it as some have argued. Kristin Hohenadel in a *New York Times*' piece on Timothy Spall, which appeared concurrently with the U.S. release of Leigh's *All or Nothing*, quotes this veteran Leigh performer's somewhat hyperbolic "take" on the filmmaker's special gift in this regard:

> He [Leigh] presents this tapestry of the least aspirational, the least successful people in the world, and builds a solar system of a magnificent interior life. These people are almost majestic in their despair. It raises it to the pitch of almost Shakespearean tragedy. (AR 13)

In an interview with Alan Franks in the *London Times Magazine*, Leigh describes his own youth as a privileged life on underprivileged streets:

> The point is that I did have a direct awareness and experience of both a working-class and a lower-middle-class environment. It was a world where I was at school with working-class children, but would also be taken by my parents to see the Halle [Manchester's distinguished symphony orchestra] and the D'Oyly Carte, and Stratford, and I make absolutely no bones about having had an ambivalent or plural background. It was a rich mix, but as I say, it was not an uncommon one for the children of doctors, or dentists, or vicars. (31)

At the beginning of the twenty-first century, Leigh, now viewed as a world-renowned *auteur*, invites and does not suffer from comparison with acknowledged influences and models from his past like Chekhov and Dickens in literature and Yasujiro Ozu, Satyajit Ray, Ermanno Olmi, and Jean Renoir in film. His realism, like theirs, goes way beyond notation that merely reproduces the surface of life within the conventions of plausibility to the valid creation of art of straightforward vigor, occasionally casual lyricism amid unlikely situations, and recognition of the mysterious, and even the spiritual, concealed within the ordinary. For Mike Leigh, currently hailed, as Richard Porton judges him in the Movshovitz volume as "Britain's most consistently provocative contemporary filmmaker" (62) or as "the maestro of the mundane," as Lahr terms him (50), it has been a slow but steady ascent. Leigh's output reflects how the realistic narrative film has been identified and valued during its first century. Leigh's prestige has often been fueled more by recognition and honors conferred outside England rather than within his island nation although he was named Officer to the Order of the British Empire in 1993 "for services to the film industry." Leigh may only be half-facetious when he describes his film, *High Hopes*, in a conversation with Peter Brunette reprinted in the Movshovitz volume as "an ethnic, foreign-language, Third World movie from a small island off the French coast. And if you couldn't understand it, that's why" (33). In this same interview collection Leigh replies to Mirra Banks' query of whether his work is better understood in England or abroad: "Sometimes it does seem to be better understood here [in the United States], France, Australia, in Germany, and other places.... I think what that's about is some of the self-loathing and self-deceiving manifestations of English culture" (120).

He was never a particularly distinguished student academically; however, Leigh attended such venerable institutions as the Royal Academy of Dramatic Art, where he won a scholarship, the Central School of Art and Design, and the London International Film School. He has expressed particular indebtedness to what he learned at Camberwell School of Arts and Crafts in 1963, especially in life class. Paul Clements in *The Improvised Play: The Work of Mike Leigh* quotes Leigh's impression of this experience: "I was in a life drawing class at Camberwell one day when I suddenly had this clairvoyant flash. I realized that I was experiencing as an art student was that working from a source and looking at something that actually existed and excited you was the key to making a piece of art" (8). In a similar vein, Coveney describes the young man's epiphany: "The material was all around—as obvious and evident as the nude body of the model whom he was drawing—and it was the artist's duty to get out there and experience it, and then absorb it into the creative process" (64).

While this discovery may have occurred in life class, Leigh bears testimony throughout his films to the value of perceptual drawing. It is the kind based on perception of the real world. As an art student Leigh was exposed to and absorbed the philosophical side of drawing that lies in its empiricism and visual epistemology, the experience of certain facts about the world together with teaching artists how they know what they know. It can be argued that this early training in the visual arts contributed to Leigh's ability to look afresh at the world. Only extraordinary, cultivated powers of observation and perception could create Leigh's filmed world. One can see in Leigh's work what Raymond Durgnat noted in Jean Renoir as "a certain sensuousness, that reflex wholeness of intelligence, affect and tactile imagery more common in visual artists (since seeing is a preliminary to touching) than in verbal ones, who are quicker to blot out the world around so as to follow the verbal thread of a purely mental thought" (10).

People have a tendency to look at the world and verbalize their responses by substituting what they know about it instead of describing how something actually appears at a given moment. Leigh, from what he may have learned in his early perceptual drawing and life classes, deliberately disrupts that practice in his films as he carefully avoids substituting signs and symbols or rushing to judgment. These early lessons at Camberwell complement Leigh's other antecedent influences. Among these influential givens are the British realistic novel, the sense of authenticity from the legacy of the British documentary film as named and practiced by John Grierson, and the larger philosophical context of the British empiricists themselves, who prized reality. Peter Brunette, for example, reports Leigh's comments about respecting a sense of preexisting reality in the fiction film:

> Whenever I occasionally teach film, what I say to student directors is that... we should aspire to the condition of documentary. By which I mean that when you shoot documentary you do not question that the world you're pointing a camera at actually exists in three dimensions and it would exist whether you filmed it or not, and if we can aspire to that condition with what the actors are doing, so that it really is in three dimensions, and really does go around corners, then the bit we actually see, the tip of the iceberg, is going to have that solidity to it? (C2)

Leigh desires to have his films aspire to the condition of documentary: "you want the event to feel like it really is happening whether you're filming or not." But, at the same time, as reported by Ray Pride in his *New City* essay reprinted in Movshovitz, Leigh also wants "the film to aspire to the condition of theatre, or circus. Is he or she going to fall off the tightrope? The only way to get that to happen is just to be very, very thorough" (112).

Leigh's Collaborative Method

Without the reliance and security of conventional filmmaking on a developed screenplay from which producers can secure production funding, Mike Leigh has always worked outside the Hollywood development or studio systems. He proudly claims that he and collaborators make films rather than scripts, and Leigh's very method of doing so seems as if he goes at each film as a fresh start in the business of filmmaking. Lahr quotes Leigh's conjecture on the imagined Hollywood response to his way of working: "If you were to pitch one of my films as though you knew in advance what it was, none of them would ever have been made" (50). In "Mike Leigh's Original Features, an interview by Graham Fuller," a preface to his book, *Naked and Other Screenplays (*the others being *Life Is Sweet* and *High Hopes*), Leigh again underscores his opposition to the standard way films are financed and made: "Then, in my case, I'm the man who doesn't have a script, won't say what it's going to be about, and doesn't want to discuss casting—not by any standards a viable, commercial proposition!" (xvii).

The collaborative accomplishments tend to be intensely personal ones derived from huge amounts of exploration that lead to precise structuring on the part of the director. Paul Clements in *The Improvised Play* divides Leigh's exploratory period into the category of pre-rehearsal with two basic areas of work:

"narrative" and "behaviour" that embrace the characters' biographies narratively: "Their culture, their consciousness and their physical characteristics: how they walk and talk; their bearing and posture, manner and mannerisms and the interrelationship between all these things" (33). So much of Leigh's film-making is to let behavior speak for itself as he goes along with the mystery of human complication. The "structuring" that follows is the period when "sequences of action are polished prior to their being filmed" (33). "My job," as Lahr quotes Leigh, "is to gather the resources, then go out there and find the film by making it" (51). Leigh spoke to me with quintessential British understatement and modesty about working with actors during an unpublished interview in 1997:

> With the actor I get around to deciding precisely what we're up to during the course of working.... It's a combination of all kinds of things to be honest. I've always got an objective, but, as in all art, there is an interaction of ideas—an order—yet you change, expand, and subtract according to things that evolve with what emerges and happens. I may be more receptive to such things than some other directors.

His achievement is recognizable in the completed film, however impossible it is to say exactly why and how it was achieved from outside the group's rehearsal activity. "What I'm after," as Alex Lewin quotes from the director about his approach to auditions, "is actors who can sit and be real without the need to take on the role of a dramatist" (60).

Leigh's famous collaborative method based on extensive improvisations with his actors during prolonged rehearsals for his films (typically twelve weeks to as much as six or seven months) began as early as his theater piece, *The Box Play* (1965). It has continued without much alteration ever since, followed by extensive weeks of location shooting. He assembles a select group of actors with whom he works individually to develop a character based on a dozen or so people the performer knows from life. Hence, fictional characters in his films are constructed by Leigh and his actors from real people in testimony of his interest in life as it is really lived and people as they really are. This technique he first employed in his stage work with *Individual Fruit Pies* (1968). "Leigh's process," as John Lahr describes it, "is a kind of treasure hunt, in which his collaborators bring stuff back from their lives and pick over it with the director to make up a story whose general parameters are growing in Leigh's mind but which is unknown to the group. The generic term 'improvisation,' while it's not wrong, is not exactly right, either, for the epic undertaking whose rules Leigh sets out at the first company get-together" (54).

Leigh chooses a character from discussions for the actor to work on in collaboration with him. In contrast to John Cassavetes, who would not discuss parts with his actors as a group, Leigh does work with his actors as an ensemble. When moving beyond the one-to-one phase, these characters meet one another only in situations Leigh devises. The actors know only as much as their characters would know. In the midst of improvised scenes, the director might suddenly interject a surprise plot element to see how the actors will react within their characterizations and the relationships they are improvising with others. In this way, Leigh considers that he provides actors with their own creative space, which would be foreclosed if they knew all about their characters' actions or destiny as they would from a completed screenplay. "Since one of the themes which is consistently explored in Leigh's work," as Paul Clements explains, "is the way in which people in their behaviour and relationships are limited by the physical and emotional circumstances of their lives, it is entirely natural that the rehearsal process will explore the outer material world of the characters as fully as their inner motivations" (43). With few exceptions, Leigh, unlike Ken Loach, has always worked with professional actors, and he exacts enormous commitment, even sacrifice, from them with the happy result that their performances for him often are defining ones in their careers. Leigh has his own indeterminacy principle that operates at many levels in his filmmaking, embracing even the content of his finished films and their effect upon audiences with things to resolve as a result of his frequently inconclusive outcomes. Unlike in so many film narratives, in Leigh the problems of every single major character will not be resolved by the end.

The characters that the actors bring Leigh become integrated into a film narrative devised collaboratively through research, discussion, and especially abundant improvisation as they interact with one another as they would in reality because of what the director asks them to do. Details and interpersonal relationships that become consciousness are the stuff of Leigh's films and really the only plots; revelations of social structures, of course, emerge from these elements, but his principal interest remains character. Ray Carney in *The Films of Mike Leigh: Embracing the World* submits that in Leigh "drama is generated out of states of being more than acts of doing.... Rather than competing in the realm of action, Leigh's figures are placed in situations in which their ways of feeling and thinking are compared" (15). What sustains Leigh's actors the most is that they can dig deeper and deeper into characters as complex as the people they are and live with on a daily basis, making the fiction they are working on as rich and contradictory as life itself. In a sense, then, a Leigh film is a documentary of its actors and their characters as the product of their collaboration with him. Leigh gets these results by working with the actors, not dominating them. He does ask his actors after they have been requested to go "into character" to remain there until he gives permission to come out. He brings everyone into a shared conception of the film's narrative, rousing each person to join in as an individual to realize a united vision. Leigh's ensemble players never act out roles without believing in them.

Leigh insists that everything be carefully constructed, not only physically and technically but also emotionally. In this process Leigh helps his performers to discover the humanity of their characters and rediscover perhaps through that pursuit a renewed depth of their own humanity as well, which accounts for why people in his films have texture, not merely attitude in their presentation of self. Jonathan Rosenbaum testified in an American tribute to Leigh's work early in the filmmaker's career appropriately titled "England on the Inside" that his characters "always seem to have lives that extend beyond the borders of the work" (215). Thus Leigh's casts, having invested so much of their own talent and imagination in the creation of the characters, appear to move beyond roles to actual beings in narrative situations they have, in part, devised, do indeed seem to live their characters' lives on the screen. They act with their characters' lives. Brenda Blethyn, for example, gave witness to Gerard Raymond of *The Village Voice* of the benefit of Leigh's workshop approach to her award-winning portrayal of Cynthia in *Secrets & Lies*: "I knew precisely when a particular thought was coming into Cynthia's head. There was no interpreting; there was just no other way of doing it" (64). Timothy Spall, as quoted by Kristin Hohenadel, similarly observes about his character who feels his common-law wife does not love him in *All or Nothing*: "I'd been building this character for 10 months, and I felt so connected with his despair.... I think you sense that in the film. When I look at it, I think, Oh, God, that's not me, that's the character" (24). Leigh scrupulously observes his characters from without: no voice-overs and the like reveal them from within to secure audience empathy through exposed thoughts. Audiences may almost forget they are watching acting, but, if they do not see the acting, they surely feel it and know it is good.

On the fraught question of authorship for his films, Leigh explained to Graham Fuller: "I create scenes distilled from improvisations. But I don't go away and sit in a room and write the script. We do it by going through it and building it up so that it is being written by actually rehearsing it" (xv). Moreover, in a conversation with Judy Bloch excerpted in *Film Quarterly*, Leigh explained how the credit "Devised and Directed by Mike Leigh" evolved, much to his regret, from this procedure:

> I think one of the biggest mistakes of my career was to use that phrase, and I wish to hell that I had always put "Written and Directed by..." earlier than I did. For various historical reasons, I thought because I didn't sit in a room and write it, it was better to say "Devised." Eventually, I realized this is the biggest red herring of them all. The truth is that this is a medium in its own right, it's a plastic medium; everything I do that's worth talking about happens in conjunction with the actors. Obviously I make decisions. I have ideas of who the character's going to be, but then it's different from what happens. I create the characters and the actors create the characterizations. (53)

Leigh has taken a somewhat different approach to the plays he has done in the theater. Rick Lyman in a *New York Times* piece reports that Leigh "never felt they were his alone. Indeed, he said, he still shares half the royalties on any revival of his plays with the actors who appeared in the original production" (Section 2, 4).

The director is responsible as author for the material of the film that he dramatically constructs. Accomplished Leigh performer Philip Davis says of the director's method, as reported by Michael Coveney in Movshovitz: "It's not a democratic process. All you ever concentrate on is your own character. The rest is down to him" (41). He orchestrates the talents and contributions of all his collaborators without forcing on them a preconceived ideal film of his own devising. Leigh writes a scenario of three or four pages at the end of the long preparatory period. Coveney explains that this artifact indicates "the number of the scene, the location, characters involved and a one-line summary of either what happens or what is discussed" (214). Leigh is able to proceed with such seemingly simple outlines because by this time in the extended rehearsal process, his characters have been developed to such a measure of completeness and complexity that they will not hazard reduction.

The dialogue shot is not improvised. It is fixed and scripted through the invaluable efforts of Leigh's continuity and script supervisor, Heather Storr, who has worked with his ensembles all during the decade of the nineties. But Leigh does not write in the conventional way, as he explained in an inteview with Rita Cook for *Screentalk* with reference to *All or Nothing*: "I write it by directing it, sequence by sequence, scene by scene, moment by moment" (47). Perhaps something of the improvisatory way Leigh works throughout the prolonged process remains in the finished film, and audiences react to it accordingly. He is far more disposed to cultivate a disjunctive narrative form than most filmmakers who embrace clear cause and effect for their presentations. Terrence Rafferty articulates the nature of that element of seeming spontaneity in his review of *Life Is Sweet*: "Leigh's unconventional storytelling gives his movies a strange kind of suspense. Every scene and every new character seem to give rise to a fresh set of narrative possibilities, and there's no way to predict which of them will be elaborated upon and which will remain, to the end, suggestive diversions" (102). Buddhists speak of learning to see the world with "beginner's mind," and an analogous starting point underlies each of Leigh's film projects. One aspect of Leigh's realism is his alacrity to use the adventitious detail that Alan Spiegel describes, which I apply to Leigh who separates "phenomenal appearances from preconceived mental categories and expectations, to create the illusion of chaos and indeterminacy, and to use *this* as a dramatic device" (258). Similarly, Susan Sontag in her 1966 essay "Theatre and Film" observed that "a little-remarked fact about movies is that the moments that are plastically and emotionally most successful, and the most effective elements of characterization, often consist precisely of 'irrelevant' or unfunctional details" (106). This orchestration of seemingly inessential details as guarantors of authenticity constitutes what Roland Barthes termed "reality effects," as Robert Stam observes in *Film Theory: An Introduction*, persuading "spectators to take what was really nothing but constructed effects as transparent renderings of the real" (143).

In Mike Leigh progression usually catches up to digression, but it is often a combat, a circumstance that may be related to what John Hill in *British Cinema in the 1980's*, borrowing from Brian McFarlane and Geoff Mayer, calls a general "dawdling tendency typical of British cinema" (80). Notwithstanding the importance of improvisation in the development of a Leigh film and his affection for the peripheral as well as the central, the adventitious together with the necessary, the director trusts that his finished film does not feel or look improvised. Certainly for Leigh film had not used up the conventions of realism as he redefined them in collaboration with his actors, cinematographers, and designers according to his own method of application. Indeed, he seeks a fairly classical final product in the film itself: mimetic representation of a discoverable and discovered world, but one that Leigh constructs quite deliberately. It is shaped by the selectivity and design of collaborative art, which somewhat qualifies what he does not so much as rendering the world as creating his own world, as the title of Coveney's biography suggests, from the medium of which he is master, that is, filmmaking. However, it is worthwhile to remember what Adam Gopnik reinforces in his analysis of the art of Joseph Cornell that "in the root sense" a "realist is an artist preoccupied with the world he finds rather than with the world he wants." And like Cornell, Leigh "is on the side of the real" (184).

So much of what goes on during the months of improvisational workshops with Leigh comprises the back-story for the characters and is never directly represented or seen in the completed film. As the actors construct entire histories of multiple decades for their characters, these workshops become, in effect, collaborative work-in-progress quasi-novels that never get written, for only the novel can address the effects of the passage of time upon characters more comprehensively than either drama or film. So if Leigh presents a story in "real time," and its horizon seems tiny and limited, the perspective of the felt life in the actors' embodiment of the characters is often quite long. In this way, the actors become the bearers of memories beyond what is represented in the film, and that, in turn, makes what is portrayed on the screen especially memorable for viewers. Leigh's method lets us draw on deeper feelings about these people than they themselves are shown to feel, which may account for why Leigh's films feel as spacious as a novel. All of this is quite different from an invitation to patronize these characters. His films seem intensified episodes from these work-in-progress novels. It has been said that Jane Austen knew her characters so well that she would narrate to her family incidents in their lives that did not occur in the books, and Leigh's actors have that profound knowledge of the characters they portray. The collaborative workshops provide time, conceived for artistic purposes rather as a novelist would, via Leigh's long preparation period for the nuanced development of character or germinal scenes from a linear sequence of a narrative history that was never intended to be incorporated in its entirety into the finished film. The small portion that a film shows of characters' lives is informed by the sense of their whole lives. This larger narrative has been developed in the process of trying to understand the full potential of the material. Leigh discussed in his interview with Fuller the effect of this strategy on his actors and their characterization in his films, as was confirmed in the testimony on *Secrets & Lies* by Brenda Blethyn:

> [The films] seem so real because the actors are not doing what actors in a film normally do, which is to simulate artificially, with no foundations. The way we work, the actors have confidence in what they are doing and saying, because they really know who they are and how to play the character, because a history is built into the relationship. (v)

Leigh does not do exposition in the usual manner of film narrative; often the story begins in the middle of action without any prior hook to get his audience interested or informed. The back-story, although it does not appear directly on screen, helps to hone and define what Leigh's camera does capture. Thus, his films imply that he and his collaborators are privy to a great deal more about the characters than has been recorded. They could supply far more, if necessary. Rather than filming a slice of life from the world outside or from a completed prose fiction narrative, Leigh films a slice of life from the world that he, his actors, and the production team actively create without foreknowledge of what the ending will be or, more significantly, mean. In this way his art becomes less conceptual than contextual. He glories in leaving the matter of interpretation to his audience and challenging viewers to keep abreast of contradictory moods and changes of pace. The distinguished British novelist John Fowles has commented that "one of the greatest arts of the novel is omission—leaving it to the reader's imagination to do the work" (368). Leigh follows something like this strategy by offering his audience the possibility to exist and think, as it were, in front of his film without foreclosure of their own thought process and inferred conclusion, as in the Hollywood movie that often conspicuously tells its viewers what to think. His characters do not so much develop exactly. They reveal instead more and more of themselves over the course of the film.

Through the months together, the actors fully inhabit the fictional world of their constructed characters and consequently bring to every interaction filmed deeper nuance, texture, and subtlety than most screenplays provide. Charles Eidsvik's comments about ensemble acting, while referring to Ingmar Bergman's, not Leigh's, seem apt for the latter work as well: "The actors conspire to live together in a story as if it were real. They thereby reinforce one another's ability to convince and reinforce the viewer's willingness to take their play world as an imaginative entity" (93). The fictional world generated by these exercises of Leigh's ensemble cast draws the viewer into the nearly novelistic solidity of reality that underpins what is shown. Kenneth Turan in his piece in the Movshovitz collection cites Alison Steadman's description of Leigh's "Quiz Club" for his actors:

> We all gather in a room and he asks us questions which we answer only in our heads. 'What does your character think about Margaret Thatcher?' 'What does he or she think about sex before marriage?' 'What did you give for Christmas presents?' When you realize you are secure enough in your character to answer all these questions, you know that everything's clear and watertight. (94)

Leigh has testified to his preference for film over what he sees as the claustrophobia of the stage. Film lets him get out into the world as he has always done through location shooting. His collaboratively developed characters interact in something and someplace that is real. His final rehearsals never occur until he gets out on location, where he refines and distills the material for shooting in lieu of an actual written script, although one may be created post-production. Leigh's approach to filmmaking in the preparatory phase likewise suggests the spaciousness of form as his films are assembled into satisfying, multilevel tales closer to the novel than to dramatic literature. This study appropriates for Mike Leigh a similar position to what Anthony Lane has given to the portraits made by August Sander, the famed twentieth-century German photographer. "You are struck," Lane writes, "by the daunting realization that to look at a Sander is not merely to consult a social record of this times, however thorough that may be, still less to be charmed or amused. The experience is more like entering a novel" (97). A novelist must mediate between his or her characters and the reader through the language chosen to represent the world experienced in the fiction as populated by the novel's characters. Leigh makes similar mediative choices in his film techniques but with the end of advancing, insofar as it is possible, the appearance of a seemingly more unmediated approach to characters than is customary in filmmaking. Homer Croy in *Star Maker* quotes D. W. Griffith on the relationship between film director and audience that anticipates Leigh: "A film is a cooperative effort between between the director and the audience. A director shows a bit of human emotion; the audience fills in the rest. The better the film, the greater the cooperation between director and audience" (75). His collaboration with his ensemble and the cooperation he envisages from his audience determine both Leigh's content and his film technique. Ray Carney argues for the distinctiveness of what Leigh does contrary to what prevails in most mainstream films, which Carney imputes to typical Hollywood movies: "...the consciousness of the main character or characters is not the organizing center. That is to say, the drama is played out, not in the character's mind, but the viewer's" (16) with the corollary that Leigh's plots, "such as they are, are less something that happens *to* the characters than expressions of what the characters are" (17). Hence Leigh's characters seem observed rather than invented, which generates a distinctive suspense, if not of the Hitchcockian variety, in its own way as compelling as more deliberate Hollywood devices.

Leigh's Visual Style

Leigh's films feature a plain, patient, and direct visual style, correlative to and sustaining of his pure and direct ensemble acting that has remained very consistent over the years. He has successfully solved the dilemma raised by

Erwin Panofsky years ago in his classic essay, "Style and Medium in the Motion Pictures," when he wrote, "The problem is to manipulate and shoot unstylized reality in such a way that the result has style" (292). As in painting, about which Peter Campbell has written "there is an English tendency to find the first impetus to picture-making in personalities and narrative, rather than in formal values of tone, shape and colour" (26), Leigh's cinema eschews familiar cinematic tropes and obvious camera rhetoric. His core of human truth might be destroyed with greater artifice. His style grows so near to the subject that a viewer no longer thinks of it as style unless one takes stock of how successfully Leigh's meaning has determined the functional quality of the look and experience of his films. As a filmmaker Leigh's technique is directed to avoid the need for attention-getting, let alone eye-popping, techniques. He encourages an unmediated perspective on his characters that we understand principally through their social relationships and their being in a particular context, not from audience identification with their consciousness or internal states of mind via frequent point-of-view shots.

Louis Giannetti and Scott Eyman in their textbook, *Flashback: A Brief History of Film*, describe the look of Leigh's films in the following blunt way: "Leigh's visual style is usually plain: a meat-and-potatoes documentarylike functionalism. No pretty pictures here" (528). Many viewers do find beauty but certainly not conventional prettiness in Leigh's minimalist, crisp images and the physical expressiveness of the characters' faces, bodies, gestures, and voices that he captures in his careful, well-placed shots of them. Leigh's deft camera placement usually supports the neutral-observer point of view "best known," as Stuart Klawans identifies it, "from the work of another great director of acting ensembles, Howard Hawks" where "neutral does not necessarily mean unengaged" (718). On the other hand, Carney merits some credibility when he observes boldly that Leigh's "figures repel identification. His camera placements don't encourage the viewer to see things through their eyes. His music and visuals don't allow the viewer to participate in unmediated states of feeling and thought" (16).

Without striking visual effects to manipulate viewers' responses, Leigh relies on the human face and voice and trusts the patience of his viewers to work through his long takes. He alternates these with spare, eloquent movement of the camera for what may be discovered within a deep focus frame that usually preserves the integrity of space. Ray Carney argues that from *High Hopes* and on into the later films, "close-ups are used to cultivate consciousness; in the early films they aren't" (197). Leigh's art of film is closest theoretically to the work of the French theorist, André Bazin. Robert Stam neatly summarizes Bazin in the following capsule comment that seems apposite to Mike Leigh's cinema as well: "Bazin particularly valued the down-to-earth, relatively eventless plots, the unstable character motivations, and the relatively slow and viscous quotidian rhythms characteristic of early neo-realist films" (76). It takes little adjustment to see these characteristics in the films of Mike Leigh. Like Jean Renoir, Leigh seems to avoid the imposition of absolute meaning in portions of his films by encouraging viewers to explore his images. Nevertheless, Leigh's visual acuity conveys and matches his subtle acumen about people, and if he offers less that is spectacular to watch, he gives more room for his actors and audience to inhabit.

There are admittedly distinctive aspects of Leigh's style, such as his total avoidance until recently of dissolves in favor of decisive cuts and holding a number of shots at the end of scenes. Leigh explained the latter attribute in his interview with Fuller: "Very often events are taking place that will carry on, even though we're leaving them. There are times when you cut from something right into something else. It's just a function of what's going on" (xxix). Even as Leigh frequently expresses gratitude to his excellent editors like Jon Gregory and Robin Sales, it appears that he frequently shoots his films the way he wants them cut.

Stylistically, Leigh and Dick Pope, his cinematographer, have employed formally inventive ways to explore characters and their emotion with somewhat more visual bravura in films like *Naked*, *Careers Girls, Topsy-Turvy*, and *All or Nothing* than in the substantial body of work that preceded them. As recently as 1991 when *Life Is Sweet* was released, Terrence Rafferty wrote of Leigh's style:

> It's just about impossible to detect any advance in technical sophistication from his earliest works to his most recent ones; neither his visual ideas nor his sense of dramatic structure has become noticeably more "professional" over the years. One film, from whatever period, looks much like any other. (101)

In no sense should such remarks be taken as a negative assessment of Leigh's clean and effective visual mastery that seems to capture life as it happens. His visual style never seems intent on consecrating itself rather than the moment it represents. In the most recent film discussed here, *All or Nothing*, his and Dick Pope's often-favored elegant medium shots, mirroring the filmmaker's nonjudgmental approach to content, may have become more obvious to experienced viewers. Moreover, Leigh goes so far outside his usual practice in *All or Nothing* as to use a dissolve or fade as a final stylistic fillip.

His abiding concern for relationships is often worked out visually in terms of spatial relationship in his *mise en scène*. Juxtaposition creates formal relations, and to a degree the world (not only according to Mike Leigh) is nothing except juxtaposed forms. Viewers must attend carefully to even slight registrations, or else the drama or narrative, deprived of external theatrics, will be missed altogether. With his audience, no less than with his collaborators in making the films, Leigh invites and expects participation toward the goal of emotional and maybe also cognitive discovery as well. At the very least, Leigh's visual style enlarges the interpretive dynamics of the interaction between film and viewer in films of moments, bleak and otherwise, that both capture and transcend the flow of time. What may be taken in Leigh at first as a simple report of the truth, upon closer inspection, comes to be seen as the product of delicate cinematic choices in the act of filmmaking used to achieve an artistically constructed meaning.

CHAPTER ONE
First Feature and Deferred Second: *Bleak Moments* and *High Hopes*

Bleak Moments

Having staged ten collaborative theater pieces, Mike Leigh opened his film career by directing a feature-length movie, *Bleak Moments* (1971), derived from its theatrical performances at Charles Marowitz's Open Space Theatre in London. With the original cast who had worked with him on the play, Leigh and this remarkable ensemble, the first of many, turned a character-driven slice of life into a consummately well-realized film, not simply photographed theater. In Leigh's discussion with Stephen Lowenstein on this film in *My First Movie: Twenty Celebrated Directors Talk about Their First Film*, the director explains the one advantage this project had over subsequent ones in his career:

> Apart from anything else, here was a narrative I could describe—at least we could say what it was about, because normally my problem was—and has been ever since—that I could never say what the film was going to be. The usual premise was, there's no idea I can talk about yet, and no script—just hand over the dosh. (144)

Through the cumulative power of small details, Leigh convinces us that even stalled lives are worth knowing. Significantly, the running time of the film is somewhat longer than that of the stage version, permitting the film audience to experience sustained silences and the tension of the actors' eye exchanges to powerful effect possible only with film techniques.

This first feature film from Mike Leigh was financed with a small grant from the British Film Institute's Production Board, and the considerable balance, fourteen thousand pounds as Leigh reported to Lowenstein (144), from actor Albert Finney, Leigh's secondary school classmate from Salford. *Bleak Moments* won the Golden Hugo prize at the 1972 Chicago Film Festival and the Golden Leopard Award at the Locarno Film Festival. Lahr refers to Roger Ebert's enthusiastic *Chicago Sun-Times* review of the spectacularly promising young

British director's *Bleak Moments* as "a masterpiece, plain and simple" (51). *Bleak Moments* is almost an urtext in Leigh's canon besides being a minor masterpiece in its own right. Here and in many of the films that followed, Leigh deals with people who, in one way or another, are cut off, alienated, isolated from the world. Leigh defies the most basic theatrical and film convention that something should happen, preferring to capture the quotidian rhythms of his characters' lives with almost Chekhovian simplicity and precision of detail, finding in the ordinary pained comedy underlaid with compassion but not sentimentality.

When *Bleak Moments* was shown at the Edinburgh University Film Society as part of its 1992–93 season, Danny Carr cryptically observed that "part of the interest of the film is seeing just how many terminally repressed introverts Leigh can squeeze into a plot." He concludes his brief but amusing observations by asking if his readers are up to the challenge of a film with "moments (bleak) that are so excruciatingly embarrassing that it will take all of your will-power not to curl up into a ball and make grunting noises" (Carr, EUFS Programme 1992–93). In a similar vein, Kenneth Turan reported that backer Albert Finney humorously suggested as a possible title *Carry on Gloom* (90). Leigh, having apparently forgiven his benefactor this quip, has consistently praised Finney for permitting him total *carte blanche* in *Bleak Moments.* He expressed his salient impressions about this premiere film in his Lowenstein interview:

> To have the luxury of making a film that is so personal and idiosyncratic and that you're free to expand and contract as you go along means that there's no tension between you and the material. You're not enslaved by somebody else's idea or an idea that you don't really believe in or something you're merely doing in order to advance your career. It really is organic and it really comes from your bowels and your soul and it appeals to your sense of humour, it's all of those things. It was also an object lesson in how backers should behave. (155)

Early on, Leigh seems to have subscribed to Chekhov's notion that the more elaborate the plot of a story, the less effective it tends to be as a work of art. In this film, Leigh simply presents life as the quality of the immediate present as his characters live it from moment to moment. The protagonist of *Bleak Moments* is Sylvia, who works as a secretary in an accountant's office and cares for her mentally challenged twenty-nine-year-old sister, Hilda. Anne Raitt and Sarah Stephenson, respectively, bring chilling veracity to their portrayals of the two sisters. The plot focuses on Sylvia's interactions with two men: Norman, played by Mike Bradwell, a would-be folksinger who mimeographs an alternative newspaper in the garage behind her home, and a teacher, Peter, played by Eric Allan, who attempts a date with her, which proves mutually unsatisfactory. In addition, Joolia Cappleman as her colleague at work, Pat, and Liz Smith, as Pat's mother, contribute some robust, animated, dramatic tension to the largely quietist proceedings. Leigh explores the themes of isolation, lack of communication, frustration, quiet and, especially in later films, not-so-quiet desperation. Leigh described the theme of this first feature film in the following way in his interview with Lowenstein:

> It's a film about non-communication, in fact a film which puts somebody who simply cannot communicate, Sylvia's sister, Hilda, amongst others who should be able to, but can't. In some ways Hilda was communicating in the most honest and direct way of any of them. So, yes, it was very much about the pain of sharing and communicating and being able to articulate and be honest. (145)

Moreover, perhaps with an unacknowledged debt to literature, Leigh demonstrates in this film as well as later ones a degree of irresolution, ambiguity, and elusiveness that typically separates his work from mainstream film narrative. For Leigh human relations and social transactions are necessarily oblique, and a film narrative can make its points by indirection without filling in the blanks left in ordinary conversation.

Anne Raitt's hauntingly attractive Sylvia resembles a creation from the mind of Emily or Charlotte Brontë, assuming with her hair often in a severe bun a Brontësque appearance complemented by the volumes by the Brontës that Peter picks up and holds for a long time. He grasps *Wuthering Heights* during a brief scene with Norman when Peter asks Norman if he reads much, which hints at a degree of sexual rivalry over Sylvia. Although never coming close to the intensity of what might be called a "Heathcliff moment," Peter, armed with texts of presumed high culture, faces off Norman, embracing his guitar, a symbol of popular culture, as they discuss formal education and Norman's failure to go for A-levels. The Apollonian Peter in his relationship with Sylvia differs sharply from the easygoing Dionysian Norman, whose folksongs give the delighted Hilda rapt pleasure and contentment. Sylvia tells Norman about Hilda's fondness for his songs: "You have a fan." Sylvia herself seems far more relaxed with Norman than she does with Peter. Likewise, Hilda is particularly taken with Norman's "Run and fetch the pitcher and get the baby some beer."

Allusions to British literature appear throughout Leigh's films almost as often as his references to and sequences about food. Both serve him well in *Bleak Moments*. Leigh's parallel cutting between Peter and Sylvia at an unusually deserted and unwelcoming Chinese restaurant complete with surly waiter (Ronald Eng) and Pat serving tea to her bedridden mum, who leaves her dentures exposed on the furniture much to her daughter's horror, achieves notable counterpoint. The strained silence of the couple at the restaurant contrasts the mother and daughter shouting match that brings Hilda, the observer of this scene, to tears. The restaurant scene is less dramatic but no less telling, as the only other customer (Reg Stewart) in the establishment consumes his dinner while observing the less-than-ebullient Peter and Sylvia increasingly disengage themselves one from the other. At first they are seated side by side; after Sylvia visits the ladies' room, she returns to the table and sits opposite Peter with her back to the one other patron in the restaurant. Few films have offered up as bland a menu of Chinese cuisine as this one: vegetable curry, boiled rice, chop suey, and sweet and sour rice. This undemonstrative British couple is not yet very far removed from the traditional Sunday joint, two "veg," and potatoes or similar tribute to Britain's traditional food choices that Leigh reflects in many sequences in subsequent films.

Later, over sherry back at her house, Sylvia asks Peter if he would like some nuts and then confesses that she does not have any. The conversation betrays a certain anxiety. Peter obviously is unsure how to deal with Hilda, as he says her name three times and observes that he must learn how to communicate with her. Leigh shows that Hilda is someone Peter patronizes. In a stumbling effort to make conversation, Peter inquires whether Sylvia likes to "watch television or the radio." Sylvia with wry mockery responds that she finds watching the radio easier. Carney develops persuasive contrasts between Peter and Sylvia on the matter of humor wherein he equates the woman's comic tone with that of Mike Leigh (48):

> For a character like Sylvia (or for the viewer) to be able to see the wacky humor in a situation (rather than being offended, wounded, or morally outraged by it, as Peter invariably is) is to inhabit the same imaginative position that Leigh does as an artist—half-inside the experience, slightly above it yet still in touch with it, emotionally exposed and vulnerable to it but not overwhelmed by it. (49)

Later, as Peter pursues the problems of communication, to the extent of even evoking Marshall McLuhan, Sylvia counters his claims about conversational gambits by arguing that such devices are rarely of much use: "They seem evasions." Leigh suggests a passionate and emotional, even erotic, however deeply repressed, subtext beneath the vacuous meaninglessness of the couple's conversation, but as a filmmaker he does not pretend to see into his characters' inner depths. His characters present the same opaque surface viewers experience with real people. At the same time, Leigh's dramatic realism stirs viewers' associations of physical and emotional experiences rather than ideological ones so that we share almost physically through identification with these characters their painful sensations and embarrassment.

Subsequently Sylvia notes that she was just saying something to him in her head that was quite amusing : "I was imagining you without your trousers. Take your trousers off." She follows up this observation with a further serious question, "Would we ever get around to touching each other?" With a low-angle shot the camera records Peter's slow rising from his seated position, giving focus to his lower body as the extension of his masculine self into potentially sexual space. He comes toward her; she rests her head on his chest. He slowly raises her head to face her in a not quite realized kiss on the mouth. He elects not to stay for coffee, but Leigh frames Sylvia in the kitchen through the serving hatch that separates the kitchen from the dining room as she prepares additional coffee. Paul Clements in *The Improvised Play* reports that this "tortuous love scene in which Peter and Sylvia fail to connect was based on fourteen similar occasions in the pre-rehearsals including one in which they had sex" (52).

Leigh's use of the frame within a frame as well as framing with mirrors in this film conveys a sense of erotic loneliness and underscores the detachment of his female characters from the desired world of romantic connection. They serve almost as visual restraints, reflecting the psychological check the women impose on themselves. Similarly, the situation of a character surveying the limits of her life from a room with a single window has obvious symbolic import, suggesting a deterministic, even fatalistic, lack of choice. Leigh's chosen and limited *mise-en-scène* reveals his characters' situation spatially, in depth, rather than through more traditional linear progression of overt action. This sequence captures the nuances and banalities of common speech but also, as is common in Leigh's films, the unspoken, the dialogue of dreams, longings, and intimations that people fail to utter, often even to themselves. Anne Raitt with her watchful waiting brings the viewer to accept a human being of enormous submerged depths and desires without seeming to act a character. That his actors are frequently filmed behind objects further suggests how emotionally introverted and reclusive Leigh's characters are. At her job, Sylvia is filmed behind her typewriter in numerous shots, and Norman is typically seen behind his guitar.

The only time Leigh ever created a storyboard was for a sequence in *Bleak Moments* when the principal characters appear for tea, and nobody talks, and the director performs a series of close-ups. He describes what he did in Stephen Lowenstein's volume:

> They're all looking at each other and twitching and it goes into absolute catatonia. We took off the blimp so the eye-line was clear and you really hear the camera motor.... I storyboarded for that sequence, yes, but normally I don't do it. My working method is to run the action and then talk with the cinematographer and go through it and make decisions and try bits and plan the shots. (151)

During this sequence Leigh expressed pleasure in his arrangement of Pat and Peter on either side of the kitchen hatch, which some of his collaborators objected to because the characters were both at the edge of the frame looking in opposite directions. Leigh liked the significance of the tension created thereby, as he reported to Lowenstein (151). Shot composition often emphasizes a character's detachment from others. Pat, feeling alone and ignored, is seen from slightly below; she's juxtaposed with Sylvia, Hilda, and Norman clumped together, seen from slightly above. Peter sits reclining with one knee crossed over the other, pointed toward the camera. The exterior scenes function in much the same way. The camera does not follow Sylvia on her way to work but rather shows only the intersection she passes through and lets her walk out of sight.

Sylvia demonstrates her unease with cigarettes and frequent nips of alcohol. Her topping off Peter's sherry anticipates Beverly's obsession with this maneuver in the future *Abigail's Party*, another film adaptation of a Leigh playscript but essentially a film transfer of a stage version. The exterior shots in *Bleak Moments* may offer an alternative to the claustrophobic interior tale; however, Tulse Hill outside the house appears other than comforting. The distancing deep focus of the opening sequence where Sylvia meets Peter as they appear to go off to their respective workplaces and talk briefly in inaudible dialogue anticipates their final detachment from each other at the end of the film. Leigh returns to this species of street scene in numerous later films, and, retrospectively, the setting in this initial work becomes evocatively familiar in his world. In the film's interior decor, the Japanese print on the wall may subliminally point to Ozu, the Japanese master Leigh venerates and to whom he has been compared on occasion. The low-angle shots Leigh often favors in *Bleak Moments* as well as parallel actions and the creative use of silence and void may amount to a kind of homage to Ozu with his exquisitely rendered emotional truth.

The physical intimacy between the sisters as Sylvia combs Hilda's hair and dries her after a bath affords moments of something other than bleakness. At the end of the film Sylvia gives a rendition of "Two old ladies caught in the lavatory" to her and Hilda's amusement. The two women share a united relationship that no outsider except possibly the spaced-out Norman can appreciate. Peter is clearly uneasy about Sylvia's sibling, and Pat cannot understand why Sylvia will not permit her to take Hilda to a faith healer.

Some moments in this film seem reminiscent of Arthur Penn's *The Miracle Worker* (1962) in its portrayal of the relationship between Helen Keller and Annie Sullivan. One remarkable sequence finds Hilda in her bath with her yellow rubber duck. She is prone in the tub, sucking in and spewing out water, most contentedly. Leigh has an affinity for characters like Hilda, and Sarah Stephenson sets a standard for such portrayals, which subsequent performers in Leigh's films meet but do not surpass.

It is doubtless nothing more than a coincidence in 1971 amid the craze of the mini-skirt that Leigh invests women's knees with erotic content in his own way, if not to the extent Eric Rohmer does in the same year with *Claire's Knee.* He contrasts on several occasions the well-turned, stocking-covered knees of Sylvia with Hilda's less attractive bare knees. With the often dimly lit backgrounds and the dark dresses Sylvia wears, the film's lighting emphasizes the attractive skin tones of Sylvia's face and legs in a number of key setups. This detail contrasts with the unflattering effects of Leigh's highly naturalistic lighting, which often makes the actors look tired, old, and homely. At times, Sylvia's luminous face appears almost to be floating in a pool of darkness. As Carney asserts, "Leigh's presentation in all of his work is radically *embodied*" (53).

A typically digressive Leigh sequence takes place late in the film when Peter is found in the teachers' lounge of his comprehensive school and a fellow teacher (Susan Glanville), an attractive woman, seeks his collaboration on what she terms the humor project. She wants students to analyze why they laugh and to categorize jokes. Peter, as usual, seems perplexed by this query and fails to be forthcoming. Throughout *Bleak Moments*, Peter has been a comedian who did not know he was funny, as Leigh hints with this fillip. Mike Leigh's films develop what I call the Bergsonian approach to comedy, from Henri Bergson's study of laughter arising from a too-mechanical response to the challenges and vagaries of existence. Both Peter and Pat become laughable as well as somewhat pitiable insofar as their self-imposed rigidity prevents their accepting new life possibilities or full expression of their own personalities. Perhaps their tragedy is that they are capable only of comedy. The tragicomic nature of the whole film becomes recapitulated here with the uncomprehending Peter, for whom life is a conundrum of self-consciousness.

Peter and Sylvia meet by accident for the last time outside the public library, where Sylvia remarks obliquely to Hilda that it's "just like Romeo and Juliet all over again, isn't it, Hilda?" Peter again registers nothing like a shock of recognition about his failed relationship with Sylvia. Norman, the wandering minstrel, suddenly vacates the garage at the back of the sisters' home; Hilda presses her face against the rear window of the departing van, and Pat has another bout of hysterics when queried about her mother before taking Hilda off to the pictures. Sylvia has been endeavoring to play a Chopin nocturne, the same composition used with the titles at the beginning of the film, but after her sister and Pat leave, she bangs out a one-finger rendition of "Freight Train," in commemoration of the departing Norman. Sylvia's Chopin and Mike Bradwell's arrangements of folk songs are the only music in *Bleak Moments*, but the effect puts one in mind of the orchestra and Chebutykin's "Tarara-boom-dee-ay" at the close of Chekhov's *The Three Sisters*. Leigh commented to Lowenstein about the absence of a score for this film:

> I had this notion that not having music would somehow be purer and actually that made some sense. Though now when I think back to it, you think, well, actually the right music would have been rather interesting for it. But it was a kind of philosophy at that time to make a film where the action came without any vinaigrette. (155)

The intricacies and failures of the human relationships in the film yielded something other than unrelieved bleakness. It progresses from realism to a special quality of lyricism without dependence on illusion. Sylvia produces a melody that in its own way is surprisingly far reaching and sustains her without recourse to escapist movies that her sister and Pat require. She manifests a measure of bravery and self-reliance that echoes Chekhov's sisters without imitating them. Unlike Peter and Pat, Sylvia has more independence and a relaxed will similar to Norman's. This is captured in Sylvia's still moment at the end. It is replete with emotion, not exactly specified but almost palpable. Skeptical humanism is no enemy of positive values or even of resolute action, as Leigh suggests through Sylvia at the end of this resonant film. If, as it is said, Russians theatergoers attend productions of Chekhov's play as if visiting the three sisters themselves, *Bleak Moments* likewise almost demands re-visitation and re-visioning for full appreciation of Leigh's delicate humane understanding of people simply living with their moments. As one of my students wrote after viewing it: "The thing that struck me most about this film was the feeling I got when watching it. I felt as awkward and uncomfortable as the characters, which helped me empathize with them more."

Leigh discussed with Lowenstein the difficulty of making this film, and his comments reveal some fundamentals of his storytelling and filmmaking applicable to all that has followed in his distinguished career:

> ...you look at it now and you think it's not epic really. Not much happens. But actually it was hugely epic. The camera is placed in a very considered and heightened manner. You could shoot the same subject by getting in there with 16 mm black and white film and doing it hand held and very rough. That's not what this was about. It was very composed and controlled and that made it a very tough operation. (153)

Leigh found his art in characters who are rich and evocative despite their seeming drabness and in details of their lives and how they respond to living. As the foregoing quotation implies, there is something almost epic in such carefully composed intimate experience rather than immense, impressively grandiose and polished delineation, where more may indeed be less in terms of conviction and credibility.

In filmmakers of the stature of Ozu or Olmi, Mike Leigh found touchstones for the kind of films he wished to make, as evidenced by Ray Pride in his "The Leigh Way" in Movshovitz. Pride quotes from an essay by the filmmaker about Ermanno Olmi's *Tree of Wooden Clogs* (1978):

> This remarkable and wonderful film, which I love deeply, is one of the few true epics... This masterpiece succeeds effortlessly and with monumental simplicity in getting to the essence of the human experience. Directly, objectively, yet compassionately, it puts on the screen the great, hard, real experience of living and surviving from day to day, and from year to year, the experience of ordinary people everywhere. (112)

In this first theatrical release, Leigh brought his own English art from the ballast of real life to a film of genuine emotional resonance and intelligence.

High Hopes

After eighteen years, during which Leigh refined his method of creation in a series of accomplished films for television, the director returned to theatrical features in 1988 with *High Hopes*, which won the International Critics Prize at the Venice Film Festival. Appropriately, in light of his extensive television work, this film was partly financed by Channel 4. It became something of a breakout work in Leigh's career as far as the interest and enthusiasm it garnered from an appreciative coterie worldwide and particularly in the United States, where leading critics proclaimed Leigh a major world-class director on the strength of this film. Unlike the credits on his television films until the 18-minute long *The Short and Curlies* in 1987, this theatrical release had on the opening credits, "written and directed by Mike Leigh" rather than "devised and directed."

Figure 1. Shirley (Ruth Sheen) and Cyril (Philip Davis) at Karl Marx's Tomb in Highgate Cemetery from *High Hopes*. (Courtesy Jerry Ohlinger Archives)

The film was generated by Leigh's own feeling of inertia in the midst of Margaret Thatcher's revolution in Britain, but, as usual in Leigh's films, its point is not primarily political. The filmmaker commented to Jay Carr in the Movshovitz collection that "*High Hopes* was on one level a lamentation for socialism being something that maybe has gotten lost somehow" (56). The prime minister herself is alluded to through a cactus named for her described as "a pain in the ass" and in a poster, featuring a waving Mrs. Thatcher on two panels, with the caption "Crime Wave." Cyril's (Philip Davis) and Shirley's (Ruth Sheen) activist leftist friend, Suzi (Judith Scott), charges Thatcher directly but only refers to her with a pronoun: "She's taking away the basic right of the working class. I mean, you look at what she's doing to the unions." Cyril, then, berates Suzi for aspiring to be a capitalist with her jewelry-making business: "One minute she's talking about revolutionary Socialism, the next she's starting a business. Think." Cyril, in his nascent ideology, resists working-class reformist attitudes and policies in favor of radical, revolutionary ones. Leigh illuminates the division between rising yuppies and nostalgic socialists in the course of *High Hopes* among other details of class and society in Thatcher's England through the perspective of three couples in modern London.

Cyril and Shirley, leftists and unmarried but much in love, smoke grass and live on the edge of poverty while he works as a motorcycle messenger and she is employed with a grounds crew for public works, planting trees and other horticultural pursuits. If one continues thinking of Leigh as a latter-day Chekhov, inevitably associations arise linking the tree-planting Shirley and Astrov's avocation in *Uncle Vanya*. This vocation for Shirley contributes to her potential "earth-mother" role, which she reveals by her nurturing behavior toward others throughout the film and in her desire to have a child despite Cyril's reluctance to father one in such an imperfect world. Cyril's sister, Valerie (Heather Tobias), lives in an upscale neighborhood of detached houses with an unfaithful husband, Martin Burke (Philip Jackson), who as a beneficiary of Thatcher's new "enterprise culture" owns a used-car lot, and a hamburger joint, and drives a Mercedes. The mother of these antagonistic and combative siblings, the aging and increasingly senile Mrs. Bender (Edna Doré), lives in solitude in the last council flat on a street that has undergone considerable recent gentrification. For example, the embittered old lady's neighbors are the insufferably haughty wine-merchant and his opera-loving wife, Rupert (David Bamber) and Laetitia Boothe-Braine (Lesley Manville).

To Shirley's speculation that old Mrs. Bender, Cyril's mum, voted Tory in the last election, Cyril affirms the correctness of his girlfriend's surmise,

"Working-class Tories, stabbing themselves in the back." Rather than the Brontës as allusion in *Bleak Moments,* another author from the nineteenth century receives recognition in *High Hopes*, namely, Karl Marx. Cyril stands before Marx's grave in Highgate Cemetery and says, as printed in the published screenplay, that "What'e done was, 'e wrote down the truth: people was bein' exploited. Industrial Revolution. They was forced off the land into the factories. There weren't no working class before then. He set down a programme for change" (231). Through Cyril, Leigh seems to suggest that the moral and social judgments of ordinary people are necessary for good political decisions. To Cyril, capitalism produces an unjust society, in which economic values drive out human values. Greed and consumerism prevail at the expense of spiritual wholeness and human relationships. The unrelenting pursuit of profits undermines familial and communal bonds; therefore, capitalism debases human morality by corrupting the rich and brutalizing the poor.

Cyril shows himself an opponent of the free-rein market economy of the Thatcher era and demonstrates at least an acquaintance with *The Communist Manifesto*. Like Marx himself, Cyril may be weakest in his political theory, his conception of political human beings, and the political state, yet he is consistent when he tells Shirley that he wants everyone to have enough to eat and places to live and "then you 'ave babies." He is concerned with what makes a society just. Shirley, the realist, demonstrates her love for Cyril even as she acknowledges "the world ain't never goin' to be perfect." Indeed, within Cyril's own family, the proletariat itself appears as a Marxian myth for his sibling, Valerie, through her entrepreneurial husband, has become a member, albeit with special vulgarity, of the bourgeoisie. It is Ray Carney's contention that Marxism "represents a fundamentally different understanding of experience than the one Leigh offers" because, unlike Leigh, "Marx believed that the most important aspects of life would yield to a totalizing, impersonal, and systematic analysis" (201). In contrast, Carney summarizes the particular effect of Leigh's films:

> But the greatest difference from the Marxist position is that, in scene after scene, moment after moment, *High Hopes* asks us to acknowledge the absolutely overwhelming importance of butterfly flutters of feeling and thought, of private inward turnings and meditative moments of mind that will never be made part of an ideological system of understanding or control. In this sense, the entire film might be said to be Leigh's meditation on the limitations of political understanding of experience. (202)

Roger Pratt's photography of Ruth Sheen does not reduce her malocclusion or provide her with a chin. However, with equal attention to her hair and fine eyes to complement her accomplished portrayal, the camera allows Shirley to achieve a rare kind of natural beauty, which contrasts with the carefully constructed appearance of the equally brilliant Lesley Manville in her portrayal of Laetitia Boothe-Braine. Manville's multiple roles for Leigh exemplify the range of characterization he is able to achieve with talented contributors in a variety of films; she validates her different characters superbly in every appearance she makes in a Mike Leigh film. Manville is the embodiment of his successful working method although other performers from his ensemble are surely as versatile and adaptable as she is. Her character in *High Hopes* is especially memorable, if perhaps less plausibly a real person than is usually the case in Leigh, and an extremely entertaining caricature. She is like a latter-day Dame Edith Evans as Lady Bracknell in John Gielgud's stage production and Anthony Asquith's 1952 screen version of Oscar Wilde's *The Importance of Being Earnest*.

The interaction of Mrs. Bender and Laetitia when the old lady seeks help in getting back into her house after she forgot her keys provides a poignant comic scene nearly unrivaled in British cinema. Confronted on the steps as she returns from a shopping trip to Harrods, Mrs. Boothe-Braine most reluctantly admits her aged neighbor to phone one of her children. Laetitia will not permit Mrs. Bender to bring her grocery cart into the house and advises the old woman to "chop-chop!" as her aged neighbor slowly ascends the front stairs. The two women have a conversation while waiting for Mrs. Bender's deliverance from her yuppie neighbor. Laetitia suggests the great desirability of Mrs. Bender's "buying…a nice little modern granny-flat." In a wonderful exchange of verbal ambiguity, Mrs. Boothe-Braine asks whether Mrs. Bender has all her original features. She means, of course, things like cornices and fireplaces. Unbeknown to her, Mrs. Bender's house remains a council property, that is, housing for the poor. Gentrified owners of adjacent properties may not want to recall that fact. Undeterred by this announcement, however, Laetitia Boothe-Braine continues, as the published screenplay expresses it: "Oh? Well, mercifully, you people do have the opportunity to purchase your council property nowadays. I'd snap it up if I were you. Then, of course, one resells" (212).

Throughout this dialogue in the kitchen, Leigh has a tape playing quietly in another room a trio from Mozart's *Cosi Fan Tutte*, "Soave Sia Il Vento." In Da Ponte's libretto for the opera, this passage supplicates for gentle winds, calm waves, and all the elements responding benignly to human wishes. It's an ironic contrast to Mrs. Bender's worsening circumstances. On the other hand, if Mozart is the most stylistically and technically exacting of composers, the trio is analogous in a way to Mrs. Boothe-Braine, who reveals a certain fondness for the eighteenth-century master. Intertextually, this same Mozart passage was used extensively in John Schlesinger's sophisticated and stylish *Sunday Bloody Sunday* (1971) released the same year as Leigh's *Bleak Moments*, which in some quietist respects it slightly resembled. Whether or not Leigh intended any possible reference, Mozart as emblem of culture and restraint enters the context of *High Hopes* as a teasing and suggestive presence. Mrs. Boothe-Braine consistently patronizes and ridicules her elderly neighbor, delaying showing her the lavatory after she has heard Mrs. Bender's rather urgent request and making remarks like "We are an old scatterbrain today, aren't we?"

Valerie at last shows up, appareled in a too-fancy red dress that contrasts markedly with Laetitia's understated red dress and black accents to complement her black hat with a pronounced reddish ornament. These are all testimony to the superior costume work done by Leigh's long-term costume designer (and future Oscar-winner for another Leigh film), Lindy Hemming. Valerie observes to Laetitia, "It's amazing what you can do with a slum, isn't it?" In the same vein, after she has wormed her way into Rupert's study, Valerie calls to Mrs. Bender, "Oh! Look what they've done to your coal-hole, Mum!" Shortly thereafter, Cyril reappears to salvage his mother whom he fears has been hurt and receives the following response from Rupert (David Bamber): "Now, look here. I really have no idea where your mother is. Whom she may be, or indeed whether you have one." To which Cyril replies "You wanna a fat lip?" and Rupert rejoins "Now…what made this country great was a place for everyone and everyone in his place. And this is my place" (221). Cyril, later, will imitate and mock Rupert's sentiment and delivery of the line in conversation with Shirley.

Leigh provides three parallel bedroom scenes of the Boothe-Braines, Valerie and Martin, and Cyril and Shirley the night after the incident in Mrs. Bender's neighborhood. These provocative sequences become a gauge to morale and value as a means of assessing the several couples. In their bedroom, after the Boothe-Braines have attended *The Marriage of Figaro* at Covent Garden, Laetitia sings in English "Voce Sapete" while vainly trying to enlighten her confused husband on the vocal registers of the women he has just heard in that Mozart opera. The drunken Rupert thinks the aria his wife is singing is a "bloody awful hymn." Their bedroom sequence ends with Laetitia avoiding her husband's cold hands and rejoicing: "I thank God every day I've been blessed with such beautiful skin. You really are a very lucky boy. You take me for granted" (228). There is little forgiving warmth of Mozartian comedy in this bedroom.

Valerie and Martin are discovered bickering over who is to initiate sexual overtures. Valerie wants her husband to be Michael Douglas, whom Martin fails to recognize as Mr. Boothe-Braine failed to identify Mozart. Valerie, still determined to pursue her erotic fantasy, avers she is a virgin to which Martin roars with laughter, turning away from her, and succumbs to a coughing spasm. This sequence parallels an earlier one of sexual game-playing between the Boothe-Braines, where Laetitia, sitting on the stairs in her underwear, speaks as "Mr. Sausage," inviting her husband to come and get her. He quickly disrobes, runs up the stairs, jumps on her, while she declares "jolly good" and roars with laughter as their legs intertwine. Leigh himself has said of the Boothe-Braines in the interview with Graham Fuller, "Mike Leigh's Original Features," that they "are only unsympathetic in their disregard of the old lady, Mrs. Bender. When you see them in their private world, being vulnerable, having feelings, having sex, sending each other up, they are perfectly sympathetic. I try to show people in a rounded way, in a layered way" (xxiii).

Finally, Leigh shows us Cyril's and Shirley's bedroom as Shirley takes off her lover's boots as if the scene were in an American Western. When Cyril and Shirley, after she plays "this little piggy" with his toes, move on to "unzip a banana" and ultimately to sexual intimacy in this sequence, she expresses a desire not to use contraception, and this leads to a discussion of families and their effect on offspring. Unlike the damage caused by Cyril's family on him, Shirley insists that her family "didn't fuck me up," perhaps a nod to Philip Larkin on Leigh's part. Although Cyril argues that families are out of date and "two's company," this sequence ends with warmth and mutuality, intimating that an act of conception may not be too distant in the future. Cyril and Shirley are learning how to be actors in a biological process, which contrasts with the other more self-absorbed couples in *High Hopes*; they are learning to think with emotion, a condition frequently endorsed in Leigh films. They are not cut off from natural growth like the Boothe-Braines or Valerie and Martin. What Leigh sees is how the qualities that save us in one way have the power to destroy us in another, and consequently he often deals in doubles, pairings, and parallel contrasts. So while we identify with Cyril and Shirley as the most compassionate characters in *High Hopes*, who transcend the limitations of materialism and pride in possessions demonstrated by the other couples, Leigh does not wholly excuse their lack of ambition and their reliance on hashish. Nevertheless, this couple act far less in a moral vacuum as parallel to and reflective of the market economy espoused by the film's other couples.

In *High Hopes* Leigh creates an odd, but wonderful, mixture of sentiment and irony, which, operating in tandem, produce a further extension of the doubleness so often featured in his films. Leigh does not permit his impulse toward satiric exaggeration to overwhelm the bounds of verisimilitude. An especially endearing sequence that crystallizes Leigh's mixture of sentiment and irony is the departure by bus back to Surrey on the part of Wayne (Jason Watkins), the lost innocent whom Cyril and Shirley befriended in the beginning of the film only to have him ineluctably reappear. Leigh shows Wayne looking out the back of the bus, and Shirley concludes the young man reminds her of "E.T." Earlier, after she had bid goodnight to Wayne in his sleeping bag, she expressed to Cyril her hope that she not have "a kid that's a bit thick."

What finally distinguishes Cyril and Shirley from the other couples is their human capacity to love anything and each other, an irrepressible Eros that eludes Peter and Sylvia in *Bleak Moments* despite intimations of such a capacity on the part of Sylvia. Cyril and Shirley have acquired an inclination, desire, and ability to consider people for the qualities they possess and to react emotionally to those qualities, whether in the aimless and lost Wayne or the equally vulnerable Mrs. Bender. Such attributes anticipate the virtues and traits that will enable them to become loving parents and compassionate caregivers to an elderly mother. Leigh posits these principles against other characters' blatant acquisitiveness, exhibited, for example, by Cyril's brother-in-law, Martin, whom Cyril terms "the jerk in the Merc."

The last set piece in *High Hopes* is the birthday party Valerie hosts to celebrate herself and her affluence rather more than her mother's seventieth birthday. Leigh often brings people together for family reunions and festivals with mixed results that stand in sharp contrast to the companionship and love commemorated by greeting cards. Notable instances of these troubling affairs are demonstrated, for example, by this film and the later *Secrets & Lies* (1996). For this gathering, Mrs. Bender is picked up by her son-in-law, although earlier in the film when the invitation was extended to the old lady, Valerie promised her mother that she would chauffeur her. On the way to the family gathering, Martin leaves his mother-in-law in the Mercedes while he pays a quick visit to his unnamed mistress (Cheryl Prime). Despite Martin's self-proclaimed arousal, a sexual episode does not take place except for her submitting to a bruising forced kiss. Interestingly enough, Martin does ask her if she has seen her kids, and the woman responds, "No…ain't seen neither of 'em since before Christmas." This detail from Martin seems somewhat out of character, but it does reinforce the parent question underlying much of the film.

Valerie's attire for this family party parodies Laetitia Boothe-Braine's dress in the earlier episode of the lost keys, even to a vulgarized version of her hat. Leigh brings an artist's eye to such material details of costume and décor. Shirley and Cyril seem ill at ease in Valerie's house; "We're detached!" announces Valerie to her brother, who cryptically replies "Are you?" Immediately thereafter Shirley notes the incorrect placement of chess pieces on the ornate set, to which Valerie insists, "Look. I like it like that, all right?" Similar sequences of sibling tension are familiar in Leigh's films from *Meantime* to *Secrets & Lies* and *All or Nothing.*

Mrs. Bender appears her usual bewildered self in this setting. She rejects both sherry and champagne for a cup of tea much to Valerie's disgust. Valerie observes that her mother spoils everything and manifests far more affection toward her dog, which she calls Baby, than to her mother. Cyril's sister ridicules his gift of the shawl to Mrs. Bender, but she discovers her mother did not receive her present and mutters "Typical Harrods!" to which Martin retorts, "Why don't you shut your gob?" John Hill in *British Cinema in the 1980's* goes so far as to claim that "Martin's disdain for Valerie is shared by the film and, thus, runs perilously close to colluding with his behaviour towards her" (194).

This "happy" occasion deteriorates into increasing acrimony and chaos. Leigh tracks in slowly on the sleeping Mrs. Bender at the table and holds on her for the entire scene, as we only hear the others in their intense squabbling. We see Valerie's arm and hand as she tries to force-feed birthday cake to her resisting mother. Brother and sister accuse each other of addictions, Cyril to drugs and Valerie to alcohol. In the course of this unseen action but audible dialogue accompanied by evocative musical score, Valerie accuses her brother of preventing their mother from buying her house. He replies that Valerie wanted to purchase the house only to make a huge profit after Mrs. Bender's demise: "you think of no one but yourself!" (253). As the published screenplay directs for this memorable sequence, "*we remain close on* Mrs. Bender *and her thoughts and memories, sad, alone and confused*" (253).

In an earlier scene just prior to the key episode with her neighbors, Leigh similarly focused on Mrs. Bender slowly making her way down a busy city street. The open form of urban life shown slightly out of focus surrounds her as figures pass out of the film frame. These setups reflect Leigh's attempt, as he explained in his interview with Graham Fuller, to find "a shooting style that absolutely investigates the spirit of what is happening" (xxviii). Andrew Dickson's musical score for this street scene with its insistent bass notes likewise captures the increasing tension impinging on Mrs. Bender.

Lest excessive pathos overtake his narrative, Leigh cuts from the dining-room scene of the reflective Mrs. Bender to Valerie staggering upstairs with her champagne bottle and dog. Shirley elects to take the old lady home in a taxi; Cyril leaves on his bike, and we shortly find Valerie, still wearing her hat, drinking from the champagne bottle in a lavish bubble bath while her dog looks on. "Valerie's drunken collapse," notes John Hill, "has clear echoes of a similar scene in *Meantime* when Barbara (Marion Bailey), who also cannot have a child, sits huddled and drunk in the corner of the room she had been planning to redecorate" (198).

Shirley brings Mrs. Bender to the flat she shares with Cyril, where his mum seems to relish the steak and kidney pie they serve her and even expresses satisfaction with the shawl they had given her. In her conversation she returns to her own distant past with remembrances of sibling rivalry between herself and her sister Freda, including a suggestion of possible sexual rivalry with another sister, Rene, over the man who became Cyril's and Valerie's father. The back-story Leigh and his actors created during their prolonged rehearsal period remains in *High Hopes* in such elliptical details. While this penchant continues to be criticized by some viewers, it contributes significantly to the felt life that Leigh's films are famous for. Suddenly exhausted after her long day, Mrs. Bender collapses on the couple's bed before she can be returned to her own home. Cyril and Shirley repair to the spare room and discuss fear of aging and their future parenthood; Cyril declares that from twenty-five to thirty-five are the best years of one's life. This sentiment Leigh will return to later with *Career Girls* (1997). He makes Shirley feel under the covers, and she retrieves a brass banana from Valerie's fruit bowl, which Cyril assures her that he did not steal because "it followed me home." The scene ends with their kissing and cuddling with covers pulled round them. Ray Carney interprets this scene as an "inward voyage of consciousness" for the favored couple in the film: "Cyril and Shirley pursue independent reflective paths, respond to each other's unspoken thoughts, turn on their own premises, criticize themselves, and react to their own statements" (197). Stylistically, as noted earlier, Carney finds a strategic change in the way Leigh uses close-ups and pregnant pauses to denote what he terms "inward turning, far more than events" (198) in the delineation of character consciousness that he thinks distinguishes Leigh's later films from his earlier ones.

After breakfast, the two socialist lovers bring Mrs. Bender up to the roof of their apartment building, where Shirley has a small garden. St. Pancras Station, where Mr. Bender worked, is close by and in the distance, as Cyril points out,

St. Paul's Cathedral "looks like a tit, dunnit?" Finally, he points out to his mother where she lives beyond the gas works, a view that is, as Eric Allen Hatch in Baltimore's *City Paper* observes, "entirely new to her, of her lifelong town" (26). Mrs. Bender with unaccustomed exuberance gives the film's last line, "I said, it's the top of the world." Beside her, Shirley and Cyril stand together, enjoying life, thereby to validate without irony the film's title. To an extent this trio of characters does achieve high hopes at least temporarily. This acknowledgment contrasts with the Thatcheresque high hopes of small business entrepreneurs satirized elsewhere in Leigh's film via Cyril's scorn of Suzi's proposed business and Martin's advice to Cyril that he has "gotta speculate to accumulate." John Hill in *British Cinema in the 1980's* takes a contrarian position:

> . . . *High Hopes* ends up conforming to a conservative ideology of "familiarism" that is little different from that associated with Thatcherism. Moreover, in celebrating the virtues of the privatized family as a kind of escape route from political impotence and passivity, the film, for all its apparent "socialism", appears to end up reinforcing the very scepticism about more collective (or "socialist") forms of political action that was already such a feature of this era. (198)

What distinguishes the progress of *Bleak Moments* to *High Hopes*? Certainly the filmmaker's preference for two-word titles remains unchanged, and his choice of milieu endures. The contrast in the degree of optimism conveyed by the titles is striking, but in Leigh that sort of inference cannot be taken too transparently or unironically. As Cyril and Shirley speak, joke together, and share inner states of being, in effect, self-consciously narrating their lives to each other and to themselves, they effectively invent those lives. The bourgeois characters seem more dependent on received roles and style such as the Ralph Lauren coordinated accessories purveyed to Americans in the early twenty-first century.

This second theatrical release of Leigh's career demonstrates much of what the director/writer had learned during the interim years in television drama. His mastery of comedic nuances and subversions stems from the television work rather than from *Bleak Moments*, but his formal construction and moral force, while perhaps richer in *High Hopes* than elsewhere in his body of films, are readily recognizable and even familiar. Leigh's dialogue in this film goes further to demonstrate that speech is what characters do to each other, even as the filmmaker steadily developed skill in the speed and saltiness of good spoken language. *High Hopes* stands as Leigh's indictment of Thatcher's England presented typically through individual lives and personal relationships. To that extent it became a touchstone in his canon, different in kind perhaps, if not necessarily greater, than *Bleak Moments*. This is the territory Leigh makes his own in presenting what is happening and has happened in England.

The structure of *High Hopes* features for a more deliberate causal approach to narrative that will characterize most of Leigh's subsequent theatrical releases in contrast to the cumulative method irrespective of clear-cut cause and effect in many of his television dramas. David Barker in "'It's Been Real': Forms of Television Representation" has argued that television drama has not adopted very readily the cinema's narrative form that favors linearity and motivational credibility. Like John Fiske and John Hartley whom he cites, Barker suggests that television's structures are often more like those of speech than of writing. Thus, television drama often demonstrates a "logic" that is oral and visual as opposed to the consistency and narrative development from cause to effect found in the classic realist text (48). To be sure, Leigh's collaborative method without an actual script would seem curiously amenable to such television structures in films.

Figure 2. Cyril (Philip Davis) and Shirley (Ruth Sheen) point out London landmarks across from St. Pancras Station to his mother, Mrs. Bender (Edna Doré), the day after her seventieth birthday from *High Hopes*. (Courtesy Jerry Ohlinger Archives)

CHAPTER TWO
Leigh's Television Plays

In "The Middle Age of British Television," published in 1977 in *American Film*, David Thomson observed that "the quality of British television drama does something to make up for, and may be stimulated by, the dearth of a contemporary British cinema" (50). Film, like the British nation itself in the 1970s, was widely believed to be in a chronic state of relative, if not absolute, decline. The prevailing assessment of this time period is that British film industry, as Desson Howe quotes from an unattributed source, "was alive and well and hiding out in television" (Movshovitz 48). Thomson included an impressive catalogue of directors and writers by way of example from the decades before the seventies until 1977. Unfortunately he does not mention Mike Leigh.

Interestingly enough, in the British Film Institute's TV 100 List, published in October 2000 in *Sight and Sound*, two of Leigh's television films for the BBC's "Play for Today"—*Nuts in May* and *Abigail's Party*—films produced and shown in the time period that Thomson covered appear (3/10). Thomson's evaluation of British versus American television is convincing: "British television is subtler than American; it expects more involvement from the audience. Yet, within this island, I am dismayed by the way television seems happy merely to mollify an uneasy people" (50). Thomson continues with an impassioned lament:

> Television is not so much entertainment or information as a habit, perhaps even an alternative to living life to the full. In both Britain and America, I believe, it is to be endured, like poverty or bad weather. We watch its insipid, neurotic flicker and the shriveling of our own sensibility with equal bitterness. (50)

Leigh had already challenged such mollification with *Hard Labour* (1973) as well as *Nuts in May* (1976) and *The Kiss of Death* (1977). He would continue to do so in his wide-ranging series of television films through the mid-eighties before returning to theatrical features with *High Hopes* in 1988. One characteristic that links these television films to his theatrical releases is Leigh's avoidance of easy escapism and a soap-opera declension between good guys and bad guys, which limited character development through predictable and established bounds. It is regrettable that American television audiences did not have an opportunity to see these Leigh films for television during the decade of their release in England. Leonard Quart, in a note for the initial chapter that he contributed to Ray Carney's study of Leigh's films, explains their absence on American broadcast television in the following way: "PBS clearly felt that Leigh's low-budget, idiosyncratic films were unable to provide the literate escape to which an audience looking at handsomely mounted, nostalgic, impersonal works like *Brideshead Revisited* was accustomed" (247). Such high-minded prestige-mongering was not for Mike Leigh, and consequently his television films were unseen in the United States. In fall 2001 the Museum of Television and Radio in New York City included Leigh's *Abigail's Party* along with television films by Stephen Frears, Ken Loach, and Alan Clarke in a retrospective appropriately titled "Disruptive Directors of British Television."

Hard Labour

The innovative producer Tony Garnett, who provided several films a year for the BBC in the early seventies, gave Leigh the opportunity to do his first television film, *Hard Labour* (1973), set and filmed on location in Higher Broughton, a working-class section of Salford, the director's Manchester-based home. The story about a hardworking and aging Roman Catholic cleaning woman is based on an employee of Leigh's family, and consequently the autobiographical material of this film is doubtless greater than usual in his work. Additionally, this film represents the first time Leigh worked with Alison Steadman, who subsequently became his wife and valuable participant in his later projects. The subject matter of older adults seems unusual for a young creator like Leigh, although there are intriguing precedents like the boy wonder John Updike's first novel, *The Poorhouse Fair*, which featured the elderly. Leigh's *Hard Labour*, his first 70-minute television film, complements his first feature film *Bleak Moments* in several ways beyond their rather dour and severe titles, most notably in the sense of lived experience enacted through patient and nuanced detail. Neither film affords much time or occasion for comedy. Yet both embody something real and truthful that escapes being depressing. Both are remarkably mature and complete artistic achievements for such a young filmmaker; however, it will be remembered that Leigh was by this time already a seasoned stage director/writer.

For his protagonist, Mrs. Thornley, Leigh chose Liz Smith, the character actress who played Pat's mother in *Bleak Moments*. Vincent Canby in "Down from Hopeless, to Hilarious" calls her "the great Liz Smith, who has the pointy impassive face of a saint on the façade of Chartres" (C1). This practice of using actors in multiple capacities in Leigh's films would add distinction to many actors' careers and that of the filmmaker because of the quantity and quality of their work. Smith's collaboration with Mike Leigh, for example, resulted in her becoming a beloved and recognized featured player in a variety of films and television series after *Hard Labour*.

The Thornleys, husband and wife, are used to hard labor. He works as a night watchman, a job Leigh himself held briefly early in his life and to which he returns later with a character in *Naked* (1993). The film opens with Jim Thornley (Clifford Kershaw) returning home after a night of work at a toy warehouse with evocative high-angle shots over the labyrinth of Salford back-to-backs. In the interior of their house, Mrs.Thornley raps her broom handle on the ceiling to awaken their adult daughter, Ann (Polly Hemingway), who still lives with her parents. Ann and her parents have a largely silent breakfast, but she does bid good-bye to her mother.

Mrs. Thornley runs a hand sweeper and asks her disagreeable husband to raise his legs so that she can clean under him. Leigh focuses on legs and feet in this brief sequence to suggest fragmentation and disengagement among characters as he will with the same device in later films. Mrs. Thornley, then, goes to her for-hire domestic work for Mrs. Stone (Vanessa Harris). "The scenes in the Stones' house," Coveney explains, "were shot in a house (on the brink of demolition) just two doors along from where the Leighs had lived in Cavendish Road" (53). Here Mr. Stone (Cyril Varley) unexpectedly returns home in the middle of the day, much to his wife's dismay, because he has forgotten a patent book. Mrs. Stone's response to her husband is every bit as complaining and bereft of civility as Mr. Thornley's usual discourse with his wife.

This shared tone denies any significant difference based on class in such husband-wife exchanges except the Stones seem more equally matched in their complaints. In contrast, Mrs. Thornley suffers in silence before her husband, and her depression, which viewers hear articulated as religious guilt at the end of the film, may well be the anger she feels toward him turned inward. Her lack of verbal expression becomes almost unbearable in the face of the negligent and indifferent treatment she receives from nearly everyone in the film from her employer, husband, and children to finally her priest. Leigh spares Mrs.

Thornley the tics and mannerisms that are often associated with other lonely and pitiable characters in a number of his films.

One of the most disturbing sequences in *Hard Labour* occurs when Mr. Thornley comes home from a pub on a Saturday night and imposes himself sexually upon his seemingly sleeping wife, whose body he pushes and shoves as if she were a rag doll. Mr. Thornley tosses his wife's hot water bottle out of the bed and forcibly turns her over on her back as he growls "Come on" and other less intelligible inducements. Earlier in the pub Mr. Thornley has been advising a younger companion to marry so that he would not return home to a "stone cold bed." Leigh then provides a scene of the Thornleys' connubial bed that appears far from wedded bliss. Equally repellent in an almost physical way is a brief sequence where Mr. Thornley has his wife massage liniment into his arthritic shoulder, and his hairy back temporarily dominates the screen.

Ray Carney provides a telling anecdote and perceptive inference about his students' reactions to the liniment scene after he has shown *Hard Labour* in his Boston University film classes:

> Students who sit impassively through a slasher movie cringe, squirm, and squeal in disbelief at Leigh's scene. The physicality of the moment disconcerts them precisely because it refuses to be intellectualized. It would be so much easier if it functioned metaphorically or abstractly. It would be "about" something. It would be thinkable. It would be safe. (56)

Leigh's recognition of physical needs includes the frequency of visits to and flushing of toilets in *Hard Labour* and elsewhere throughout his canon. Similarly, with respect to the physical (and another sense of labor), Mrs. Thornley and Ann, her daughter, discuss pregnancy and childbirth. Without her mother's knowing the reason for Ann's interest, the young woman thinks about Julie (Linda Beckett), her friend who has become pregnant by her married boyfriend and undergoes an abortion in the course of the film. Mrs. Thornley informs her daughter that "you have to suffer to bring children into the world." Her daughter seems shocked to learn that her mother was in labor for two days prior to her own birth and in twenty-four-hour labor with the birth of Edward, Ann's older brother. She plays with the wedding photograph of Edward during this conversation while her mother dusts.

When Mrs. Thornley visits her auto-mechanic son Edward (Bernard Hill) and his wife Veronica (Alison Steadman) in their new housing estate (more upscale than the residence of Edward's parents if not so posh as the area where the Stones reside), Leigh begins a pattern frequently replayed in his later films. These journeys between material spheres serve as reflections of character as much as demonstrations of taste in Leigh. Steadman's Veronica embodies the attributes of the controlling woman who will loom so large and fierce in *Abigail's Party*. Here she demonstrates care in her preparations for tea, complains about her husband to her mother-in-law, and registers the same exasperation as Mrs. Stone does about the length of time their respective husbands spend in the bathroom. She nags Edward about chewing his fingernails and putting his elbows on the table. Despite all evidence to the contrary in her neighborhood, Veronica expresses pleasure in the fact that "every house is just a bit individual," although significant variations are hard to recognize.

In this film pioneering Mike Leigh deliberately, without flash, gives a matter-of-fact portrayal of the emerging multicultural and multiracial society in the post-imperial world of the late twentieth century and celebrates before most other English filmmakers the mixed-race nation that Britain is increasingly becoming. Mrs. Thornley, for example, helps a Sikh woman who cannot quite comprehend which English coins to use in a laundromat. Barry (Alan Erasmus), Edward's co-worker in his auto-repair business, is West Indian. Furthermore, as Ann's boyfriend, the Pakistani cabdriver Naseem (Ben Kingsley) is the most sensitive man in the film in his dealings with the woman he cares about.

This couple's sequence in the taxi office as they wait to hear how Julie has come through the procedure to terminate her pregnancy is the most delicately conceived in the film. They are subordinate characters in the narrative, but Leigh invests them with surpassing decency and affection. "Know what it reminds me of?" Ann asks Naseem. "Torture," she answers and then adds "I hope it never happens to me." In halting English, Naseem explains why she is a different kind of girl who has someone who cares about her. The edgy Ann by way of response to Naseem's declaration smiles for once in the film and looks contented.

Throughout the film Mr. Thornley bickers with his daughter about church attendance; she counters by charging him with equal neglect of such duties. Richard Corliss, in an overview on Mike Leigh in his *Time* review of *Secrets & Lies*, observes about *Hard Labour* that "even the nun to whom the saintly lead character offers charity is snarky and ungrateful" (67). The only member of the family seen in church for confession is Mrs. Thornley at the film's close. Shown in fairly tight profile but with the camera far enough back to include her hands clasped together in supplication, Mrs. Thornley, two weeks since her last confession, displays no emotion apart from a definite hesitancy in speech, and confesses to the priest: "I just don't love people enough." Considering how much of Leigh's film is given over to showing how Mrs. Thornley generously and unstintingly meets the needs and expectations of others, this remark comes as a revelation of paradox. She continues by explaining: "It's my husband; I don't love him." Leigh expects his viewers to remember the earlier bed and liniment sequence, as Mrs. Thornley further qualifies: "I don't like to touch him when he wants me to do something for him." She does not answer when the priest asks her if she has spoken to her husband about these thoughts. She does affirm her guilt when the priest asks her: "Did you feel guilty?" He recommends praying to God for help in these matters, encourages her to make a good contrition, assigns penance of "Five Hail Marys, one Our Father and one Glory Be" and absolves her. His final request to Mrs. Thornley is for her to pray for him. She readily responds, "I will."

The priest resumes reading his newspaper with the banner headline on the back facing the camera elliptically and ironically referring to "the love of my life." While the closing credits roll, Mrs. Thornley is seen back at Mrs. Stone's house polishing a window. Her labor on behalf of transparency has been duplicated by Leigh's film, since viewers now have, as it were, a clearer window on the soul of Mrs. Thornley to augment any comprehension gained throughout the film as to the externalities of her daily life.

Leigh shows himself at the end of *Hard Labour* and his earlier first feature film, *Bleak Moments,* as the consummate realist filmmaker, unsentimental in his sympathy for his deprived characters but combining elements of comedy with fundamental seriousness. Unlike in his later films, he pays scant address to comic possibilities or comic relief in the portrayal of these bleak and hard lives. He shortly will redress that emphasis in his television films, bringing to that medium what he had been pursuing in his stage work during the seventies and into the eighties, that is, social comedy and satire on social pretensions. Nevertheless, Leigh will remain capable of sympathy even while seeing the ironical and satiric implications in character and situation.

His effective drama, as with his satire, requires the same levelheadedness soberly demonstrated in *Bleak Moments* and *Hard Labour.* He does not consort with rage, notwithstanding close proximity to it. Comedy lets him seize further latent possibilities in familiar things. Leigh's new leavening ingredient of laughter mixed with his continued clear-sighted perception of dysfunctional relationships compounded by misguided social mores permits a wider range of tone in later films than was achieved in these initial distinctive, if rather severe and monochromatic, efforts.

Nuts in May

In the last five years of the seventies, Leigh devised and directed two perennial favorite television films, both featuring his wife, the talented and versatile Alison Steadman: *Nuts in May* (1976) and *Abigail's Party* (1977), which were two major works for the BBC's "Play for Today" series. On the BFI TV list of top 100 titles, these two Leigh features came in at #49 and #11, respectively. *Nuts in May* is very loosely based on a Leigh play, *Wholesome Glory*, performed at the Theatre Upstairs of London's Royal Court during 1973. Although the action of the play is confined to a bed-sit, Leigh's film takes the characters in their Morris Minor convertible on a camping holiday near Corfe Castle in Dorset, using exterior settings almost exclusively except for brief claustrophobic scenes inside small tents and a short pub scene. The pleasure and appeal of *Nuts in May* seem solidly within the expectations of superior television situation comedy. Ray Carney makes something far more portentous out of this material with what he considers its exploration of "problems of selfhood and identity, and the major problem with taking your feelings and opinions from outside yourself" (82). He further finds a pattern in Leigh's work from this point forward of a "justice structure." "Characters," in Carney's view, "who are socially inadequate or insensitive are made to pay a narrative price for their shortcomings" (84). Such an interpretation, while provocative, seems to beg hyperbolic ethical and moral questions at the expense of Leigh's patent and accessible comedy.

The urban-based Pratts are from Croydon near London in Surrey: Keith (Roger Sloman) works in social service and plays a banjo; his wife, Candice-Marie (Alison Steadman) works in a toyshop and plays a guitar. While these two people embrace a concept of sanguine nature, regarding themselves as temperate and gentle folk in touch with their landscape, they both bring along to the country disadvantageous mental baggage that equips them poorly to deal with the camping experience. Their worst difficulties arise not from nature so much as their strained relationship with other people. This couple is extremely smug and self-righteous about their vegetarianism, health regimens, and conservationist practices. They boast, for example, that there are no "killer whites" in their portable larder, that is, no refined sugar and processed flour. Keith trusts instrumentation and systems; he carefully logs the weather on gauges he brings with him. He tells Candice-Marie that "there is no point in having a schedule if you don't stick to it" and admonishes her to chew her food seventy-two times. Rather than converse as in ordinary discourse, Keith makes pronouncements in a strange throbbing vibrato. Not for him who stores and delivers dry facts a conviction that true knowledge is a spiritual journey, even though he may have deluded himself into believing he is successfully pursuing such a quest. Without realizing what he is doing, Keith bullies everyone with his assumed superior knowledge, especially poor Candice-Marie. This couple endures as recognizable types even at the start of the twenty-first century because, as Michael Coveney aptly described them, "they are historically and hysterically poised between the weekend hippie syndrome of the late 1960's and the New Age ecological freak-out of today" (103).

The first antagonist to the Pratts' bucolic fantasy appears in the person of fellow camper Ray (Anthony O'Donnell) from Cardiff, who attends a teacher training college where he is studying to become a physical education teacher. His radio disturbs the quiet that the Pratts seek: "everything was peaceful until you came along." They later befriend Ray by offering him a ride back from Lulworth Cove after they had all been caught in the rain. This act of generosity leads to increased intimacy between Candice-Marie and Ray, much to Keith's displeasure, as she shows Ray the rocks she collected on the beach at Lulworth and they lend each other books. She gives him a guide to Corfe Castle, and he provides her with a booklet on Ancient Purbeck, where fossilized stone with dinosaur tracks embedded in it is still being quarried. Candice-Marie and Keith later find evidence of this geological fact during a visit to a Purbeck quarry scene that Coveney opines "has Beckettian overtones" (62). At the quarry site, a taciturn, if not exactly Hardyesque, quarryman (Eric Allan from *Bleak Moments*) "dresses" the stones for a future wall at the new Corfe post office.

Leigh effectively carries off a particularly excruciating scene that tests the patience of actors and audience alike as both participate in an experience consisting of many more beats for a limited action than is usual in film practice. Keith and Candice-Marie force Ray to join in with an interminable rendition of a song Candice-Marie has "composed" about wanting to visit the zoo complete with all of Keith's directorial asides of how it should be performed. We share Ray's misery with ever tighter close-ups on him as the Pratts blithely continue this repetitious and stupid song that makes everyone yearn for a rock-and-roll station on Ray's radio. Keith and Candice-Marie follow up this performance by having Ray photograph them by their tent with Keith constantly and patronizingly querying Ray about his ability to carry out the task. Ray Carney sees Keith here as functioning "like a bad movie director, who dictates the most minute details of Ray and Candice-Marie's blocking (where they should stand for the photograph), line readings (in the song), and feelings about and interpretation of their roles (in the talk about nutrition)." Furthermore, Carney specifically links Ray's behavior to the "pardigmatic Hitchcockian artist who...takes the spontaneity, surprise, and fun out of experience—the play out of play" (83).

Honky (Shelia Kelley), with inappropriate high heels, and Finger (Stephen Bill), a plasterer, arrive on a noisy motorcycle at the campsite. They are neophytes to this camp scene, and Ray helps them set up their tent. The three of them become friendly perhaps partly as a defense against the sour and judgmental Pratts. The threesome noisily return to the campsite after a night of drinking and darts at a pub near Corfe Castle, singing "It's the rich that gets the pleasure/It's the poor that gets the pain." Keith becomes irate at being disturbed as Honky and Finger drunkenly make their way to their tent and continue talking loudly into the night. Keith goes over to their tent and tells them, "You get back to your tenement."

The antagonism escalates at a time of crisis. Finger attempts to start an open fire contrary to the rules and regulations of the campsite and the law of the country code solemnly invoked by Keith. Unable to convince Finger to desist from his fire-building, Keith attempts a citizen arrest. Wielding a substantial tree branch, Keith goes on a savage, atavistic offense against Finger, made all the more vivid and disorienting by the handheld camera work. "Come on, I'll knock your head off," screams the enraged Keith. Honky, in turns, kicks over the Pratts' outdoor table.

Suddenly, Leigh has catapulted the film at least temporarily into the world of *Deliverance* or *Lord of the Flies*. As a survival-game movie, *Nuts in May* offers only a glimpse, but the sobbing Keith (who retreats and tells Finger "I was only trying to advise you for your own good") has experienced a savage horror. For a moment Leigh exposes the fear that civilized behavior is only skin deep, and someone like Keith under fairly minimal provocation could turn feral. From the vantage of the new millennium, we can look back on this sequence as a harbinger of such recent disturbing phenomena as road rage and violent behavior on commercial aircraft. Finger tells Honky that Keith "could have killed me, you know." After Keith has absented himself by taking a walk, Finger proceeds to light his fire and heat up beans and sausages. Finger explains what happened between him and Keith when Ray returns; the latter observes of their fellow camper, "I think he is some kind of nut case."

At Keith's insistence, he and Candice-Marie decamp in search of another site. Leigh emphasizes the portable propane stove Keith places in the trunk of his car in contrast to the controversial open fire Finger requires to heat his dinner. On the road they are stopped by a local motor policeman (Richard Ireson) who examines their car and Keith's papers, and finally issues only a warning to Keith about his nearly bald spare tire and the necessity to keep the rearview mirror from being obstructed by objects in the back seat. In light of Keith's brief potentially murderous attack on Finger, the sudden appearance of the policeman could be used to suggest something like the finger of fate in Thomas Hardy's Dorset. Keith, however, exhibits no sense of guilt beyond silencing his wife repeatedly with "Leave it to me, Candice-Marie" in response to all questions the policeman poses.

After the Pratts reject alternative campsites, the film ends with their setting up camp in a field on the property of a chicken farm with the approval of the owner for a mere 25 pence. Candice-Marie waves a long chiffon scarf in the breeze and reminisces about a dancing class of her youth. (Amusingly, Alison Steadman as Wendy in *Life Is Sweet* [1990] will revisit such a class as its teacher at the beginning of that film.) She expresses wonder and delight as the wind makes melody over the strings of her guitar in the field. Keith waxes poetic over this aeolian harp effect with references to "child-like elements in the universe," the "joy of life," and "...in harmony with the birds." This last avian reference elicits from Leigh a witty Ernst Lubitsch-like cut to a chicken in a pen. Candice-Marie breaks into a final original folk song with such lines as "litter makes me shiver."

Keith obeys a call of nature, carrying a shovel and roll of toilet paper into an adjacent field through a barbed wire fence. Little pieces of paper adhere to the fence, waving in the wind to parallel his wife's chiffon scarf. He must pass large sows on his way, and the film's last image is that of a substantial pig happily chewing. The alimentary reference affirms the fundamental conditions of life that Leigh's works never stray from for very long. Candice-Marie and Keith, misfits and self-imposed exiles from all commercial campsites, are now isolated to the tedium of being alone together with the pigs for their remaining holiday in the country. And yet in their own way and to the extent they can be, they seem happily English with an emotional response to climate, land, region, and their imperfect relationship.

Abigail's Party

Alison Steadman moves beyond the vacuous Candice-Marie, speaking with what speech pathologists term an r-distortion and behaving at most ever so slightly passive-aggressively, in *Nuts in May* to become much more like Keith as the loud, opinionated, peremptory, and overtly aggressive Beverly in *Abi-*

gail's Party (1977). She commands the set like a Sherman tank. This stage piece became, in the description of Michael Coveney, "not a television film, but a hastily compiled television studio play which merely replicates the Hampstead Theatre production" (112) as another BBC "Play for Today." As a location filmmaker, Leigh objects to this kind of videotaped studio transfer of a stage production, and he has not been persuaded to yield up any other of his numerous theatrical stagings for video posterity after *Abigail's Party*. Its continued almost cult popularity has proven in some ways satisfying but also dismaying when it may have interfered with adequate acknowledgment of Leigh's subsequent excellence and achievements. As Alan Franks notes in an interview with Leigh in the London *Times Magazine, Abigail's Party* was aired during an ITV strike at a time when Channel 4 did not yet exist and there was no competition on BBC2. The film was seen by an audience of 16 million viewers; "it was an exposure beyond Leigh's dreams" (32).

Perhaps because it was meant as a work for the theater, *Abigail's Party* calls attention to theatricality in everyday life via a hybrid vehicle reminiscent of Sartre's *No Exit* and Edward Albee's *Who's Afraid of Virginia Woolf?*. Coveney sees it as " an extremely cunning subversion of a West End boulevard comedy" or, in a darker tone, "more akin to Greek tragedy than to most television comedy" (114–5). The piece is funny, with an edge of hysteria, as it moves to a gripping climax. Leigh's characters who rely on ready-made phrases and exhibit sensibilities derived from popular culture and commercialism show the conversion of the human into the mechanical as Henri Bergson's formulation of the source of comedy would have it. Accordingly, like a number of Leigh's plays with their emphasis on farce, in contrast usually to his films (for the most part) *Abigail's Party*, on occasion, drifts too easily into the realm of caricature.

The film's action takes place in real time. Beverly (Alison Steadman), former beautician and wife of Laurence (Tim Stern), a real-estate salesman, invites new neighbors, Angela (Janine Duvitski), a nurse, and her husband Tony (John Salthouse), a former professional soccer player for Crystal Palace who now works with computers, to their house for a drink. In addition, the genteel Susan (Harriet Reynolds), whom the overly familiar Beverly, of course, calls "Sue," stops by for the unsuspectingly brutal social hour. This divorced mother of two has a fifteen-year-old daughter, the unseen Abigail, who is giving a party that night in the flat below. Early in the evening prior to Susan's appearance, Laurence offers olives only to have Beverly tell him that nobody wants olives. He rejoins that he likes olives, and "that's twenty-five percent of the assembled company." Their verbal battle continues throughout the evening much to the discomfort of their guests. Beverly is a true vulgarian; she anticipates later characters in Leigh in the pride she displays toward her downstairs bathroom. Having topped off Sue's gin and tonic once too often, Beverly watches Sue go off in the care of Angela to be sick in this bathroom.

Laurence has pretensions, maybe even legitimate aspirations, to higher culture with his received discourse on art, his supposed fondness for classical music recordings, and his boxed set of Shakespeare, "our heritage" as he boasts and then qualifies, "of course, it's not something you can actually read." "They are lovely," purrs Angela. Rita Felski comments on this facet of behavior in George Orwell's portrayal of the lower middle class, and what she observes could apply equally to Laurence here: "One manifestation of this status anxiety is a craven respect for high culture accompanied by almost complete ignorance of its content" (36). Tony seems to smolder silently as his wife babbles good-naturedly. As she reports to Beverly while her husband is away in response to her hostess's question of whether her husband was ever violent: "No, he's not violent. Just a bit nasty. Like the other day, he said to me, he'd like to sellotape my mouth."

The unctuous Beverly does nothing to allay Sue's fears about Abigail's party when she hears there may be as many as twenty-five young people. "There will be older boys at the party," she reminds the anxious mother. She remembers from her own youth the fact that "a glass of cider, she's anybody's." Since she learns about a couple "snoggin" in the bay window, she helpfully suggests to Sue: "It starts with one kiss, and then they find their way to the bedroom." When Laurence and Tony "pop down" to see how things are going at Abigail's party, Laurence returns alone, and Tony's late re-appearance with a wet shirt remains mysterious. To be sure, the alternative party offscreen must be more festive than what is transpiring in Beverly's living room. During his absence, Beverly had indecorously suggested that Tony might be sustaining sexual assault from fifteen-year-old girls who, she assumes, would wisely choose him over Laurence. Beverly is equally insensitive in expressing her views on divorce and a woman's need for "a bloke." Both she and Ang (pronounced, as Coveney explains, "dipthongally, with a soft 'g,' as in 'sponge' or 'Angela' without the 'ela'" [117]), as Beverly calls her neighbor, acutely embarrass Sue, who has been divorced for three years while Beverly and Ang have been married for the same period of time.

Upon Tony's return, Beverly and he do a bit of seductively intimate slow dancing, which further infuriates her husband. He and Sue are goaded into dancing themselves through Beverly's hectoring. Tall Sue and short Laurence look mismatched physically, reflecting the greater disparity manifested throughout the film of Laurence and Beverly, both physically and mentally. Leigh permits Laurence a poignant moment of reflection where he expresses envy for musicians and artists because they are born with talent: "They got something to cling to." As Laurence notes, in a Thoreau-like insight that may be construed as also self-reflexive, "most people drift through life without aims." He finally asserts himself against Beverly whom he calls "ignorant." She, in turn, tells him to "drop dead."

Trying to gain control, Laurence plays a recording of Beethoven's Fifth Symphony, while Beverly repairs upstairs to bring down her "erotic" canvas that her husband has termed "pornographic." With the fateful initial chords of Beethoven's first movement reverberating in the room, Laurence, perspiring and looking unwell, enacts the imperative Beverly earlier expressed and suffers a fatal heart attack. However inane and twittering Angela has appeared during the evening, she demonstrates her professional competence as a nurse in attending to Laurence. Beverly descends the stairs with her banal nude study in shades of blue, which the audience is permitted to see, to find her collapsed husband. The symbolic convergence has classic Leigh resonance. With what seems like genuine grief, Beverly embraces Laurence, although in her movement she drops ash from her cigarette in her husband's face. This action horrifies Tony, who rebukes her for carelessness.

Just before these baleful events occur, Tony has raised his hand to his wife but does not strike her. He tells her to get up so they can leave. Now in the midst of a medical emergency, he yields to her superior knowledge, phones for an ambulance, and, finally, rather touchingly, holds up his wife's long hair so she is less encumbered as she attempts unsuccessfully to resuscitate the expiring Laurence. Everyone addresses reproofs to the unhelpful but increasingly distraught Beverly during this sequence. Even the passive Sue says to her, "Will you just shut up?" Angela gets a major leg cramp, an affliction which, according to Coveney, actually happened to Janine Duvitski during rehearsal, and Leigh recommended keeping it in the piece (117). Tony abandons the bereaved Beverly, who has been embracing him, to go to his wife in pain. Her former soccer player husband, who presumably knows something about muscle aches, massages her leg and tells her to "stretch it." Sue tries to phone Abigail, as the film ends, with the ineffectual and plaintive "Abigail, it's mummy here."

Deliberately hackneyed and humorous parentheses of predictability constitute much of the dialogue and action of *Abigail's Party.* Steven Vineberg describes Leigh's method in what he terms chamber-plays such as this one as building "on Pinter's idea of using the banalities of workaday language as a code for conveying the buried emotions of men and women of limited imaginative scope. But Mr. Leigh is both more of an entertainer than Pinter and more of a psychological realist" (AR 3). At the ending of *Abigail's Party*, Leigh's move beyond passing intimations of mortality in the script to Laurence's sudden death generates the distinctive interplay of the comic and the serious that becomes a hallmark of his later films. It is probably not coincidental that the same year of this television transfer of his stage play saw the release of Leigh's *The Kiss of Death*. Visitations of mortality are integral to the comic processes of these two works with characters in need of but not searching for a moral compass. The result is that sudden death enters the two television films with the jarring quality that it has in real life. By accident, *Abigail's Party* became a test case for discrimination in the evaluation of it and some of Leigh's controversial later films.

The late Dennis Potter, renowned for his groundbreaking television dramas, wrote a notoriously negative London *Sunday Times* review of the television production. He accused the director, as Coveney reports, of "immense condescension" toward "the dreadful suburban tastes of the dreadful lower middle classes" and concluded that "as so often in the minefields of English class-consciousness, more was revealed of the snobbery of the observers rather than of the observed" (35). Potter's screed seemed to influence a number of subsequent critics about Leigh's work even though he had provided virtually no evidence to support his claims. Leigh remarked to me during an interview that this kind of charge is never brought against Harold Pinter in his plays. Leigh argues that critics often paradoxically privilege drama and the institution of the theater to permit greater latitude in treatment of class than is granted to the more popular and democratic media of television and film. Significantly, in retrospect from the twenty-first century, Leigh's television dramas before and after *Abigail's Party* have gained acclaim comparable to those of British dramatists like Alan Bennett and Dennis Potter, who have done some of their finest work for television.

The Kiss of Death

Leigh's 1977 BBC TV film, *The Kiss of Death*, according to Michael Coveney, is one of the director's favorites partly because the character of Trevor, played superbly by David Threlfall, who rather disturbingly resembles "Dr. Who," "contains certain autobiographical elements" (107). It is set on Leigh's more or less native grounds, the Pennines in Oldham, Lancashire. This film is another in Leigh's series on the season of youth moving toward socially adapted, sexually functional adulthood, but the young people in this film are gainfully employed. Without contempt for the bourgeois world of work, these characters are preparing themselves in ways they may not fully comprehend for adult responsibilities. The filmmaker here does not necessarily imitate Shakespeare's challenge to "move wild laughter in the throat of death" as Berowne is asked to do in *Love's Labour's Lost*. Nonetheless, the presence of mortality darkens and informs much of the film's comedy although Leigh's vision is anything but elegiac and not quite so dark humored and adrift from real life as *Six Feet Under*, Alan Ball's HBO series first broadcast in the United States during the summer of 2001. Here the reticent, one might even say "dead quiet," shambling young man is Trevor, an undertaker's assistant to Mr. Garside (Clifford Kershaw), an older man played by the actor who portrayed Mr. Thornley so forcefully in *Hard Labour*. To the credit of Threlfall and Leigh, because Trevor does not say very much does not suggest that he is thinking nothing although precisely what he is thinking is left undisclosed.

Leigh shows the activities of a mortuary housed in what appears to be a church-like structure: the two men talk casually while they prepare a body, and Trevor drills holes and attaches handles to a child's casket. Their business is partially about concealment, embalming and touch-up to soften the inexorable fact of mortality. Mr. Garside offers his opinion that Trevor enjoys an enviable position as he projects his young assistant through a full life cycle and ends with what his employer views as Trevor's ultimate benefit, a free funeral. Nonetheless, his boss is unwilling to lend Trevor a car from his funeral establishment, claiming that he does not want to wipe footprints off the roof lining.

Leigh recaptilates the opening sequence in *The Kiss of Death* of the funeral procession moving into a cemetery years later at the beginning of *Secrets & Lies*. Despite his callowness in matters of the heart, Trevor is surely not uninformed about death or unprepared to encounter it, and this awareness confers a measure of implied maturity upon him. Throughout his films Leigh often shows his characters in cemeteries, where the living walk every day among the dead. Here in one scene young people pleasantly meander through a cemetery with the distant cooling towers of an atomic-powered electric generating plant in the background, which conveys a sense of tradition, of continuity, and a realism about life and death, the past and the present.

Leigh in this film neither constructs exciting scenes nor exhibits character in the usual cinematic way through goal-setting actions and examination of causes and effects. Rather he conjures up the dramatic color and shape, the absurdity and hope of youth itself, especially seen in the first tentative movement toward sex and love. Once more Leigh provides a quartet of characters. Trevor and his diffident chum, Ronnie (John Wheatley), who stocks shelves in a food market, are paired off with two blossoming, nubile girls. Petite, Betty Boop–like Sandra (Angela Curran) has apparently been involved with Ronnie for a period of time, but shoe saleswoman Linda (Kay Adshead) has only just become acquainted with Trevor. The gum-chewing Linda seems somewhat predatory and aggressive in contrast to Trevor. Paul Clements notes of this performance that Kay Adshead's Linda with her chewing gum takes on "the quality of a specific mannerism and a cultural activity" (85), which the filmmaker returns to in the recent *All or Nothing*. Leigh introduces one of his oblique and humorous visual clues to an understanding of her. He shows her sitting outside a movie theater where the current attraction is *Jaws*, and we see the famous gaping mouth and pointed teeth of its iconic poster. Trevor has stood her up while he shoots pool with Ronnie. She takes off to find him engaged in his pool game and physically assaults him for failing to meet her as scheduled. After she leaves, Trevor tells Ronnie that he will not be seeing her again.

Before he changes his mind about that resolve, as he does subsequently, the film takes Trevor and his mortician boss to the comfortable middle-class home of a young couple, the Bodgers (Frank McDermott and Christine Moore), whose infant child has died presumably as a result of Sudden Infant Death Syndrome. The couple is in the care of a youthful policewoman (Karen Petrie), because this kind of death necessarily requires police attention. Trevor removes the small corpse, which looks like a doll, not plausibly like a human infant. Coveney reports it was made by medical artists at Manchester University and that if it looks unreal, as it does, Leigh acknowledged that then "we shot it wrong" (109). The policewoman casually tells the couple, as she takes her leave of them, "I'll probably see you at the coroner's office tomorrow." The sequence continues to the morgue, where the tiny body is deposited for later examination. In typical Leigh fashion, understatement characterizes his handling of this material, and the effect is curiously that much more powerful.

Trevor and Linda appear to be on the brink of a reconciliation when a neighbor, Christine (Marlene Sidaway), calls Linda to help her with her aged mother, Mrs. Ball (Eileen Denison), who has fainted following an outing in the car. Linda and Trevor run down the street to offer aid. The old woman marginally revives through Trevor's ministrations. He carries her upstairs to her bedroom and continues to offer her care until a doctor (Brian Pollitt) arrives and asks the couple to leave. She asks Trevor his name and tells him hers is "Dolly," to which he predictably replies with a winning smile, "Hello, Dolly." Linda chastizes him for sitting on the bed as he cares for Dolly, and Trevor replies, "I always sit on the bed." In a Tennessee Williams or Edward Albee play, Trevor might be seen as the angel of death in such a sequence, but Leigh presents him as simply a caring young man.

These episodes contribute to our understanding of Trevor as more sensitive than was perhaps first supposed. In addition, Trevor's persona throughout the film is that of someone who reads with avidity and seriousness, but he rarely even reveals the title of any book he is reading. We see this same attribute in the character of Rachel in *All or Nothing* (2002). Linda, following their charitable visit to their neighbor in distress over the mother, wrests a volume from Trevor to discover he is reading *Dracula*. She, in turn, shares with him her reading material—illustrated romance magazines—and asks him if he thinks one of the women pictured is pretty. According to Andy Medhurst in "Mike Leigh Beyond Embarrassment" in *Sight and Sound*, Trevor "already reads too many books and if he decides to throw in his job with the undertaker (a knowing nod here to *Billy Liar*) he could decide on a career of alienation and sexual violence and change his name to Johnny [the misogynistic protagonist of Leigh's later *Naked*]" (10/11).

This claim that Trevor is a precursor of Johnny may be too convenient and overdetermined as pursued by some Leigh interpreters in response to the filmmaker's open-endedness. Carney, for example, titles his chapter on this film "Existence without Essences" and waxes philosophical about Trevor and the contingencies of existence that almost require the later Johnny of *Naked* as exegete. What follows from this exchange on reading over the coffee that Linda serves thc two of them is a prolonged *pas de deux* beginning with Linda's invitation to Trevor, seated across from her, "You can kiss me if you like." This less than fulfilling amatory sequence is a more extensive version of a similar encounter between Peter and Sylvia in *Bleak Moments*. The ill-at-ease Trevor, whose face mirrors that part of him unready for this encounter and competing with the part that is trying to catch up, laughs inappropriately. This response puts Linda off her seductive stride. When he finally does kiss her, it is a brutal coming together of mouths as he squeezes her face. Nevertheless she invites him to come upstairs even though that invitation ends without consummation and in more giggles from Trevor. Ray Carney extrapolates an interesting pattern from this sequence:

> Almost all of Leigh's major scenes have the same step-by-step quality as the "kiss-of-death" scene. To remember any of the great moments in Leigh's work is not to recall a

> static effect...but a sequence of temporal events. Over and over again in his work, Leigh presents two or more figures feeling their way toward, away from, and back toward each other in time. (76)

Earlier Trevor had arranged for Ronnie to use his mother's bedroom for an assignation with Sandra that proved abortive because Ronnie could not articulate the reason for a sudden visit to Trevor's house when Sandra thought they were going for an afternoon drink. Now at Linda's, Trevor likewise cannot act on his own and her desires. Michael Coveney writes well of this sequence at Linda's house:

> We glimpse, as if in a series of intuitive flashes, an entire catalogue of human emotions in the mating game: anxiety cruelty, affection, wonder, contempt, and playfulness. This is how love scenes are endured in life, not in the movies, but distilled and refined for *this* movie. This sequence, camera tight in on the two faces, with no long shot and no trickery, is one of the highlights in the Leigh canon, and all about the performances, which are fresh, funny, completely original, and entirely truthful. (111–12)

Although Linda and Trevor do not go to the bedroom after the kiss, he does agree to go with her to a disco, a destination he had rejected in the past. The evening there further alienates him from her. Linda dances with Ronnie but not with Trevor; in the car returning home, he rejects her advances and leaves the back seat next to her to go around the car to sit beside Ronnie. Homosociality between men temporarily supersedes heterosexual pairing off, the essential part of male friendship being a kind of mute and merciful understanding that Leigh privileges at the end of this film. Andy Medhurst suggests a possible link between *Kiss of Death* and Leigh's later *Naked* in "their shared, specific gendering of the trap motif Leigh uses so frequently: the trap is female, women are out to get you, and domesticity equals a kind of death" (10/11).

In the film's final sequence, the funeral car has been called into service for a wedding. Trevor starts a conversation with a beguiling young flower girl (Elizabeth Ann Ogden), who, having vacated the interior of the church, waits impatiently for the rest of the wedding party. She tells him she does not like boys and will never marry. This exchange in some ways seems less inane than Trevor's colloquies with the adult women in the film. Trevor and Ronnie drive back to Ronnie's flat. Ronnie apologizes for the unsatisfactory disco evening the night before. Trevor shares with Ronnie the view from the highrise of neighborhood children milling around the large black car on the street below. The two young men return to the street, both laughing, and drive away in an aerial shot, another effective, God's-eye view in Mike Leigh's cinema.

Coveney explains that originally Leigh wanted a final scene in which the boys take to the highway en route to Blackpool where they would pick up two hitchhiking girls who would be contrasts in dress, appearance, manner, and ease of conversation with Linda and Sandra. Leigh is quoted on this scenario: "That would have told the story of escape from this small-minded, rather bone-headed girls in Oldham and their middle-class aspirations" (112). However, time did not permit this conclusion.

The Kiss of Death was the first Leigh film with a full musical score, composed by Carl Davis, who later would serve the director in such exemplary fashion in his actual movie musical, *Topsy-Turvy* (1999). Davis's score, performed by a woodwind ensemble of flute, oboe, clarinet, and horn, is a marvel of what could be termed the antagonism of styles, a tonal range, as Coveney aptly describes it, "both jaunty and plaintive, light and melancholic" (111). The greater range of expression in the music—exceeding that of the characters themselves—contributes to the film's subtext that Trevor and Ronnie and the girls, too, have depths not yet plumbed, hinting at healthy and uncomplicated high spirits of the future. Wind instruments are well chosen to sigh forth yearning appeals as Leigh shows his late adolescent protagonist undergoing an initiation into maturity. Apart from Davis's score, at one point when Ronnie and Sandra are making out, a passage from Gilbert and Sullivan's *Iolanthe* is heard, presumably on the radio, a tiny aural foretaste of things to come in Leigh's canon as soon as *Who's Who* and much later in *Topsy-Turvy*.

Who's Who

Leigh followed up *The Kiss of Death* with another narrative of working youth, *Who's Who* (1979), one more BBC TV "Play for Today," but now the young people are primarily junior stockbrokers in the City who come from the right schools (like Charterhouse, which is referred to). These scions of the old order are preparing to take their rightful places in Margaret Thatcher's England. The film Leigh devises is different from its predecessors because Leigh usually considers emotions more than manners and avoids the superciliousness of much British social comedy. However, *Who's Who* plays as a comedy of manners with the associations to a privileged class and an obsession with the surface and facade traditional to that established genre. Here, as George Meredith might have it, comedy is a game played to throw reflections upon social life, and it deals with human nature in the drawing rooms of civilized men and women. Hence this television film promulgates social satire more overtly than Leigh's usual working-class and lower-middle-class studies, but his skeptical, mischievous style is ingratiating partly because it is a different modulation. For example, the film opens with a figure seated in a wing chair, back to the camera, smoking a pipe and listening to John of Gaunt's enduring speech on England as the blessed island nation, "this scept'red isle," from Shakespeare's *Richard II.* "This blessed plot, this earth, this realm, this England," comes replete with William Walton–like musical accompaniment, evocative of life in "parody Britain."

The listener is Nigel (Simon Chandler), who shares an expensive London flat with Giles (Adam Norton), and Celia who, while alluded to, is never seen in the film. The two young men display an "odd couple" dynamic, with Nigel being more domestically attuned than the rather careless, puerile Giles. Friends at one point refer to Nigel as Giles's nanny. These housemates are preparing for a small dinner party for which Nigel will do the main course, and Giles will ask his mother when he next visits her to prepare an apple crumble for this social event. The absent Celia is supposed to do the hors d'oeuvres.

At the brokerage firm where the young men work is Alan Dixon (Richard Kane), a clerk who ironically becomes the film's diminished and democratic John of Gaunt, celebrating his native land by writing to the rich, famous, and titled. Celebrity has become the new "happy breed." After unsuccessfully trying to obtain autographs from the royal family, he constructs a "Tree of Great Britain" of the current royal line. Moreover, Alan plans during his vacation to visit royal seats like Balmoral and Windsor and displays on the walls of his home portraits of Victoria and Queen Elizabeth II as well as British memorabilia. This character shares more than a slight resemblance to Charles Pooter, the comic protagonist of George and Weedon Grossmith's *Diary of a Nobody* (1892). Leigh will pay considerable attention to George Grossmith in *Topsy-Turvy* as a performer in Gilbert and Sullivan operettas but not as the coauthor of a Victorian comic masterpiece.

Alan's eccentric wife, April, played by Joolia Cappleman, who had proved so memorable in the role of Pat in *Bleak Moments*, raises and sells chinchilla cats. Her concern for feline pedigrees exactly parallels her husband's obsession with and veneration of privileged lineage. Throughout this film Leigh employs his customary parallel structures but obtains satiric bite through the double activity of inflation and deflation, as with the Dixons' shared interest in bloodlines albeit in different species.

Tellingly, Alan receives a reply from Mrs. Thatcher's secretary early in the film, informing him in boilerplate of the pleasure the prime minister took in receiving his letter and enclosing a signed photograph of herself. April observes that she likes Mrs. Thatcher's hairdo, and Alan affirms she is a handsome woman. Leigh prophetically witnesses in this exchange to Mrs. Thatcher's ability early in her tenure to attract and retain affection and dedicated loyalty from people who individually might not be particularly important but collectively assured her a large majority. How grateful Alan is for those "little havens of intimacy" that Mrs. Thatcher became famous for. One such experience can be observed in the elevator sequence where he and Francis (Jeffrey Wickham), a senior partner in the brokerage firm on his way, much to Alan's nobility-obsessed delight, to an appointment with Lord Crouchurst, exchange commonplace pleasantries about their respective wives using their first names. This scene implies more familiarity between the two men than they actually have.

Leigh parallels scenes at the Dixons' with scenes of the young men hosting their staged event, that is, the dinner party. In one hilarious sequence Alan returns home early to find a cat photographer, Mr. Chakespeare, played by the redoubtable Sam Kelly, who reappears in 1980 in Leigh's *Grown-Ups* as well as the more recent *All or Nothing,* and a potential cat-buyer, Miss Hunt, (Geraldine James) of Sloane Square. She has been disappointed by Harrods' failure to secure a cat for her. The laconic Miss Hunt registers as distinctly upper class on Alan's radar. He immediately excuses himself and changes his clothes for a blue monogrammed blazer and ascot in order to offer sherry to Miss Hunt, although she declines. He now wears a lofty and knowing expression that powerless people hoping for power affect. Coincidentally, the young men at the dinner party are also attired in ascots; however, sartorially, they do seem more to the manor born than does Alan. He learns that Miss Hunt rides and hunts on her own horses at her family's country estate.

At the dinner party, we learn that Samantha (Catherine Hall), who resembles a young Judi Dench, had first met Nigel shooting on his father's farm in Norfolk. Alan, upon learning that Somerton-Friars was Miss Hunt's mother's maiden name, pulls out his handy copy of *Debrett's* to check further. The young women who visit Nigel and Giles all sport hyphenated names. Meanwhile, her husband's insistent inquiries disrupt April's preparations both for handing over "Tiger-Lily," a hyphenated feline, to her new owner and the photographic setups she and Mr. Chakespeare are endeavoring to complete. The ensuing chaos takes us into familiar farcical Leigh territory as Miss Hunt leaves with admonition to play with her new cat and feed her, as April feeds her brood, "lamb's heart, ox heart, chicken gourmet menu and a little fish." With the departure of Miss Hunt, Alan turns his attention to Mr. Chakespeare, who denies he has any ties with the Bard of Avon and informs the disappointed Dixon that there are forty C/Shakespeares listed in the London phonebook.

Leigh offers quieter, but no less pungent, comedy in an earlier scene at the Kensington home of Lord Crouchurst, a family name curiously Evelyn Waugh–like. His lordship (David Neville) and Lady Crouchurst (Richenda Carey, who portrayed the campsite supervisor in *Nuts in May*) go through a week's worth of social engagements, including such worthies as Prince Philip, who is having lunch at Lord Crouchurst's club. Robin Strubbs's suit for her ladyship together with the actress's slightly mannish haircut embodies a satiric thrust without caricature. When she says goodnight to her young daughter (Francesca Martin), who is being cared for by a youthful, engaging nanny (Lavinia Bertram), Lady Crouchurst seems something less than maternal in contrast to the solicitous April affectionately caring for her cats. Alan has told his wife that the motto of the Crouchursts is "Wealth is strength." Unbeknownst to Alan, the current lord is seeking advice from Francis at the brokerage firm on how to manage the dwindling resources of his mother. The concatenation of these details across locales and among different groups of characters results in multiple layers of signification for viewers to reflect upon. Leigh does not force a rush to judgment even in satire. Like others, this film with its echoes and iterations requires the cooperation of the viewers' memory for the stew to be at its most piquant.

Hence, with that food metaphor, we briefly look at the dinner party chez Giles and Nigel. What endures from the eating rituals of Mike Leigh (and he may yet do a film titled "Mealtime") is the love embodied in the preparation and presentation of food. Nigel's efforts as a chef are considerable. Despite the necessity of his serving "tinned soup," as Giles maladroitly reminds the assembled guests while they are consuming it, Nigel's main course of the crown pork roast "with its socks on"and "apricot and prune stuffing" looks good and is well received, as is the apple crumble courtesy of Giles's mum. Some mocking sport attends the group's recognition of Nigel's "placements" of the silverware, but this solecism is forgivable. Earlier at the Dixons', April had rebuked her husband for not properly placing his eating utensils to indicate that he had finished his dinner. Later an incipient food fight appears to be developing with the tossing of dinner rolls across the table. Leigh derives droll comedy from a sense of social error and absurdity.

Coveney reported that Nigel's dinner party in Leigh's estimation was "more improvised than almost anything else I've done, and it shows"; the director felt it needed a week or so more of work to be fully realized (133). Its aleatory quality, nevertheless, correlates well with the unsteady maturity of the young people. The young women, played by Catherine Hall and Felicity Dean (Caroline), reveal a slightly feline manner and even cat-like visages further subliminally connecting this action with earlier scenes at the Dixons'. In shooting the farewell of Nigel's guests, who have become increasingly drunk, Leigh has them finally appear only as legs, hands, and bodies without faces. They thank their now-languid host, who remains on the sofa filmed in medium distance, not really connecting with anyone: all of which may connote an absence of mature individuality and wholeness. Ray Carney infers a more profound seriousness in how the filmmaker works with this material: "...life becomes a kind of dumb show in which everyone is mimicking a set of preformulated attitudes and prefabricated poses. In this orgy of publicity, privacy disappears. Life becomes its outside. Experience becomes generic. Its mystery and wonder and interiority are erased" (122). To Carney *Who's Who* becomes for Leigh a cautionary tale from a director who, "most committed to deep definitions of selfhood has created a film of the shallowest possible selves" (123). Or with less gravity, this film may be seen as Leigh simply presenting an affectionately satiric vision of the fashionable world without neglecting its implicit moral shallowness.

A down-to-earth character in *Who's Who*, Kevin, played by Philip Davis, who will go on to do similar but larger roles in later Leigh television dramas and feature films, becomes a model of normality in his role as observer of behavior in the brokerage office. He, likewise, observes the hanky-panky in an opposite office building by actors Roger Hammond and Angela Curran, an alumna from *The Kiss of Death*. Kevin is a clerk, sharing an office with Alan Dixon, listening to Alan's trivia, gently teasing his older associate, and demonstrating an alternative to the other characters' discourse and pretensions. In that capacity he serves almost as a stand-in for the director and a remembrance of Leigh's usual social milieu. Kevin smiles broadly and Alan smirks as they view the couple across the way with perhaps just a little shared envy. Carney's final judgment on most of the characters treated satirically in this film is that "*Who's Who* is a sinking ship on which the only survivors are the servants, menials, and secretaries" (129).

Leigh's film ends suddenly at this juncture with the appearance of the royal seal behind the credits accompanied on the sound track by a reprise of the melody for "Loudly let the trumpets bray!" from Gilbert and Sullivan's *Iolanthe*. This music was heard earlier in the film; Giles listened to it prior to the arrival of the guests for the dinner party. Gilbert's words for this choral number for the entrance of the peers of the realm capture some of the satiric tone and content of the now-concluded Leigh film as dedicated Savoyards might recall:

> Bow, bow, ye lower middle classes!
> Bow, bow, ye tradesmen! Bow ye masses!
> Blow the trumpets, bang the brasses!

Who's Who assesses present and future pillars of the English nation in a manner that W. S. Gilbert would doubtless understand. Like the much later *Topsy-Turvy*, this film seems a departure for Mike Leigh when compared to what went before and, in the case of this television film, what comes after. The environment is different, but Leigh continues here as elsewhere to exhibit relative control and understanding of the spuriousness and artificiality of some strata of British life.

Grown-Ups

Setting his television film for the BBC in Canterbury, the more-than-slightly-Chaucerian Mike Leigh creates his own latter-day "Canterbury Tale" in *Grown-Ups* (1980). Always eschewing analytical portraiture, Leigh, like the Chaucer of the tales, specializes in direct presentment but with the pleasure of observing and understanding. He reveals his characters' private lives and behavior, their changing moods, and their moral qualities, both good and bad. The exigency underlying this choice of setting, as Coveney explains, was the BBC rule that a film crew could be considered as being within London if they were in a radius of thirty miles of Charing Cross; otherwise they were viewed as on location (144) at appreciably higher cost.

Canterbury seems an ideal choice for the material of this often very funny film that anticipates Leigh's later feature, *High Hopes*, in some shared plot premises and in the fortuitous presence of Philip Davis (Dick) and Leslie Manville (Mandy). *Grown-Ups* can also boast the first appearance in a Mike Leigh film of Brenda Blethyn (Gloria). The actress and director succeed spectacularly well in this initial effort and will go on to greater acclaim in *Secrets & Lies*. The wonderful ensemble cast is rounded off with the Butchers played with remarkable control and about-to-explode British reserve by Sam Kelly (Ralph) and Lindsay Duncan (Christine) together with Janine Duvitsky, the accomplished comic actress whom Leigh first used in *Abigail's Party*. The latter actress turns in a convincing and uncomic performance as Sharon, a fellow store clerk with

Mandy who longs to leave "sweets for dresses" but laments her subsequent sales position in shoes.

Schoolmates and now married young people, Dick, a dishwasher, and Mandy take up residence in their first home, a council-owned house, and discover their next-door neighbor in a privately owned semi-detached house is "old Butcher," who taught their Religious Knowledge class at school. Their teacher, less than overjoyed to have former pupils living next to him, has himself married since their years in school. His wife is the slow-speaking Christine, who presides over physical education classes at the same school as Mr. Butcher. Theirs is a desiccated marriage, however superficially polite. The film is organized to explore the parallel lives of these two childless couples, a design common in a number of Leigh films.

Despite their verbal battles—Mandy often chides Dick, "Don't be so stupid"—this couple adopts a builder's perspective for their marriage. They can construct a marital relationship even if things are a trifle shaky, and they stay connected with their partner's goals and values as evidenced by Dick's willingness to father a child. The scene where she confesses she has not taken her contraceptive pill as they are about to make love, a development Dick accepts, saying to his wife "It's what you want, innit," is contrasted with a parallel scene in the Butchers' conjugal bed. Ralph Butcher is reading *Life before Man*, and his wife petulantly remarks, "I hope there aren't any human beings in that book. They might upset you." He, in irritation, queries his wife, "What do you want?" Coveney treats Christine's response in the following excellent summation: "The reply is stunning, the one moment Lindsay Duncan brings Christine to full emotional self-exposure. 'I want sex. I want love. I want a family. That's what I want.' Checkmate, and lights out. Butcher thought it might be something he could do something about" (148). This scene, from the more recent vantage of Leigh's *Topsy-Turvy*, prefigures his portrayal of the relationship between W. S. Gilbert and his wife, especially their final sequence in her bedroom.

Sam Kelly's Ralph Butcher is a notable Leigh character that trails certain Chaucerian associations. As a teacher of Religious Knowledge, he bears some resemblance to Chaucer's paradoxical clergy, whose behavior seems at odds with their calling. While on two occasions, Mr. Butcher charges two women, his wife and Gloria, with insufficient faith and affirms to the latter that his "is a decent Christian household," his typical interests take him to prehistoric times, monsters like the Loch Ness one, and self-absorbed grunts and muttering. In one characteristic non sequitur, he demonstrates how a figurine in the shape of a dinosaur is really a nutcracker. Despite his endorsement of Christian charity, Mr.

Butcher demonstrates little love or sensitivity toward anyone in the film. If viewed, however, as an example of the uncharitable, this character makes an important contribution to a topic Leigh's film shares with Chaucer's pilgrims in their constant thematic return to love, marriage, and a renewed sympathy for sexual love.

Another somewhat Chaucerian character that illuminates *Grown-Ups* is Mandy's older sister, Gloria, a typist who lives disagreeably with their mother, a character never seen in the film, and attaches herself to the young married couple in the guise of wanting to help them. Eventually, she seems to hope to become their live-in baby-sitter. She arrives on one occasion with a gift-wrapped Hoover vacuum cleaner for them, but her presence becomes increasingly intrusive and desperate even as she stops by only for her stated "cup of tea." Brenda Blethyn's Gloria is projected, to borrow Coveney's accurate and succinct characterization of the actress's performance, "as a pathetic monster in the same class of performance as Alison Steadman's Beverly [in *Abigail's Party*]" (145). Or, somewhat more expansively, Andy Medhurst's formulation gives the totality of this character in a plethora of coordination: "Brenda Blethyn's Gloria is pathetic and tragic and maddening and vulnerable and shameless and ludicrous and grotesque and heart-breaking all at the same time" (8/11).

As the agent provocateur who disrupts both the adjacent Canterbury couples and the transversal that brings their parallel lives temporarily together, Gloria precipitates the film's greatest comic action when her parasitic behavior toward Dick and Mandy has resulted in her being locked out of their house. Claiming her mother has thrown her out of their house, Gloria had appeared at her sister's prepared to move into the spare bedroom. Following further rejection by Dick and Mandy, who are incredulous that Gloria has actually lost her home with her mother, Gloria in hysterics takes refuge in the neighboring Butchers' residence. Christine, who is washing a car in front of the house, has left the front door open, not in the least expecting it to be an invitation to the fleeing Gloria, who runs up the stairs and locks herself in the bathroom.

The scene that follows represents a distillation of Leigh's ability to be disturbing, hilarious, and poignant simultaneously. Gloria is cajoled after much labor to vacate the bathroom with the assurance that Dick has gone back to his own house and the promise of a cup of tea to be provided by the incredibly patient Mrs. Butcher. Exiting her haven, Gloria sobs to the point that mucus drips quite visibly from her nose in one of those memorable Leigh images of graphic, almost repellent, physiological detail, reminiscent of Mr. Thornley's hairy back in *Hard Labour*. At the front door, she complains that she has not had her tea and that Dick still stands in the Butchers' front lawn, whereupon she bolts back up the stairs. Dick runs up the stairs after her and grabs her by the waist, an action that elicits even louder screams from Gloria.

What follows on the stairs looks like an absurdist version of the *Laokoōn*—a literal pile-up of disparate characters and social world—with Dick, Gloria, Mandy, and the Butchers all embroiled on top of the hysterical Gloria on the staircase. Mr. Butcher does shortly take his place on the ground floor below the remaining group on the staircase and tries to placate the participants as Dick tells him to "piss off." Somewhat more conciliatory, Dick persuades Gloria to get up; she rises but declines to let go of the railing. He becomes infuriated again, insisting to the Butchers that all he is trying to do is get his sister-in-law out of their house. Finally, clearing the stairs except for herself and Gloria, the calm, collected, and solicitous Christine Butcher assures her uninvited guest that "we'll just sit here until you are ready." Mandy, thoroughly exasperated with her sister as is Dick, says that everybody will be at the Butchers all afternoon. Meanwhile, in a change of tempo, Mr. Butcher turns to Sharon, who has gathered up Gloria's things in the hall, and asks, "Who are you?" in the manner of a fugitive latter-day caterpillar from *Alice in Wonderland.* Sharon identifies herself, to which Mr. Butcher flatly replies, "I thought I recognized you." Later he calls her Susan. When Mandy once more tries to force compliance on Gloria, Mrs. Butcher herself explodes, urges her neighbor to pull herself together, and actually slaps her. Mandy returns to her own house muttering, and shortly Dick brings the remainder of Gloria's possessions out of their home and deposits them on the threshold of the house next door.

Gloria has her tea with Ralph and Christine, whom she soon calls by their first name, abbreviating Mrs. Butcher's name to the more familiar "Chris." Behind Mr. Butcher on the wall next to a painting of a Venetian scene Gloria comments on is a framed reproduction of Chaucer's Wife of Bath as represented in the Ellesmere Manuscript of *Canterbury Tales*. Once more Leigh throws out a visual detail that may have relevance for interpretation. Gloria manifests some of the presumption and peremptory attitude of Chaucer's immortal character. She may not be a weaver of cloth, but she picks up Christine's knitting and takes over without being asked to do so.

To speculate a bit further on a possible unifying device in Leigh's subtly shaped structural and artistic design for this film, *Grown-Ups* opens with a removal truck arriving at the new residence of Dick and Mandy. The principal action at the end of the film is the removal of Gloria from the Butchers' in a taxi, accompanied by Mandy. She goes back to her mother's, after her "lie-down," which she has insisted on having following her tea. Moreover, Leigh supplies a corresponding aural envelope in the ecclesiastical-sounding choral passages that open and close this film in the ancient cathedral city of Canterbury.

The film's final sequence moves the action from the farrago at the Butchers' and the parallel bedtime scenes to the Christmas season. Gloria returns to the neighborhood bearing presents, encounters the Butchers about to leave in their car, and asks Mr. Butcher, who remains silent, what Father Christmas will bring him this year. Sitting on a couch with her legs across her husband's lap, Mandy is pregnant and hopes the child will not be born on Christmas Day. Gloria hopes her niece or nephew will be a Christmas baby as she bends over Mandy with her head on her sister's abdomen to experience any fetal movements. Sharon serves tea to the group. Everyone looks contented with the possible exception of Sharon. Leigh accompanies this tableau with a choir's rendition of "The Holly and the Ivy." Somehow the extremely traditional English carol punctuates the distinctiveness of what Leigh has accomplished in *Grown-Ups*. It might be viewed as amusingly ironic but not truly satirical.

Indeed, in Leigh's context "The Holly and the Ivy" seems appropriate, if ever so slightly askew, because the characters in this film are not greeting-card versions of merry England. By the same token, once we accept these characters in their wholeness of being and the freight of their human relationships, we feel somehow enriched by knowing them, because Leigh's means of presenting them has not been along the customary path of mainstream films. Leigh requires us to take the time to sort through his characters' reality, which is often more material than psychological, to get at truth. Whatever truth we ascertain resides as not so much within the film text as within what our perspective has led us to. However direct and unmediated Leigh's films appear, they are not uncomplicated in their presentation of lived experience. To paraphrase and appropriate Auden on poetry and apply it to film, *Grown-Ups* must be modified in the guts of the living and real audience. Thus, the maturation suggested by the title of the film challenges us as much as it does the fictive characters.

In his interview with Graham Fuller, "Mike Leigh's Original Features," the filmmaker made the following claim: "Historically, I regard *Grown-Ups*, in terms of its structure and depth, as being the first of my better films. I don't in any way diminish the films that preceded it, from *Bleak Moments* to *Who's Who*, but I think that they are much less assured, less thorough and polished. They also took less risks, and have less to say" (xvii).

Leigh's works for television constitute an extraordinary legacy in the broadcast medium, especially when compared to the drama on network television in the United States during the same period and later. Unfortunately, American audiences did not have the opportunity to view these BBC television films. From these works Leigh and his collaborators move on with confidence to the award-winning theatrical features of the nineties.

Home Sweet Home

In a quite different sense from the way the phrase has evolved in the United States with its denotations of sudden eruption of extreme and unsuspected violence, Mike Leigh "went postal" in his thirteenth project for BBC TV, *Home Sweet Home* (1982). His ascerbic examination of the quotidian existence of three hapless postmen and the women in their lives shot in Hitchin, Hertfordshire, is less intrinsically humorous than a number of his other television films. In tone it often resembles *Bleak Moments* and *Hard Labour* but contains intermittent hilarious moments to complement its darker elements. Leigh mentions in his interview with Graham Fuller that this film employs what he terms a "metaphor, on the go" because "it's told like it's one of the Mills & Boons stories that one of the postmen's wives, June, is reading" (xxxvii). Leigh does not invite viewers into the consciousness of his characters but sets the problem of working out their relationships in this film.

On the surface, the most normal postman is Stan (Eric Richard), whose wife ran off with another man long before the action begins. He has a fourteen-year-old daughter, living away at an institution. Tina (Lorraine Brunning), has become a "ward" of contemporary social service to which subject Leigh devotes some risible satire. Stan is presented as an average sensual man but not a sexual predator. He has a less-than-tempestuous affair with the neurotic June (Su Elliott), the wife of one of his co-workers, Harold (Tim Barker). He is, moreover, the flirtatious object of affection from the superficially attractive but shrill Hazel (Kay Stonham), the wife of fellow postman Gordon (Timothy Spall). She invites Stan in for tea when her husband is working a different shift. Later she embarrassingly presumes to act like a mother to Tina during the daughter's weekend visit with her father. She instructs her in peeling potatoes, brushes her hair while reprimanding the child for her neglect of this task, and publicly raises the question of whether Tina wears a bra.

As a currently unattached man and the boss stag, as it were, of a postal herd, who takes all females as his right, Stan exudes somewhat more masculine appeal and animal magnetism than their respective husbands do. Harold seems pathetically immature, however much he dotes on his wife, who indulges herself in claims of suffering and the assertion that her husband could never understand the depth of her anguish. "June Fish," as Paul Clements in *The Improvised Play* describes her, "compensates for the absence of excitement, love, and colour in her own life by absorbing the language and values of the paperback romances which she reads so avidly" (43). On the other hand, viewers may sympathize with her quest for an alternative to her husband's devotion to what might be called elementary school humor on the order of "Why is Prince Charles a postman? Because he's the royal male" or "What's yellow and dangerous? Shark-infested custard." Although June has repeatedly told her husband that men find her a desirable woman, Harold cannot believe his wife's assertion when she finally reveals to him that she has been unfaithful to him with Stan. *Time's* Richard Corliss describes June as "hate-filled" and "an adulterer, but infidelity with her husband's best friend gives the woman no more pleasure than anything else in her sorry life" (67). A provocative allusive juxtaposition linking Stan and Harold emerges later in the film. Stan greatly appreciates Frank Sinatra and plays a recording of Old Blue Eyes for the pleasure of sharing "My Way" with Hazel, Gordon, and Tina. After Harold has received in his marital bed the devastating news of his wife's infidelity, he sings "Maresy Dotes," which was one of the young Sinatra's early hits.

In contrast, Hazel's husband is the sloppy, heavy-drinking, and slothful Gordon who, unlike Harold, has suspicions about his wife's fondness for and casual intimacy with Stan. He sees the two of them together in Stan's house when the couple joins Stan and his daughter for tea after all of them had eaten Sunday dinner at Hazel's house. Here both June and Tina observe Stan kissing Hazel as they clean up in the kitchen after tea. June looks through a window at this intimacy; Tina sees it from the living room. Gordon is deprived of this vision. As Stan shows his co-worker and his wife around the house, he tells them about the difficulty in getting the casket of his late mother down the narrow stairs. This kind of family detail may help humanize Stan and reinforce again Leigh's never-too-distant realization of mortality as part of life, presented without sentimentality in films as diverse as *The Kiss of Death* and *Secrets & Lies.*

What follows as Stan prepares to leave with Tina is the beginning of a potentially explosive Leigh confluence of forces, this time in an outdoor setting. Harold shows up, surprised to find his wife at Stan's. Now realizing she has a sexual rival in June, Hazel becomes even more harpy-like. She verbally and physically assails June, Stan and her husband, Gordon, while the latter protests to his wife that he "ain't fat." Leigh here curtails the fracas, but it momentarily harks back to similar sequences like the prolonged ones in *Grown-Ups* and *Abigail's Party*. Judy Bloch in her interview with Mike Leigh and Alison Steadman asked the filmmaker about this sequence, as she puts it, "when the women at the end of *Home Sweet Home* turn into animals, virtually, with their name-calling." Leigh's response further validates his desire for mimetic representation through some kind of actual emotion:

> The point is, that is what *happens* [italics are Leigh's] to people. All that happens in that scene is that they are behaving like some people behave in certain circumstances. The only way I can really explain anything, in any of the films, is in terms of a real world going on, real life. (Movshovitz 21)

Leigh includes a brief sequence of Stan with another woman, whose name he learns only after having sex with her. She is Janice (Sheila Kelley), a woman he picks up at the laundromat, a locale that is used for a multitude of purposes in Leigh films. As Janice leaves Stan's house, viewers perceive she is limping. Michael Coveney remarks on Sheila Kelley's portrayal (an actress who served Leigh well as the biker's girlfriend in *Nuts in May*): "… in this desolate, polio-stricken creature she paints a whole life of someone who haunts laundrettes, not to wash clothes, but to make human contact" (161). Such crystallizing encounters add exceptional depth to Leigh's films, and they are especially surprising in relatively brief television films. Because of his liaison with the woman from the laundromat, Stan fails to make his promised visit to his forlorn and uncommunicative daughter at her institution. She, too, has been crippled by circumstances beyond her control.

Leigh's sober treatment of Tina, Stan's daughter, is qualified by humor only in the aggressively upbeat behavior of her social worker, Melody (Frances Barber), whose interventions on behalf of the child and her father somehow miss the mark despite her good intentions. Viewers at the end of the film learn from Tina's new social worker, Dave (Lloyd Peters), that Melody (who may have been his girlfriend) has suddenly departed, not unlike Tina's mother from her marriage to Stan when the child was six years old. Given the situation and the shared name of adolescent girls in distress, Tina in *Home Sweet Home* might evoke memories of another lost child in Irving Rapper's classic weepie, *Now, Voyager* (1942). Of course, Leigh provides no Bette Davis to rescue this Tina, restore order to the narrative, and achieve a sentimental closure in the tradition of classic Hollywood cinema. The less-contrived verisimilitude in which Leigh works, what he calls "heightened realism," militates against any woman among Stan's superficial relationships being able to salvage his daughter.

Stan's lack of understanding of women extends to his daughter, and the surrogates assigned to help him with Tina in the person of social workers prove disappointing and ultimately laughably unable to fulfill the tasks required. Dave delivers turgid Marxist jargon to Stan as an alternative to what he describes as the "empirically self-motivated action" and "quiche lorraine" attitude of Melody, his predecessor. In return, this new social worker provokes an ever-more uncomprehending expression from Stan, who is seen in increasingly tighter close-ups in the midst of Dave's incomprehensible phrases like "peripheral substructure," "contributing infrastructure," and "the overall macro-definition." Dave does get to articulate with a sneer the maxim that "this society doesn't cater for human need; it caters for human greed." These Marxist principles will be treated less satirically in *High Hopes* nearer the end of the eighties. The bespectacled Dave of *Home Sweet Home* somewhat anticipates Cyril in *High Hopes*.

When Dave asks whether Stan has any questions, Stan only asks why the social worker brought with him an electric teakettle. Temporarily, Dave breaks into actual communicative clarity by explaining a colleague lent him the pot to substitute for the one his live-in girlfriend, "who shall remain nameless," took with her when she left him for a merchant banker—an action, which he concedes "of course, is her prerogative." He has carried the kettle in because the locks in his car are broken, and he didn't want the borrowed device stolen. That the girlfriend took all the possessions he thought they shared elicits this remark: "It really gets on my tits. Let's not be sexist about it. It really gets on my chest," as Dave explains to Stan. However, Dave does not stay long with intelligible speech since he soon complicates his discourse and loses his listener by talking about "commodity fetishism at its most naked."

The film suddenly ends with Dave's monologue continuing, unintelligible except for an occasional word, while the closing credits pass over a lone Tina standing in a backyard. This ending bears witness to what Coveney calls "a social and cultural separation which compels him [Dave] to erect, in the hastiest and most insensitive manner, the language barrier of professional certainty" (165). Another interpreter, Ray Carney, makes a convincing case for a parallel between June, the romance-reading, self-dramatizing wife of Harold and occasional mistress of Stan, and Dave, the Marxist social worker: "His revolutionary sentimentality is a variation of June's sexual sentimentality.... In Leigh's witty presentation of it, soap-opera Marxism is expressively indistinguishable from soap-opera eroticism" (149). This ending of *Home Sweet Home* together with its opening of quaint sampler-like title cards captures Leigh's tonally complex and mixed style of compassion, ironic amusement, and satiric exposure that deconstructs the notion of ideal domesticity.

Leigh's characters in *Home Sweet Home* are also delineated, in varying degrees, through these same elements of compassion, irony, and satire that save them from either total caricature or otherwise overly determined meaning. The viewer is virtually required to become a collaborator in establishing meaning through parallels, contrasts, and inferences that alter first impressions. Unlike classic Hollywood cinema, Leigh's films do not lock viewers on a tight track and speed them to an anticipated terminus.

Part of the pleasure in a film like *Home Sweet Home* is what viewers decide after they reflect upon what they have seen and reassess the characters along the way because the director's intent and judgment are not telegraphed in advance. Paul Clements especially admires a sequence when Tina, at home on leave from her institution, aimlessly kicks a stone in her father's backyard, and Clements infers that Stan is trying to stimulate a shared memory of the past with her:

> The essence of the scene is that there is no substance to the time-present of these two people and yet that is where they exist, with her swishing aimlessly and him trying to recall the past or generate some enthusiasm for the future. Firmly fixed in a real place and in real behaviour, the scene evokes effortlessly, and almost subliminally, the exact quality of this particular relationship and its evasion of what is happening now. (85)

Leigh permits viewers to make discoveries and assign weight to them, according to their own way of thinking and seeing, which is one of the reasons Leigh's films reward multiple visits. He has the unusual capacity of not only bringing characters to his viewers but also, more significantly, bringing viewers to the characters in ways that invite response although not because of facile identification.

Closely allied to this effect is the sudden recognition of small details, often unnoticed on initial viewing, that enrich the experience of subsequent visits. One such almost random example creates the casual surprise of the physical resemblance of father and daughter as Stan drives his daughter back to her institution. Their similar noses had not been apparent until cameraman Remi Adefarasin's intimate and elegant profile shots in the car of father and daughter. Until this sequence Tina was usually shown in full-face shots. This kind of detail becomes more central in Leigh's next television drama, *Meantime*. Leigh's attention to incidental physical details not typically found even in so-called realist films extends in *Home Sweet Home* to capturing Timothy Spall (Gordon) arranging his genitalia after he gets off his bike and goes around the corner of a building at the post office. Leigh doesn't omit such details of human physicality, but he does not obsess over them either. Bodies, their appearance, functions, urges, and the like do not typically evoke distaste in his films, perhaps allying him more closely with Rabelais or Chaucer than with Swift.

As noted elsewhere, the sound of toilets flushing is common in Leigh's films, and this film is no exception in utilizing that auditory effect. On the matter of sound, the original score by Carl Davis for *Home Sweet Home* deserves mention for its deep-throated double-bass accompaniment, played by the London Double-Bass Ensemble, to action in Leigh's film, where it is used strategically if sparingly. It does contribute depth and texture to the silent physical similarity of father and daughter in the absence of much dialogue.

Home Sweet Home is representative of Leigh's achievement in his series of television films, coming as it does past the halfway mark of his works in this genre. It may not be the best, but it serves as a kind of model of how as a filmmaker and writer Leigh hints and suggests. He makes his viewers look again at the world and the individuals they come to know. Much of the labor of reconstruction and signification is left to the audience. In the process, he transfigures the commonplace without violating the foundation in social realism, for his characters are surely products of their social situation like the postmen and the frustrated women in this film. Leigh seems to be developing a more sensitive gauge of moral calculation expressed as always in sharp social-cultural details that will achieve fulfillment only later with his return to feature films. In these longer, theatrically released films, the greater length of time available for storytelling and development of fully realized characters beyond what is available in a television drama will open new possibilities for him. On the other hand, Leigh's next television project, *Meantime*, interestingly enough not for the BBC, turned out to be among his most esteemed efforts on the strength of casting and concept.

Meantime

Three years into Thatcherism, Leigh made *Meantime* (1983) as a 16mm "Film on Four" for Central Television. A bit later, Channel 4 films began to be shot on 35mm with a view to film distribution, but Leigh was not in time to benefit from this development. Michael Coveney writes that this circumstance delayed the filmmaker's return to feature films for another five years (172). *Meantime*, which won the People's Award at the Berlin Film Festival in 1994, looks at the effects of unemployment on a father and his sons. Conditions in England during the period of the film, the early eighties, were comparable to those of the Great Depression of the 1930s. The national income was dropping rapidly; manufacturing had plummeted more than 20 percent, and several million jobs had been eliminated. However, whatever political content this film or any of Leigh's works may have, it is never allowed to supplant the relationships and the characters as focus, however much the economy has exacerbated existing family problems and caused others.

The Pollocks live with a defeatist attitude and increasing hostility toward one another in a London East End council flat in one of England's morbid vertical slums. In some sense the discontinuity among generations summarized by the alienation of the young is lessened for people like the Pollocks as father and sons are part of the wide and growing breach between social and economic classes. Partly because of a poor economy, the sons are stuck as perpetual adolescents, and their parents are forced to remain as caregivers to adult children even though Mark and Colin might contribute something to the rent of their council flat. The sons are suspended between teenagers and adults, unable to move forward into the grown-up world because they cannot or will not find jobs and move out on their own. Their lives have no direction or aim save avoiding boredom, which they seemingly often fail to do. Leigh's manner in dealing with this issue is sensitive, not exploitative, and utterly real. Mark (Phil Daniels) mockingly reminds his father, John (Alfred Molina), "You don't own nothing." The film is often considered to be the best film ever made about life on the dole. Another possibility implicit in the situation might be the familial enactment of what Roland Gelatt hypothesized about England in his essay, "Is Britain Dying?," published almost a decade before *Meantime* was shown on British television. "There is a theory," Gelatt wrote, "that having pioneered the Industrial Revolution, the British are now in the vanguard of a more leisurely post-industrial world, that they have succeeded before any other Western society in shucking off an outmoded work ethic" (16). Yet the same essay also cited Tony Benn, then secretary of state for industry, speaking of the lack of fairness in British society, which he called "the last colony left in the British Empire," and urging that Britain's "problems can be solved only by means of a radical shift in the balance of power toward working people. 'Those who invest their skills, energy, and lives in industry,' he argues, 'are entitled to at least as great a say in its control as those who invest their money in it'" (15).

The mother in this family, the coarse and unsympathetic Mavis (Pam Ferris), has a more culturally refined, upwardly mobile, childless married sister, Barbara

(Marion Bailey). She lives with her successful businessman husband, Frank (Jeff Roberts), in one of the comfortable single homes on the Chigwell housing estate at the Essex end of the London Underground's Central Line. With a recognition of economic segregation, Leigh often contrasts the socio-economic and material status of siblings in later films like *High Hopes* and *Secrets & Lies* and, in the process, illuminates differences in personalities that may or may not be principally the effect of material difference. References are made to visiting the mother of Mavis and Barbara in the film although she is never seen; however, this kind of relationship to an aged parent is a harbinger of later Leigh films.

At the close of a visit the family on welfare makes to their more prosperous relatives, Mark kisses the wall of the entrance to the house rather than his Aunt Barbara, signifying the source of his relative's power and appeal. John Lahr has described how the Pollock family "gets demoted before our eyes," as the audience sees them leave their relative's comfortable bungalow and go back to their London high-rise. "Amid the fug of cigarette smoke and kettle steam," Lahr continues, " they are humiliated by their cramped quarters; they look out at a landscape as bleak as their prospects. Here dread is palpable and comparison deflates identity" (53).

It is the younger generation that garners the most interest in *Meantime*. Leigh's narrative and direction brought forth memorable performances from talented actors at the start of their careers. They include Phil Daniels as Mark; Tim Roth as Mark's nearly catatonic younger man-child brother, Colin, another in a long line of Leigh's impaired characters; Gary Oldman as Coxy, the skinhead friend of the brothers; and Tilly Vosburgh as their female buddy, Hayley. This film achieved a cult following among young people in subsequent decades. Unlike the teen oeuvre of the American John Hughes in the eighties, Leigh's film was not targeted to adolescents, but they embraced the director's portrayal of the awkwardness of life and a culture in which young people find their lives. Leigh's late-adolescent and twenty-something characters have a spontaneous ingenuousness and idiosyncratic unpredictability largely missing from the adults in the film. They are not impressed with authority, since they have been let down by too many authority figures such as parents. Leigh does not invest them with pro-social characteristics, but he also does not pursue strongly antisocial behavior either. He takes the risk of a human expression of this season of youth.

In the absence of a conventional plot, Leigh introduces us to the condition of unemployment in England as well as the complexities and vulnerabilities of family and other relationships without reliance on a linear cause-and-effect narrative structure. Instead he gives the viewer time to observe the physical attributes of the father and sons whose glasses and strangely similar behavior make it utterly plausible that they are biologically related. Leigh's verisimilitude becomes a product of engagement between the film and viewer in the process of text construction. Viewers must puzzle out the complexity of reality, confront the sometimes slightly sinister chaos at its heart, represented, for example, in *Meantime* by a character like Coxy who, as John Lahr describes him, "throws his humiliation onto others through his sadistic pranks" (53). As Ray Carney persuasively explains, "Leigh reveals the fallacy of motivational essentialism. He provides experiences that overflow conceptual containers" (170). Consequently, Leigh compels his viewers to acknowledge the impossibility of capturing the truth about any aspect of life or reality in abstractions. He deliberately and consistently frustrates film audiences' desires for clearly defined and credible motives. Meanwhile, little by little, he shows how already tenuous bonds inside the fractious family become more strained. Control and communication among family members, especially between parents and children, become weakened and eventually snap.

Frequently Mark calls his brother Colin "Muppet" and sometimes, more specifically, "Kermit," to which his younger sibling objects. Father and sons are shown watching television together, suggesting that television might undergird rather than undercut even this family, however short it falls of the domestic iconography of an ideal family form.

Also relative to some of the only action in the film that could be considered traditional plotting, can we be sure that Mark's visit to Aunt Barbara on the morning she has engaged Colin to help her with interior redecoration was actually meant to sabotage the younger brother's employment opportunity? Michael Coveney answers that question affirmatively:

> Mark destroys this pathetic "chance," or opening, for his younger brother for two reasons, one ideological, one pitiful: he doesn't want Colin to have anything to do with that dead suburban life out there; he really wants everything to stay as it is, even though the static depressiveness of it all is, he says, "doing my brain in." (22–23)

But Ray Carney's interpretation of this sequence as "a flow of verbal and visual experiences that absolutely resist being resolved into simple, underpinning intentions" (170) with a series of rhetorical questions seems closer to Leigh's own practice in this film. Mark delivers a speech about "principles" to his brother, observing that "principles are something Mom and Dad ain't got," which Carney assesses with respect to the ambiguity Leigh explores:

> Viewed in one way, especially given his reprehensible treatment of Barbara, any talk about how he [Mark] has principles and Barbara, John, and his parents do not is hogwash. Viewed from another perspective, he seems at least half-right. In his strange perverted way, Mark is motivated by some sense of ethical responsibility and does have Colin's welfare at heart.... Mark's speech is an act of manipulation, but that doesn't preclude its also being sincere and heartfelt. (171)

Because Mark arrives at Barbara's house before his younger brother, the aunt and nephew fear that he is lost and finally set off in her car to search for Colin. They stop at a Central Line tube station among other places. Leigh parallels their action with a sequence of Colin making his way across streets and through parks to his aunt's house. In a park he stops momentarily by a statue of the standing Winston Churchill resolute with curved arm on hip. Without looking at the sculptured figure, Colin unconsciously assumes a similar stance except his arms lack Churchill's sense of purpose. Colin's arms do not quite make it to his hip; they dangle as they have throughout the sequence. Leigh presents Colin almost struggling to stay upright and even minimally balanced. The ironic juxtaposition of Colin and Churchill here creates another enigmatic and poignant Leigh image, the significance of which one hesitates to interpret too easily. One of the problems in this film is the passivity of Colin, who seems always on the verge of becoming independent but lacks the motive power for the drama that would result. Mark, on the other hand, takes an active interrogatory stance toward his Aunt Barbara in this part of the film, going so far as to inquire why she never had any children of her own. She replies that she was waiting to see how her nephews turned out. When she tells Mark that she planned to serve fish fingers for lunch, he rejoins that he did not know fish had fingers. Meanwhile Colin becomes more morose and distanced from his brother, and Aunt Barbara becomes testy with him as she realizes that no redecoration will take place that day with either of her nephews.

Something of the same perplexity arises even in Leigh's handling of the possible meaning and significance of objects in the physical world; repetitions, suggestive of patterns, emerge but without necessarily symbolic content, as in the instance of the pens used in several sequences. During a sequence at the Employment Benefit Office, father and sons give an update of their common failure to find employment. Colin, having lost his card, is asked to fill out a form with a pen given him by the unemployment-benefit clerk (Eileen Davies). He places the removable top of the pen in his mouth while he completes the form. When requested to return the pen, he spits out the top and hands the reassembled pen to the woman who, with disgust, discards it. Subsequently Mark has his interview, and he, too, is reminded to return "my pen." He belligerently slams the pen down on the counter before the startled woman and screams "our pen." Later, at a bingo game, Mavis, the mother in this family of men, cannot find a working pen as she struggles to keep up with the numbers being called. Finally, the estate manager, played by Peter Wight, who will reappear for a provocative role in *Naked* a decade later, carefully and systematically places his pen on a sheet of paper. He then explains to the Pollocks why it is helpful to report maintenance problems sooner rather than later, using an analogy of grains of sands and anthills. Colin, the naïve literalist, asks his mother after this object lesson, "We got ants?"

Each character deals with writing implements in accordance with his or her personality and temperament. Colin is seen throughout the first part of *Meantime* with almost an oral fixation. He places numerous other things besides the pen in his mouth, including the top of the clothes hamper at the laundromat. Mark evidences hostility and sarcasm in most situations, so his slamming of the pen and claim of first-person plural ownership is completely in character. Mavis is sullen and ineffectual, and her inability to find a working writing implement suggests a corollary to her other inadequacies. The estate manager is irritatingly calm, cool, and well organized, attributes that he demonstrates through his handling of the pen. Leigh's simulation of reality is not without hints of symbolic design, for he does appear to invest commonplace objects with his own special imaginative quality, even while stopping short of symbolism in its usual sense until later in his career with, for example, *Secrets & Lies*.

Sometimes in Leigh it is a play on words, a misunderstanding or a joke that reveals the double nature he so often pursues in his films. The title of this film, of course, captures the aimless existence of many of its characters, their intervals between bars and the Employment Benefit Office. Indeed, Leigh builds his whole film on literalizing Shakespeare's "meantime, let wonder seem familiar." But one does not have to stretch very far to recognize *mean* as an adjective associated with a quality of life like Martin Scorsese's *Mean Streets*. The impoverishment of family life in the council estate is not at all exclusively monetary. It seems summed up by the mother and father when they tell each other to shut up, and neither one does. Their relationship and time together lack such elevating human qualities as kindness, goodwill, or civility of speech. Roger Pratt's photography ably captures the inhuman geometry of the high-rise housing project. Gary Oldman in *Nil by Mouth* (1998), his debut as film director, seems to have been influenced by this bleak visual image, which he recapitulates to strong effect.

If *means* as a plural noun is considered, then Leigh provides an especially satiric scene between the estate manager and Barbara, who is visiting the Pollocks to offer Colin a job in which the two discuss money from opposite positions. In the final scene between Mark and Barbara in her home, he mentions that she sounds like Princess Anne with her attempt at posh speech. She, flattered, remarks that she studied elocution in college as part of her secretarial course that led to her subsequent position answering the phone for National Westminster Bank. In the scene in the Pollocks' flat Auntie Barbara becomes a sort of surrogate for Margaret Thatcher, whose diction and enunciation, it might be noted, were not too far removed from those of Princess Anne. If these antagonists agree on anything, it is that money equals power, and Barbara does sound like Mrs. Thatcher when she insists that "you can't run a country without a fiscal policy." Coveney sees this scene as Leigh's "most explicitly Pinteresque moment"; however, with his description that "all the high finance never comes within a million miles of the problems of this high-rise" (175), an alternative claim may be made that it plays more like David Mamet without the four-letter words. *Meantime* is wise and full of detailed observations, but Leigh's wry imagination makes it sparkle with his distinctive species of satire in scenes like this one.

Barbara shows benevolence and kindness toward Colin, unlike most of the others among his family and friends, who often cuff and verbally abuse him. Barbara and Colin cannot pursue the redecorating she has employed him to do, but she exhibits her concern for the effect of one person upon another and upon the fabric of life, which may explain why her final scene with her husband is so bleak. He returns home to find his somewhat intoxicated wife on the floor in a corner of the room where she had planned to work. Self-pityingly, she expresses fear of aging and challenges her husband on his attraction to other women during their marriage. Her last words to him in this scene are "Fuck off." At times, Barbara seems to have a more highly developed sense than the other characters of the interrelationships as something organic, yet made up of the harmony of many different things, and always fluid and changing, the desiderata frequently advanced in Mike Leigh films. Her final breakdown evidences to the collapse of such values for her and links her to a number of other Leigh characters.

Leigh's playing of his own enigma variations with respect to his characters in *Meantime* results in pleasure and pain because, as Carney denotes in his choice of the chapter title "Challenging Easy Understandings: *Meantime*" (163) and his subsequent analysis, the film cannot be decoded like mainstream cinema fare. Cryptic asides resonate but sometimes only produce a resounding tinkle, as in the literary allusion Mark introduces in conversation with Hayley when he asks her if she has ever read *The Lion, the Witch and the Wardrobe.* Hayley's usual lack of affect extends to this question, which she answers with a blank stare. What Mark or Leigh had in mind in posing Narnia, a world unlike the one Mark knows and lives in and one that can be entered only by certain children and at certain times, eludes us. Nevertheless, the allegorical potential of the first book in C. S. Lewis'seven-volume collection of the "Chronicles of Narnia" in the context of this film remains stimulating. The only analogy that comes to mind is a literal one when Coxy, showing off, shuts Colin in a utility cupboard in Hayley's kitchen. Perhaps nothing short of Aslan, Lewis' noble lion, would have the power to salvage Colin. Mike Leigh, however, scrupulously avoids allegories despite a hint of submerged wistfulness for them, suggested by Mark's question to Hayley and the inclusion of a book title. Unlike C. S. Lewis, Leigh could not readily emphasize transcendence over immanence, eternity over time, or the supernatural over the natural, but perhaps Colin infuses here, via allusion to Lewis, the virtue of hope, which is woven into the fundamental nature of even his reality.

One also wonders what Leigh might intend with the West Indian couple he introduces casually, the woman (Leila Bertrand) in the laundromat and the man (Hepburn Graham), with his secondhand pram, who rides the apartment building's elevator with Colin and Coxy. Not surprisingly, the latter makes some racial jests by punning on *right* as if the word were *white*. Leigh appears in these moments to be implying something about the field of alterity to reflect the decolonized eighties in Britain. Perhaps he offers through the decency and caring relationship of the West Indian couple, an alternative to other more troubled couples in the film as well as a rebuke to Mrs. Thatcher's 1978–79 campaign rhetoric of England as an "alien swamp." The young mother-to-be incidentally rejects the secondhand pram, preferring a new one. This woman manifests a sad sense of pride. Even though Leigh has shown her for only a few moments in the film, and neither she nor her male friend ever shows up again, she is a distinctive individual with a story all her own. A similar bit of business over a pram takes place again in Leigh's next television film, *Four Days in July*.

Near the end of *Meantime* Colin has suddenly departed from Aunt Barbara's house. That Colin did not successfully complete this job assignment for his aunt proves instrumental in the final disputes, the contretemps between Barbara and her husband and the further disarray with the parents of Mark and Colin. The latter returns to his parents' flat wearing the hood from his jacket over his head. That he has had his head shaved remains a secret to his brother, parents, and viewers until the next morning when Mark peels off the hood of his sleeping brother to reveal the evidence. There is no subsequent scene with surprised parents although they are heard from offscreen calling Colin and bickering once more over who should shut up. Upon returning home the night before, Colin had asserted his independence by ordering his father out of the bedroom he shares with Mark, just as earlier he had visited Hayley's apartment on his own despite her refusal to admit him. With Colin now awake and sitting up, Mark good-humoredly rubs the crown of his brother's shaved head and says, with evident fraternal affection, "My brother's a skinhead" and then immediately qualifies, "No you ain't." Mark exits their shared bedroom by calling his brother "Kojak" after the eponymous bald detective immortalized by Telly Savalas, in an especially popular American television series in England during the period of Leigh's film. His brother, secretly pleased with this new pop culture identity instead of the earlier "Kermit," protests halfheartedly with "Don't call me that." Mark from the doorway smiles at Colin, who smiles wanly in return with a touch of gratitude. Colin has assured Mark that Coxy did not persuade him to get his head shaved. This fraternal exchange does nothing so sentimental as to demonstrate that Mark may be a bully on the surface but is a sweet, caring brother "deep down." In Leigh's films such a character is both a bully and a caring brother.

Before this final scene, the film gives us a last view of Coxy. He is on a road voluntarily encased in a womb-like metal drum, possibly a loader bucket or dust bin (garbage pail to Americans), beating it as he rolls away. His encasement metaphorically suggests the claustrophobia in terms of living space and bleak future economic possibilities for these young people. Carney concludes: "There is no simpler, 'real' inner Coxy hidden underneath the complex, changeable, unresolved outer Coxy" (169). In contrast, the understated, newfound kinship between Mark and Colin has potential for the brothers of development and maturity utterly lacking in Coxy. Leigh has given the fraternal relationship of the two young men a measure of integration and possible future direction, however precarious any achievement could turn out to be. Andrew Dickson's haunting recurring melody played by himself and George Khan on a "prepared" piano, stuck with drawing pins, as Coveney reported (195), and soprano saxophone as the credits roll seems ever so slightly more jaunty at the close than it has elsewhere in this incisive working-class comedy. Or perhaps this inference is only a response of wishful thinking in the "meantime" of our negotiations with Leigh's extremely provocative, elusive, yet curiously satisfying film text for which the filmmaker himself retains, as he told John Naughton in an *Empire* interview in Movshovitz, "a *real* soft spot" (128).

Four Days in July

Leigh's last television film for the BBC, *Four Days in July* (1984), was shot in the midst of Northern Ireland's fractious society on the streets of East and West Belfast, the first time the director had worked outside of England. The filmmaker creates a domestic comedy in what has been called the tragic skeleton in the British closet. Leigh and his largely Northern Ireland cast spent six months in production, rehearsal, and shooting after a six-month research period. The result is less a period piece than an enduring and distinctly Mike Leigh approach to "The Troubles," as the strife in this territory has been popularly known. In his interview with Graham Fuller, Leigh expressed his understanding of what he did in the film:

> Plainly... *Four Days in July*, deals with matters which—whatever else you could say about them—are graphically political, but looked at as objectively as possible. In making it, I simply wanted to respond to whatever I found in my investigation of Northern Ireland and all I wound up saying, really, was something very fundamental and basic about people. (xx)

Accordingly, neither partisan nor apolitical in its stance, Leigh's film is once more a humanist testament, conveying simply something of the nature of life for the people of Ulster. Graffiti found on a wall in Belfast, though not seen in Leigh's film, simply define the fatalism that innocent people endure: "I wonder each night what the monster will do to me tomorrow?"

Coveney amusingly reports that Leigh referred to this effort as his "first foreign-language movie" (176). As with some other Leigh films, the dialogue proves especially challenging to American ears, far more so than for Britons when the film was aired in 1985 on British television. The British Army still patrols the streets of Belfast during daylight hours in this Leigh film set in 1984. The four days, July 10–13, are the very heart of what is sometimes called the summer marching season in Northern Ireland, celebrating Protestant victories over Catholics centuries ago, most notably the festivities for the Battle of the Boyne (1690) victory by William of Orange.

Often outbreaks of Protestant attacks on Catholic homes and retalitory reactions to these attacks occur in advance of the parades and bonfires, but Leigh does not include any scenes of this contentious tradition. Leigh does incorporate impressive footage of both a July 11 Orange bonfire and an Orange parade. The bonfire sequence is used visually as the burning essence of the color orange, while the participants with their Union Jacks celebrate the orange sash their "fathers wore of yore." At the end of the bonfire scene, Leigh cuts to the lone damaged figure of the Catholic Eugene standing in the doorway of his modest house, which in twilight has a blue tint on the façade that makes a stunning complement to the orange of the bonfire. Additionally, in the parade sequence, Leigh discovers a child with a baby bottle of orange juice who looks down on the parade from an upstairs window. Leigh appears most prophetic in his implication that there can be such a thing as racism between people of the same color.

In classic Leigh fashion, the film examines the lives of two families, one Catholic, Eugene (Des McAleer) and his wife Colette (Brid Brennan) from the Falls Road, and the other Protestant, Billy (Charles Lawson) and his wife Lorraine (Paula Hamilton). Both couples are expecting their first child; however, beyond this shared circumstance Leigh shows not how much but how very little the two couples have in common. Billy is a soldier in the Protestant-dominated Ulster Defence Regiment, whereas Eugene is disabled from a series of physical assaults he has suffered over the years—a bullet on two occasions in 1973 and 1979 in addition to a bomb hit in 1976. Eugene reports this series of misfortunes, the consequence of political violence and British military presence in Northern Ireland, with amazing good humor to the window-washer Dixie (Stephen Rea), a former political internee, and his plumber neighbor, Brendan, who is fixing their toilet. Brendan, played by actor and later writer Shane Connaughton, argues that severely disabled victims would be better off dead. Parenthetically, Connaughton will later write the screenplay for *My Left Foot* (1989), which assumes a very different position from that of his character in *Four Days in July*.

From the opening sequence where children are seen playing in an alleyway as military vehicles pass on cross streets, life in Northern Ireland is seen against perpetual warfare that has become routine. War in the modern age has become increasingly complex, intimate, and personalized. Leigh illustrates this fact in the condition of Eugene and the environment the children play in. Not too surprisingly, given his attention to Eugene as victim, Leigh's own sympathies in *Four Days in July* appear to be rather more Republican than Unionist. He imbues his Catholic couple with greater sensitivity and amiability than their counterpart Protestant pair. These personal attributes of difference remain a moral criterion throughout his films. Coveney describes the UDR soldier and his chums as "a pretty dire and dour bunch, keeping fit, twirling batons, singing 'The Sash' and getting somberly drunk on cans of lager" (177). Paul Clements in his fine essay on *Four Days in July* in *British Television Drama in the 1980's* similarly contrasts the "languorous melody and occasional lyricism" of conversations in Eugene's household with the "staccato and often brutal" exchanges between Billy and his wife and friends (172). Leigh's use of discordant symmetry and parallel characters in *Four Days in July* suggests a pattern of characterization reminiscent of L. P. Hartley's description in *The Novelist's Responsibility* of the later Henry James. Hartley claims that James's characters "exist in virtue of their relationship to each other, and to their general predicament...the tormented quartet in *The Golden Bowl* are almost like unknown factors in a quadratic equation or lines in a parallelogram of forces" (180). This formulation seems apposite in some ways to the quartet of couples in this film, albeit less lugubrious since the characters in Leigh experience the happy event of childbirth across the political divide although the director does not film any sudden harmony for the former opponents.

Early in the film's narrative, Billy on his UDR patrol stops a battered van driven by a Mr. McCoy (John Keegan), who delivers an eccentric, often contradictory, but nevertheless impassioned plea for unity among Ulstermen. McCoy's full speech is included in Clements' essay: "We, you and me...are direct descendants of an ancient Ulster people. We have been here in Ulster since before the time of Jesus Christ himself. We heroes of Ulster have been defending ourselves against those so-called Irishmen for a million years! . . . We had our own language once. Nothing to do with the Gaelic mumbo-jumbo. It was the language of the people of Ulster" (170). Clements further points out that the members of the patrol and Mr. McCoy do, indeed, share a fundamental orientation: "they belong to a beleaguered nation at war, facing betrayal on all sides and forced into an aggressively defensive posture against the Republic of Ireland and its agents" (171).

Leigh offers his usual close attention to material details with both houses displaying, as Clements puts it, "their partisan icons: above Billy's bed hangs the flag of the red hand of Ulster; at the foot of Eugene's stairs is a photograph of the Pope" (168). The two men receive parallel sequences at one point as Billy painstakingly divests himself of his bulletproof torso protection after an uneventful patrol and later Eugene puts on his pajama bottoms, not without great effort, while lying down. Billy's physical movements are usually quick and restless in contrast to those of the handicapped Eugene, but during these two clothing maneuvers, they are remarkably similar in pace.

The climax of the film is the birth of the respective children. Both women experience early morning breaking of water in bed and deliver at approximately the same time. Meanwhile, their husbands sit uncommunicatively in a maternity waiting room with occasional sounds of the Orange parades penetrating their surroundings. Leigh never shows the uniting of the husbands with their wives the day after the birthing. To Eugene's query to Billy asking him if he would like to know what is going on within the labor rooms, Billy's response is merely "Bollocks." Both men must listen to a third expectant father. He is a misanthropic Protestant loyalist named Mr. Roper (John Hewitt), who concludes it is better never to be born at all. When Billy asks if Roper wants to emigrate, he is told, as cited in Clements' essay, "there's nowhere to emigrate to. Everywhere else in the world's as bad as this place" (174). Despite his infirmities, Eugene does not share such desolate sentiments, and Des McAleer's sensitive gaze at Roper implicitly bespeaks sympathy for the man if philosophical disagreement with his position.

As is memorable in many Leigh films, the grandeur and courage of women, here seen in the rigors of labor, receive unsentimental but telling portrayal in *Four Days in July*. Both infants arrive on July 12, the major feast in the Orange calendar. When Colette on July 13 tells Lorraine that she is giving her child the Irish name "Magraid" rather than the English equivalent "Margaret," as Clements explains, "the shutters come down. There will be no bonding and no reconciliation. These babies are named and inherit inescapable history" (174). Lorraine's son will be called Billy after his father, with distant associations, of course, to William of Orange. Leigh ends the film with the two women silently holding their newborn children. Leigh and his cinematographer, Remi Adefarasin, provide full-face views of Brid Brennan as Colette in her hospital bed, but more often show Paula Hamilton's Lorraine in profile or in three-quarter shots. These setups privilege or at least give a slight dominance to the more open and forthcoming Colette. Speech fails, but Rachel Portman's original music concludes the film with her haunting melody scored for viola and cello, perhaps the musical equivalents of the two young mothers and their newborns. As Clements notes, *Four Days in July* "begins and ends with children" (174), from the kids in the opening alleyway to the infants in the maternity ward.

John Ralston Saul in *Voltaire's Bastards: The Dictatorship of Reason in the West* submits that films "rarely enter unresolved public debates. They tend rather to illustrate resolved opinion" (570). Mike Leigh does not follow this standard in *Four Days in July* or for that matter elsewhere. Clements quotes the director on this very point: "When there's a solution, the audience forgets the film on leaving the cinema. Life goes on. It unfolded before the film and it continues afterwards. People often ask me what happens afterwards? I haven't got a clue. It's your problem" (175). And with respect to Northern Ireland, the issues are still not resolved.

In the new century, the Roman Catholics minority and the Protestant majority are sharing power in government, but gunmen and bombers still cast a dark shadow over efforts to reach a permanent peace. Sinn Fein, the Irish Republican Army's political arm, emerged from British elections in 2001 with more influence than ever before. Such success might suggest that the political as opposed to the military path is winning. Disarmanent of both sides remains the large unresolved issue; indeed the act in Northern Ireland is usually termed "decomissioning" to defuse the connotation of surrender that the I.R.A. infers in "disarmament." As Clements concludes about Leigh's film: "That it came to be made and broadcast is a significant tribute to the courageous independence of both its maker and of the BBC" (176). *Four Days in July* retains its relevance because Leigh's accustomed skeptical, generous, and tolerant spirit remains key to resolving the problems in Ireland.

Legacy of the Television Films

The legacy of Leigh's television films as well as those by Ken Loach and Alan Clarke during this period on the younger generation of English filmmakers endures. This influence was articulated well by Graham Fuller in his *New York Times* essay, "A New Generation of Realists Scrap the Kitchen Sink." He cites, in particular, Shane Meadows, the maker of *A Room for Romeo Brass* (2000), whose films, according to Fuller, in their jauntiness and poignancy, "share with Mike Leigh a fascination with quirks of personality" (AR 16). Meadows readily acknowledges the influence of the Loach-Leigh-Clarke television films on him when as a youngster he saw theatrical releases only about twice a year:

> Except for the likes of "Chariots of Fire" and "Absolute Beginners," there was no cinema culture in England when I was growing up. And yet I would come in from the youth club on Thursday night and on the telly there would be a film about a pregnant woman and the guy who has come round to read the gas meter and who obviously fancies her, and they'd sit in a room in a block of flats and not talk. And you'd think, 'Who the hell made this?' You wouldn't know if it was a story or a documentary but you'd sit there glued to it. (AR 16)

In interviews since the end of his television era, Leigh has always spoken with justifiable satisfaction and pride about these films as he did with me. What continues to impress viewers is that Leigh's characters have the same opaque surface that is presented by real people. From the testimony of Shane Meadows, televisual experiences like those provided by Leigh in their intensity of moment and the quality of their human illumination have the power to inspire and influence a contemporary young filmmaker.

Leigh found a way in these television films into what Merleau-Ponty sees as the telos of existence as quoted in Jenny Nelson's "Eyes Out of Your Head: On Televisual Experience": "The whole enigma lies in the perceptual world, in that television which makes us simultaneous with others and the world in the most private aspects of our life" (401). In a comparable statement David Thorburn explains an advantage television drama has over the big screen in utilizing the authenticating power of the film medium:

> The extended duration of most film, the camera's freedom of movement, the more-than-life-sized dimensions of the cinematic image—all these create what has been called the film's mythopoeic tendency, its inevitable effect of magnification. Since the natural domain of melodrama is indoors, in those ordinary and enclosed spaces wherein most of us act out our deepest needs and feelings—bedrooms, offices, courtrooms, hospitals—the reduced visual field of television is, or can be, far more nourishing than the larger, naturally expansive movie-screen. And for the kind of psychologically-nuanced performances elicited by good melodrama, the smaller television screen would seem even more appropriate: perfectly adapted, in fact, to record those intimately minute physical and vocal gestures, on which the art of the realistic actor depends, yet happily free of the cinema's malicious (if often innocent) power to transform merely robust nostrils into Brobdingnagian caverns, minor facial irregularities into craterous deformities. (542)

These films now available on home video have the potential of extending membership in that appreciative audience to future generations; they are valuable examples of Leigh at work in a medium that has historically been neglected, but that circumstance may yet be redressed through increased familiarity with Leigh's distinguished contributions.

CHAPTER THREE
Reinterpreting the Family: *Life Is Sweet* and *Secrets & Lies*

Life Is Sweet

The first film by Thin Man Films, the production company that Mike Leigh and Simon Channing-Williams, the director's longtime producer, formed in 1989, was *Life Is Sweet* (1990). Its United States distribution late in 1991 was also a debut for October Films, which, according to Coveney, was formed to release Leigh's film (222). This distributor has also become recognized for the high quality of its releases throughout the last decade of the twentieth century, including all of Leigh's films from *Life Is Sweet* to *Topsy-Turvy*.

For a filmmaker who usually presents life simply as it is without any predicate adjective expressing a particular quality or judgment, *Life Is Sweet* sounds remarkably like a "feel-good" excursion into domestic comedy. Of course, because it is a Mike Leigh film, that predication cannot be construed so unreservedly or without irony. Leigh has identified a common denominator in his Graham Fuller interview, linking several of his films apart from family matters: "What *High Hopes*, *Life Is Sweet*, and *Naked* are about, to some extent, is displaced, unemployed youth of one kind or another" (xxxiv). To be sure, the lower-middle-class family life of *Life Is Sweet* in another London suburb, here Enfield, Middlesex, is sweeter to a degree than what was portrayed, for example, in *Meantime*. Harlan Kennedy submits that "the family at the center of *Life Is Sweet* behave like human beings trying to escape the card-indexed fatuity of a sitcom" (19). Terrence Rafferty in his review for *The New Yorker* commends Leigh for his presentation of "by conventional standards, ordinary people, but they aren't dreary, and their actions aren't predictable; the movie doesn't treat anyone as a type" (101). Likewise, Vincent Canby in *The New York Times* who defines this Leigh film as "a contemplative comedy about people who aren't," judges that "the movie regards them [the characters], at their own level, without trying to be nice to them" (C10).

The kudos lavished on this film by the reviewers in the United States and what looked almost like a competition among critics to render praise suggest that at last Mike Leigh had arrived at the status of a modern master in world cinema. Hal Hinson, for example, in his review for *The Washington Post* captured the special quality long familiar from Leigh's previous films but given new potency in *Life Is Sweet:*

> Everything is this gently brilliant film seems to take place right before your eyes, without the intervention of aesthetic planning or direction. It simply happens in the moment, as if the characters were actually living on screen. This allows us to observe the daily life of an emphatically average, lower-middle-class Middlesex family without feeling that the events have been staged for our benefit; he [Leigh] creates a style of dramatic verite that's completely without mechanism. It's as if Leigh had quietly lifted the rooftop off their unremarkable little house and allowed us to peek in. (Cl)

The genial and comely parents, Andy (Jim Broadbent) and Wendy (Alison Steadman), seemingly have a solid marriage based on mutual love, respect, and shared levity. Both Steadman and Broadbent have sparkling eyes and expressive faces that convey a feeling of vivacity and enthusiasm for life and for each other even amid obvious family languors. Rafferty writes admiringly of Steadman's portrayal: "Wendy is hilariously tireless, but she doesn't wear her family (or us) out. She isn't self-important; she buzzes around without insisting that anyone pay special attention to her" (101). Nevertheless, to some extent, parents are pitted against their children once again in Leigh's work. Leigh is better than most filmmakers in conveying authentically just how enigmatic parents are to their children and vice versa. In this film, their parents' laughter, especially their mother's loud giggles and nasal guffaws, embarrasses the children. Types of laughter become like fingerprints in a number of Leigh's films; Wendy's gleeful chuckle harks back to Valerie's more desperate snorting in *High Hopes*. Andy and Wendy are employed, as is one of their twin daughters, the sensible, close-cropped Natalie (Claire Skinner), a hardworking plumber. In her chosen vocation, Natalie has taken her own stand against the gender-specific vocational grain, yet her career choice has apparently been validated by family and peers. Her straggly-haired sister Nicola (Jane Horrocks) with eyeglasses askew has, in contrast, become a reclusive, bulimic dropout rebel and self-defined feminist who is holed up in her bedroom, unable to leave the family home except for cigarettes. Nicola sees herself as a fighter for people's rights and worthy causes without being at all concerned with the happiness of people closest to her, such as her loving parents and sister. Her anger, however overt in her limited dealings with others, is chiefly directed at herself. Leigh shows these young women in a battle whether to become themselves or to destroy themselves based on their engagement and abilities to deal with emotions and relationships starting in their own homes.

Nicola wears an oversized T-shirt, bearing the message "Bollocks to the Poll Tax," into which she thrusts her hands and stretches the garment as if to shrink herself even further. Although the twins still live at home, they appear to have outgrown the need for mothering; however, Wendy and Nicola have a magnificent scene together near the end of the film that indicates otherwise. This scene, the culmination of their re-presentation throughout the film, links mother and daughter through the special psychological complexities of being female that Leigh does not simplify in the manner of so many other filmmakers. Wendy tries valiantly to reconcile herself to the girls her twin daughters were and the young women they have become. She, as the published screenplay presents her action, looks at photographs of her infant twins and exclaims: "They were such lovely little dolly-whatsits...sitting there in their matchin' little outfits (*On the mantlepiece, two snapshots of the twins as babies)*. My little Natalie and my little Nicola! And now look at 'em!" (107) This happy maternal reminiscence brings forth from Nicola a call for the sick-bucket. Leigh sees both daughters as nonconformists but says of Natalie in his Graham Fuller interview: "The difference is that the nature of her nonconformity doesn't preclude getting on with living and working and in some way fulfilling herself, within limited parameters" (xxxi). Nicola, on the other hand, while outwardly more rebellious, has somehow accepted society's imposition of an unrealistic ideal of female bodily perfection that has brought her to a perilous state of unhappiness.

Besides Nicola's eating disorder, food, its preparation and consumption, becomes a major theme in *Life Is Sweet*, including delicious satire on the emergence of the British "foodie" recently discovering the world's cuisines but adapting it for the indigenous palate. Andy by profession is a head chef of a large kitchen for what presumably is an institutional food service, where quantity is doubtless more important than quality. Leigh delays showing Andy as the competent head of kitchen until midway through the film. In the two scenes where he is at work, Andy demonstrates professional competence that may come as a surprise after the audience has seen his procrastination and laid-back attitude toward work such as home repair. "That construction is there," Leigh explained in his interview with Fuller, "in order to access him [Andy] as a person first, then a chef, rather than start from the chef premise; you *arrive* at the notion of him as a practical man" (xxxii).

Andy desires to become self-employed as owner of a mobile food caravan, now sadly decrepit, emblazoned with HOT SNACKS, that his friend Patsy (Stephen Rea) cons him into purchasing. Nicola refers to her father as a "Tory" when he asks the family to look at the caravan as an investment. Natalie is more sympathetic toward her father when toward the end of the film, he breaks his ankle as he carries a large tray of food and trips over a large mixing spoon carelessly left on the floor in his industrial kitchen. Andy, back home in a full leg cast, describes the object as an "evil spoon," that was "just waiting for the fatal day when it'd drastically alter the course of a man's life." In turn, Natalie amusingly hangs the spoon on a framed Degas print of a ballet scene in the living room so that they can "keep an eye on it." Although Natalie does not reveal the ebullience and verbal capacity of her mother, she shows that she possesses more than a little of Wendy's droll humor and playful tenderness.

Another family friend, the overweight, almost carnivalesque Aubrey (Timothy Spall), also a chef, boasts unusual and risible franglais specialties like kidney vol-au-vent, prune quiche, liver and lager, pork cyst, tongues in a rhubarb hollandaise, among other surprising delicacies. Leigh may be using Aubrey's body and culinary interests as a latter-day English version of Pulcinella from *commedia dell'arte* with his gnocchi, inherently comic and indigestible food. Aubrey unsuccessfully opens a new French restaurant in town, The Regret Rien, after Edith Piaf's signature song.

Wendy herself is no slouch in the proper preparation of standard British cuisine such as the joint, "Wen, this lamb is delicious," as Andy, her chef husband, proclaims, "Nice and pink...beautiful, innit?" Accompanied by a rebuke of "Mother!" from daughter Natalie (Nicola having absented herself from the family dinner table), Wendy celebrates food and, by extension, other sensual pleasure with the following: "Cut me a nice big juicy slice...I like mine nice and juicy! (*she laughs*)" (111), as the published screenplay denotes. Once more Leigh, in the tradition of nineteenth-century English novels he so frequently evokes, demonstrates Dickens' high respect for good food. John Lahr in "This Other England," called Leigh "something of a gastronome" whose "cooking has improved over the years; at first, his culinary ventures were as experimental as his theatre" (52).

Nicola's pathological relationship to food mirrors her terrible and passionate drama with her family. She gorges herself at night in her room on a treasure trove of chocolates she keeps in a locked container and then induces vomiting. Natalie, who has been reading travel brochures for a future trip to the United States, retires for the night and hears Nicola's retching through the shared walls of their bedrooms. She registers on her face the depth of her sisterly concern. Barbara and Leonard Quart in their review of *Life Is Sweet* for *Film Quarterly* comment on this distressing scene:

> It is a bold thing to confront bulimia this vividly and realistically. Nicola, however, never seems a grim case history, partly because the caricaturing makes her rather appealing and funny, and partly because Leigh's narrative method involves moving casually from plot to plot, from humor to humor, so that the scene's full anguish is almost tripped over, and then quickly shifted away from again, to a series of sequences about the other family members' work lives. (51)

Even though Nicola's unnamed lover (David Thewlis) protests initially, "Not again—it's boring," she perversely insists that he bind her wrists with silk scarves to her bedstead and lick chocolate sauce from her bare breasts. Her disregulation of appetite extends to the sexual as evidenced in her boyfriend's reaction to these erotic rituals.

Later, in a follow-up scene, Nicola tells her boyfriend she is writing a novel although she has not yet started it. It will be autobiographical as she readily admits, which may be why she has not begun her only slightly fictional contribution to contemporary confessional culture. Leigh suggests Nicola has achieved something less than empowerment through sexual self-expression when her boyfriend tells her, as she once more requests another session of chocolate fetish, "I don't want it. I want you." The Quarts call this defeat of Nicola by her smug, smart bloke, "one of the film's wittiest conceits" (51). Unable to reach agreement as a couple, Nicola remains without satisfaction as her lover leaves in response to her recommendation to him: "Well, piss off, then," and David Thewlis disappears from the film.

Leigh includes another brief parallel sequence of food and sexuality with Aubrey and his assistant Paula (Moya Brady). She is playing Aubrey's drums in his flat above the restaurant. He tells her, according to the published screenplay: "Yeah. I'm really pleased with you. You're quite a tasty little worker…y'know?" (*He licks his lips, then he leans forward and nibbles her ear. They keel over together until she is lying sideways on the big drum. He continues to consume her ear. He also feels her breasts. She remains open-eyed and expressionless*) (147). Coveney quotes Timothy Spall's opinion on the bizarre character he plays in *Life Is Sweet* who is derived from a real person he included on the initial list he brought to Leigh's preliminary planning sessions. Spall hoped the director would not choose to develop this character, but, of course, Leigh did: "Aubrey is obsessed with shagging. It's the misguided, the self-deluded that Mike brings to life so brilliantly" (220). Stuart Klawans in *The Nation's* review of *Life Is Sweet* sees Aubrey as "a social climber who has no idea where to find the ladder" and draws a parallel between him and the inept, hapless Wayne of *High Hopes.* Both drop in and out of their respective Leigh films and serve as foils for some of the other characters "to show them as caring people" (718).

The echo of the earlier food and sex sequence invites a charge of overkill against Leigh. Harlan Kennedy is not alone in his rather negative assessment of food metaphors in the film, but the political allegory he discovers therein points to a certain florid interpretive extremism:

> *Life Is Sweet* attempts to consume the consumer society. But the symbolist dinner-gong sounds too loudly. We get—we overget—the point. Everyone is gobbling; everyone is hungry for more. And the "midnight feast" ethos—secret, self-regarding, orgiastic—is runaway greed plus runaway guilt: the legacy of the yuppie Eighties. (20)

If Kennedy looks back to the eighties in interpreting *Life Is Sweet*, there is also something prophetic of the later nineties in this cinematic study of food and children. Adam Gopnik in *The New Yorker*, for example, discussed preoccupations of New Labour in England some years after the release of Leigh's film. Wendy and Andy, albeit from a lower social class than their affluent successors and without their self-consciousness, may well be harbingers: "The New Labour fanaticism about food goes hand in hand with a fanaticism about children. New Labour manners, like comparable manners in America, are punitively obsessive about childrearing. Cooking and childrearing have become substitute religion of upper-middle-class people of the late twentieth century" (28). In addition, through imaginative projection Andy may be able to engage some hitherto undisclosed entrepreneurial ability to achieve profitable status for his food caravan in Tony Blair's Britain. Mike Leigh's former vision of dogged existence in life's despite may yet become something else closer to New Labour than hard labor as it does in the later *Career Girls*.

Alison Steadman's Wendy as wife and mother is one of Leigh's most endearing and enduring female characters. It is easy to appreciate that she has a large and forgiving heart. She confesses to Andy after she sees his deteriorating caravan that she cannot muster any enthusiasm for his purchase. He replies matter-of-factly but also poignantly, as presented in the published screenplay: "I know you can't—it's obvious. To be honest with you, I'd appreciate it if you could. I could do with a bit of moral support" (136). By the time bedtime arrives, she is prepared to give him that support, rationalizing that they could go on holiday in the caravan if his canteen business were to prove less than stellar: "Stick a coupla bunk beds in it... 'ave a little bunk-up" (138). What is notable about this family, especially through the example of Wendy, is that all family members are permitted to have their own space in which to be human, even Nicola, whose mental and physical state does not allow her to repay the generosity the others extend to her. The love that Wendy and Andy manifest for each other and to their children is grounded in an unlimited generosity imparted through the infinite valuation they accord members of their family. Ray Carney enlarges on the applicability of such attributes as the basis of how Mike Leigh works with respect both to film content and audience response:

> The ultimate measure of a Leigh character, or viewer, is his or her ability to remain open to the multivalence of experience as Leigh is in his presentation of it. In this respect, Wendy and Andy are surrogates for Leigh and his ideal viewers....Their multiple-mindness about their own lives parallels Leigh's refusal throughout his oeuvre to filter his presentation of characters and their interactions, to force them to make a single point or conform to a single tone. There is a certain degree of tonal and emotional sprawl or clutter in Leigh's scenes precisely because, in his view, experience is, in fact, a little loose and messy. (216–17)

Wendy tells her daughter, who has charged her with trying to control her life, that in the medical opinion Nicola had about two weeks to live when at seventeen she had been hospitalized for eight weeks, the result, it is implied, of an earlier bout of anorexia/bulimia. At that time Nicola was doing well academically in her three A-levels, and her mother tells her about her own experience at age sixteen during which she, too, was progressing well in A-levels in English and Business Studies.

Then Wendy became pregnant with twins; predictably, her intransigent daughter asks her mother why she didn't have an abortion. To quote from Leigh's published screenplay, Wendy's answer affirming childbearing as creating the most enduring social bond and natural piety serves as a centerpiece in Leigh's canon in a number of his films:

> Because I didn't want one, because I 'ad two little lives growin' inside me. I don't believe in it—that's the easy way out. Your dad was only seventeen. 'E was at catering college, and he was workin' in hotels at night, tryin' to get a bit extra. We got a little flat together; begged and borrowed—couple o'cots. And when the two of you were born, we were thrilled to bits. Because we 'ad two lovely little babies. We came through, laughin'. (172)

After this declaration of maternal nurture, protection, and affirmation of her children, Wendy further explains to Nicola that what the family wants is for her to be happy, and she obviously is not. Nicola blurts out, "If you hate me so much, why don't you throw me out?" Nicola hears that she is loved even as her mother exasperatedly calls her a "stupid girl." The tears that follow for both mother and daughter move beyond recriminations to end with a breakthrough of mutual understanding and love. Within his familial contexts throughout his career, Leigh and his actors in their collaborative process find language laden with histories of love, disappointment, battles for control, unexpressed admiration and the pain of too readily-proclaimed recriminations.

Terrence Rafferty's remarks on this sequence crystallize Leigh's accomplishment in a manner similar to Carney's generalized description:

> [*Life Is Sweet*] ambles along for nearly an hour and a half without seeming especially concerned about where it's headed, and then, long after we've given up trying to figure out what the whole thing is supposed to mean, Leigh comes up with a stunning scene in which Wendy and Nicola discuss Nicola's dissatisfaction with life .... We sense how this moment of mutual unguarded honesty has emerged from the apparent chaos of the women's recent experiences. (103)

Jane Horrocks' Nicola and Timothy Spall's Aubrey compete over tics and fidgets in a brief scene in which he brings a pineapple for her mother. Aubrey testifies here that Nicola is really an attractive girl, an assessment that she denies with "No, I'm not. I'm too fat." Aubrey ends the scene by favorably commenting on Nicola's great knees, a detail that audiences might note intertextually with a nod either to Eric Rohmer or Leigh's earlier *Bleak Moments* and *Who's Who*. Stuart Klawans has interpreted a measure of doubleness in the characters of Nicola and Aubrey in that the latter "grotesque," as Klawans calls him, from outside the family "takes the onus off Nicola much as Nicola in the context of her family bears away the others' burdens" (718). Physically the painfully thin Nicola is the opposite of portly Aubrey, but beneath the skin they share a similar lack of ease in their persons and in their environment.

Both these notable performers built solid career for themselves after *Life Is Sweet*. Horrocks' portrayal of Nicola is the kind of sensational characterization that not surprisingly led to her success on stage in Jim Cartright's 1992 cabaret play, *The Rise and Fall of Little Voice*. She re-created her role as Laura Voss, or "L.V." for the long-postponed film version, *Little Voice* (1998). As this actress' well-deserved luck would have it, she also began her continuing role in the cultishly popular television series *Absolutely Fabulous* in 1993.

Unlike the character of Nicola, who is central to the plot of *Life Is Sweet,* Aubrey whom Spall plays is, at most, peripheral. However, the actor engagingly portrays the proprietor of the lamentable The Regret Rien Restaurant, drinking himself into insensibility as he waits in vain for the patrons to arrive for his grand opening. He keeps topping off his glass with an avidity that might shame Beverly of *Abigail's Party*. This hilarious debacle rich in physical and verbal comedy becomes a high point of the film, although, as Terrence Rafferty suggested, the scenes should probably have been trimmed by a few minutes. At the same time, as Rafferty observes, Leigh's shifts in tone and style keep "the audience off balance; we're never able to settle into a single mood, to allow ourselves the comfort of knowing what sort of reaction will be demanded of us next" (103). As for its rather slender contribution to the plot, because Wendy has come to Aubrey's aid for his opening night (volunteering as his temporary waitress), the scene also furthers appreciation of Wendy's nurturing instincts and compassion not only for Aubrey but also for Paula. Granted, Aubrey's clumsy amorous advances to Wendy seem gratuitous but consistent with his state of drunkenness and his Piaf stance of no regrets. Klawans goes so far as to describe Aubrey as "so sexually desperate his libido will attach itself to anything with a high voice" (718).

Aubrey's public denunciation of British dietary practices on the empty street in front of his equally empty restaurant displays him, as Coveney describes Aubrey, "like an absurd suburban version of King Lear" (221) before he privately asks Wendy to marry him. The published screenplay expresses Aubrey's jeremiad in the following: "Come on, you bastards! I'm open!! I'm ready, I'm waitin' for you—this is what you've all been waitin' for! Come and get it!! Fishwives! Footballers! You English dickheads! You stick to your fish and chips—go on, go and get cancer!" (160). After going back inside his restaurant, Aubrey turns over the tables he has carefully prepared with candles, flowers, and immaculate linens and subsequently passes out. Paula laments to Wendy that now Aubrey and she will not be able to go out for chips as she had been promised.

Spall delivers a memorable performance beyond even his promising initial appearance as one of the postmen in Leigh's *Home Sweet Home*. Klawans who finally judges that *High Hopes* is a stronger film than *Life Is Sweet* for its expansiveness of mood and portrayal of society, nevertheless, concludes that because of the inclusion of Aubrey, "there's still an uncommon richness of character in the film, an all-too-rare spontaneity. Sometimes in *Life Is Sweet*, things happen just for the hell of it—much as they do in real life. Wendy and

Andy understand that. By the end, Nicola is starting to understand it, too. I wouldn't exactly call that comedy, but it does lift the spirit" (718). True to his practice of re-employing actors from earlier films in later ones, Leigh awards Timothy Spall the leading role of Maurice Purley in *Secrets & Lives* and continues to employ him for brilliant effect in the subsequent *Topsy-Turvy* and the recent *All or Nothing*.

Leigh includes two scenes of Wendy at work apart from her abortive evening in The Regret Rien. The film opens on her ending a dancing class of little girls with ingratiating energy. A brief scene at a children's clothing store, Bunnikins, where Wendy clerks momentarily evokes, if less blatantly or stridently, memories of Steadman's Beverly's interaction in *Abigail's Party* with the refined middle-class divorced mother, Susan.

In *Life Is Sweet* the customer (Harriet Thorpe) seeks an outfit for her toddler, Nigel (Jack Thorpe Baker). Wendy becomes overly familiar as she describes the child as a "little chunker," who will grow up to be a boxer or wrestler. The customer tells her she does not want anything in pastels. Wendy nearly recommends a possible French outfit but stops herself, claiming "that's a little bit girly, innit?" The mother desires something more sophisticated whereupon, as Klawans expresses it, Wendy's "unprovoked good spirits and blithe acceptance of sexual stereotypes appall at least one of her customers" (718) with the following exchange: "More sophisticated, yeah—'cos 'e's not a girly boy, is 'e? D'you know what I mean? 'E's more a boy's boy—I mean, you couldn't mistake 'im for a girl, could yer?'' The customer icily replies, "No, he's a boy" and then rejects the navy-and-white suit Wendy proffers for Nigel, whose name she has learned in the course of the failed transaction, as she calls him, "little nidgey Nigel" (141). And maybe Leigh recalls at the same time the adult Nigel of the earlier *Who's Who.* How well Leigh and his actresses understand both these women and the culture of subtle class distinctions they embody!

The ending of *Life Is Sweet* recalls the potentially deepened sibling rapport between Mark and Colin at the close of *Meantime* and anticipates the backyard finale with Roxanne and Hortense in the later *Secrets & Lies*. Natalie, sitting together with her cigarette-smoking sister in front of the garden shed, reveals that she has not told their parents about Nicola's most recent episodes of bulimia that she heard through the walls of their adjacent bedrooms. She explains that she thinks Nicola should tell their parents about this condition, offering her not only money but, more significantly, commiting herself to helping her sister, "I think we should do something about it." Nicola admits that her self-induced vomiting is disgusting; Natalie acknowledges she does some pretty disgusting things herself in her line of work: "I put my hands down toilets. And on a good day, I might get bitten by a rat." Natalie speaks the last line of the film that hints of the sweetness of life despite its initial negation: "No, it's OK."

Human feelings and human faces fuse for renewed understanding as Nicola and Natalie accept each other and resemble each other more now than at any other point in the film. Rachel Portman's familiar short melodic fragment returns slowly to reinforce the young women's empathy during the sustained beat of silence that follows the twins' exchange. Leigh spoke about the composers' role with reference to this film and others in his interview with Fuller:

> What happens is that the composers naturally find a way to have the music come from the emotional heart of the film [Leigh notes that even a saw is used as part of the instrumentation for *Life Is Sweet*]. So if the music is plaintive or poignant, it's because the film is. It's not narrative, illustrational music. That would be counter-productive as far as I am concerned. Since ultimately the films are sympathetic, that's why you get that feeling in the music. (xxxiv)

The music remains to provide a bridge in the minds of the audience of the sisters' intimacy as Leigh and cinematographer Dick Pope close with a high crane shot of the backyard on a pleasant summer day behind the closing credits. *Life Is Sweet*, as the Quarts conclude, "provides no closure, just life's flow—of despair, pleasure, alienation, and human connection all intermixed" (51), but Leigh makes us care about these people and their lives. That alone secures a certain tart and unironic sweetness in a movie, as Vincent Canby expressed it, "that breathes" (C 10).

Secrets & Lies

Mike Leigh's *Secrets & Lies* (1996), with a title that sounds like a Woody Allen movie, became very quickly his most critically acclaimed and commercially popular feature to date. It won the Palme d'Or at Cannes and opened the New York Film Festival to go from there to success throughout the world, appearing on 100 "Ten Best Lists" for 1996. It was nominated for but lost in the Academy Award competition for Best Picture, as was Brenda Blethyn, who had been nominated for Best Actress. Unfortunately, *Secrets & Lies* failed to win any of the five Academy Awards for which it had been nominated. Following what some critics and audiences considered the unpleasant and controversial *Naked* three years earlier, Leigh's new crowd-pleasing film conceived as a comic family melodrama greatly enhanced the director's prestige as a world-class filmmaker. Like *Life Is Sweet*, its most similar predecessor, *Secrets & Lies* is about heredity and environment. As J. Hoberman wrote in *The Village Voice*: "...only a filmmaker this rigorously devoted to the inner-directed notion of acting-as-discovery could so imaginatively handle a situation so rife with trite comic complications. The *Secrets & Lies* premise defines the double take" (64).

Leigh explained in his interview with Graham Fuller some of his own motivation for this film:

> I wanted to do a film that in some way was about the need we all have to deal with our roots, to assert our identities and to know who we are, and to share and be truthful. The actual specific jumping-off point for me was the fact that there are people very close to me who have had adoption-related experiences....I also wanted to do a film about the generation of young black people in the world who are growing up, moving on, getting away from their ghetto stereotypes, being positive, and exploring avenues of possibility. (xlii)

Hortense Cumberbatch (Marianne Jean-Baptiste), a black, university-educated professional woman, a twenty-seven-year-old optometrist who had been adopted shortly after birth by a loving black family, buries her adoptive mother in the film's first scene. Now an orphan with only tenuous connection to her older male siblings (one owns a garage, and the other is a computer professional), she sets out to locate her birth mother through a London adoption agency. *Secrets & Lies* becomes a testimony to Mike Leigh's interest in the change in English law in 1975 that gave orphans in the United Kingdom legal access to records that reveal their biological parents. It has often been said that in every adoption there is a story of loss. Leigh affirms and celebrates in his own distinctive seriocomic fashion the resolution of losses and the mystical threads of life, physical and spiritual, that forever connect a birth parent and her adopted birth daughter. Hortense's motivation for establishing connection with her biological mother stems not from any feeling Leigh conveys of her not feeling good enough or important enough on her own. This competent young woman, who displays a clear sense of her own identity, does not pursue this inquiry because she seeks reinvention or self-discovery as a more conventional approach might present it. On the contrary, Hortense bears witness as an adoptee that a true family is created through time spent together, commitment, love, trials, and energies of the heart, not just a common gene pool and bloodlines.

Before Hortense learns about her biological parentage, Leigh includes an attractive and nuanced scene between Hortense and her friend Dionne (Michelle Austin), who tells her friend about a recent one-night stand she has enjoyed, a narrative that Hortense receives without judgment. It is unusual for a male filmmaker to get a handle so successfully on convincing scenes of female intimacy and friendship. This sequence in *Secrets & Lies* adumbrates the key relationship in Leigh's next film between former roommates in *Career Girls*. In a touching scene in which Hortense lies on a couch and Dionne, sitting on the floor, leans her head against her friend's legs, the two women talk about their respective mothers. Hortense tells Dionne that she thinks one of her friend's reasons for negative responses to her own mother is that in this woman she sees herself in twenty years. Hortense ends this scene with almost mystical speculation that "We choose our parents. We choose the parents in this life that can teach us something, so that when we go into the next life, we can get it right." This wisdom may appear ironic by the end of Leigh's film in acknowledgment of the vulnerable and needy parent Hortense discovers in Cynthia Purley (Brenda Blethyn).

Hortense has been chosen as an adopted daughter by her now-deceased parents just as Cynthia Purley chose to give birth to her and place her for adoption. The matter of choice becomes significant again as Hortense elects to pursue her records at the adoption agency. What she discovers at the agency makes her assume that an error has been made in the data because her biological mother is listed as white. Hortense has known she had been adopted from the age of seven when her adoptive mother told her.

Hortense is aided in her quest by a caring social worker (Lesley Manville), portrayed subtly once again by this versatile Leigh veteran without any of the satire Leigh visited upon other members of her profession in *Home Sweet Home,* his earlier television drama. Nonetheless, J. Hoberman in his review found this character "objectively sensitive, intelligent, *and* [italics are his] obnoxious" (64). Hortense discovers she is the daughter of Cynthia Purley, a white, forty-two-year-old East End box factory worker and single mother of a resentful, cigarette-addicted young adult daughter, Roxanne, (Claire Rushbrook). Mother and daughter live in a council house, where previously Cynthia had cared for her late parents and her younger brother, Maurice. Roxanne is a street-sweeper, nearing twenty-one, but, as the film reveals, she is not Cynthia's only daughter. Possibly a hint of near-allegory comes to mind in the respective occupations of Cynthia, boxed in by her life, and Roxanne, who desires a clean sweep; however, such symbolic concepts are doubtless too fanciful except subliminally for the reality-based world of Mike Leigh. A well-kept family secret, and one of those from which the film derives its title, is that, when she was a teenager, Cynthia became pregnant. She gave the baby girl up for adoption without ever actually seeing her after giving birth and never knowing the child was biracial.

Secrets & Lies conforms at least initially more fully to conventional movies than is typical in Leigh's more episodic and less traditional works. Leigh establishes the plot as a quest, and much of the film's early action is presented as a narrative of the process whereby Hortense systematically traces the steps to establish her biological origin. Bert Cardullo offers an astute analogy between this film and Leigh's own method:

> Leigh's focus in rehearsal primarily on the life of character or the character of life, on the artistic examination in detail of people's existences, is unusually germane to the subject of *Secrets & Lies:* the search of an adopted child for her biological mother. For the movie's questions are "Who am I?" and "How are these people related to me?"— which are exactly the questions an actor asks in the exploration of a character and his life. (114)

Alan Riding, reporting in *The New York Times* when *Secrets & Lies* opened at the New York Film Festival in 1996, noted Leigh's bristling at the suggestion that "his latest and most acclaimed movie to date is less bleak and disturbing than most of his previous work" (Section 2, l).

Leigh keeps adding complications and further layers to the emotional content in his context of secrets and lies. Cynthia never disclosed the birth of her first out-of-wedlock child to her other daughter, who was also born without benefit of a mother's marriage. No one in the family except Cynthia knows the full particulars, and her knowledge, too, is incomplete. Her brother, Maurice (Timothy Spall), a professional and reasonably successful portrait and family photographer, and especially his wife, Monica (Phyllis Logan), had hoped Cynthia would have informed Roxanne that she had a half-brother or half-sister somewhere in the world. This couple has their own secrets: the wife's infertility has nearly destroyed their loving marriage and contributed to the distance that has arisen to separate Cynthia and Maurice as brother and sister, although Cynthia does not learn this cause until the end of the film. Indeed, Leigh's subject becomes the pressing need to connect truth to identity and personal relationships.

Adoption shrouded in secrecy is used as a catalyst to other revelations and renewed openness within a family that serve to make people less afraid of each other. While truths have the capacity to alienate, divide, and condemn members of a family, secrets and lies can be equally damaging to genuine family relationships and connections. Thematically, *Secrets & Lies* revisits concerns from a number of earlier Leigh films, including race, class, and gender issues, but the balanced combination of familiar elements together with the compelling dramatic thread of adoption here exerts an appeal to a broader audience than elsewhere in his canon.

Leigh employs metaphor and symbol more directly in *Secrets & Lies* than in most of his earlier films. Both Hortense as an optometrist and Maurice as a photographic portrait artist are professionally concerned with ways of seeing, literally and figuratively, "with the ability to see (through frames) and the desire to be seen (in a frame), by means of the ocular as well as the camera lens" (114), to borrow Cardullo's expression of their professional connection. Thus the parallel becomes metaphoric for the imminent discovery about family and homecoming that forms the plot of *Secrets & Lies*. Indeed, like novelist Joseph Conrad and movie pioneer D. W. Griffith, Mike Leigh wants to help his audience to see better as his own artistic vision has continued to sharpen but has also mellowed over the years. It is not surprising, therefore, that the most observant of all the characters in the film is Hortense, whose eyes have been trained to see more than they give away.

Although it is always risky to speculate on autobiographical connections in Leigh's work, the fact that his paternal grandfather, Mayer Liebermann, an immigrant to Britain from Russia, was a portrait miniaturist who colored photographs may have influenced the role Timothy Spall plays so well in this film. Maurice endeavors to capture in still photography not only the faces but also the essence of married couples, families, children, and even beloved cats and dogs. The camera does "what the eye in itself,"as John Berger writes in *About Looking* "can never do, is to *fix* the appearance of that event. It removes its appearance from the flow of appearances and it preserves it, not perhaps for ever but for as long as the film exists.... And before the invention of the camera nothing could do this, except, in the mind's eye, the faculty of memory" (50–1). Maurice's process is very similar to Leigh's strategy in filmmaking except that Leigh becomes, as the term itself denotes, a maker of experience more than a recorder of it. Both wait patiently, watching and working with their subjects until they find an image they want to capture or a story worth telling.

The inevitable parallel between Maurice with his camera and Mike Leigh's career with the moving image is further strengthened by the parade of familiar faces from his past films that the director brings to Maurice's studio for photo sessions. As a still photographer Maurice need not worry about continuity between shots and the secrets and lies of withheld information required by a narrative as Leigh has to maintain in every film. Moreover, at Maurice's studio or in his on-site photo shoots, these subjects exist autonomously and not, as in a Leigh film, only in the context of the others within a respective film.

Full identification of Maurice's photographed folks and their ancestry in Leigh's oeuvre doubtless necessitates repeated viewings, which in itself is a kind of inside, self-reflexive *jeu d'esprit*. Sometimes these performers appear against the type of character they played in Leigh's previous films or occasionally as an implied extension of their earlier personae. Peter Wight from *Meantime* and more recently the night watchman in *Naked*, for example, appears as the paterfamilias in a three-generation grouping of the first family portrait Maurice photographs in the film. Few initiated Leigh viewers would fail to recognize toothy Ruth Sheen of *High Hopes*, who is posed with grinning husband (Paul Trussel). Likewise, distinguished Leigh alumna Liz Smith, here a cat owner, formerly of *Bleak Moments* and *Hard Labour*, appears now far more stylish and better coiffed; Maurice says of her and her cat, "He looks good and so do you." Her canine fancier counterpart is none other than a glamourous Alison Steadman in red sweatshirt decorated with Scotties. She can barely stop combing her pampered pooch.

Leigh offers up for Maurice's camera Su Elliott, the romance-reading adulteress of *Home Sweet Home,* as one member of a trio of raunchy women in a group portrait. Sheila Kelley from *Nuts in May* and *Home Sweet Home* is seen here with her young triplet daughters dressed in blue tutus. She explains to Maurice's assistant, Jane (Elizabeth Berrington), that she did not expect to have any children, but, thanks to fertility treatments, she is the mother of these triplets. Angela Curran from *The Kiss of Death* returns as mother of a young son (Dominic Curran) who will be photographed if he can just keep his finger out of his nose long enough to complete the picture. Philip Davis, so often scruffy and unkempt in the earlier *Grown-Ups* and *High Hopes,* wears a suit for a group portrait of a quintet of men of distinction in *Secrets & Lies*. Anthony O'Donnell, the Ray of *Nuts in May*, looks rather uneasy and unsmiling as a new father before Maurice's camera. Linda Beckett from *Hard Labour* and other Leigh films poses self-consciously, finally laughing at her absurdity, in fishnet stockings as a pin-up housewife who evokes momentary associations with *Naked* for those familiar with Leigh's work. This listing does not account for all the photographic subjects out of Mike Leigh's past, but it conveys the idea of his reflexive artifice, which links him via Maurice with the human subjects and the image, still or moving. We have archival evidence of the actors who have made earlier Leigh appearances that contributes to memories of the Leigh output.

Leigh is neither wholly anglocentric nor neglectful of a global perspective in his portrayal of Maurice's subjects. He acknowledges the presence of a black prize-fighter (Gary McDonald), Asian nurse (Lucy Sheen), and a potential Indian husband (Nitin Chandra Ganatra), who will send his photograph back to his future bride in India, among other representations of multicultural and multiracial Britain in Maurice's studio.

Maurice as a photographer exhibits craft in his chosen art and enormous empathy as well as real respect for the people he captures on film. These attributes also characterize Leigh's career and surely never more impressively than in *Secrets & Lies*. Leigh's approach, especially in his television films, eschewed conventions of photographic idealism to render exact and seemingly unmediated experience insofar as an illusion of such transparency was even possible in fictionalized drama. Such a practice may be distinguished from Maurice's more commercial enterprise, where he often urges his subjects to "put on their best face" for the camera and to convey an impression of greater happiness than either they or their arranged photographic relationships actually possess. While it is said that photos do not lie, they can tell only partial truths. Maurice at work consequently negotiates between the veracity of the portrait and photography's capacity to become almost emblematic of the significant themes of the film itself. Such a photographer who turns a profit via his art may to that end on occasion misrepresent as well as represent his subjects in their frozen moment. Beth Tauke has described Maurice with accuracy: "He spends his life trying to make people happy, or trying to make people look happy. He knows what happiness looks like. He knows how to pose people and just when to click the shutter so that the delusions they so desperately want to maintain continue" (190).

After the first meeting of Hortense and Cynthia, at which secrets and lies begin to be dispelled, Leigh presents an especially harrowing, poignant, and well-crafted sequence of Maurice photographing a young woman who has been in an automobile accident. Leigh places this sequence strategically to suggest an analogy with what is happening in Maurice's family, although the photographer himself does not yet know it. "The self that feels ugly, unworthy, and incompetent," writes John Lahr, "wants to call no attention to itself. The shamefaced hide themselves away, which is what Cynthia...the mother in 'Secrets & Lies,' does in her East End hutch" (53). What will be revealed and even ways of seeing both undergo change at this crucial juncture in *Secrets & Lies*.

In the revealing sequence at the photography studio, Maurice's first point of view is a side shot of his attractive subject in which she (Emma Amos) appears as a beautiful, unblemished blond with full, sensual red lips. Then Maurice has her turn to a full frontal view. She asks him, "Can you shut the door please?" As she turns, a large, jagged, and deep scar becomes visible on the other side of her face. Maurice moves the camera a bit closer, expressing the hope that his subject is not claustrophobic, which she affirms she is not. Apologizing for his next move, he brings the lighting instrument closer to illuminate more fully the damage to her face. She says, "I want to look as bad as possible." Her father had taken earlier photographs, but her lawyer thought it advisable to have professional photographs.

She explains the accident that resulted in her disfigurement and the subsequent loss of her job. At this point she tells Maurice that her former position was that of beauty consultant. Her seat belt had failed, and she went through the windshield. She no longer has any association with the uninjured man who was driving her car. Maurice observes that "life isn't fair, is it? Someone always draws the short straw." As a husband he makes the same observation to his barren wife when she is in the throes of yet another extremely painful menstrual period, but the commonplace does not trivialize either victim. On the contrary, Maurice's consistently supportive personal and professional approach to all the characters who in some manner or another have been hurt becomes a standard of decency and honesty in *Secrets & Lies*. This sequence with the accident victim demonstrates Maurice's belief that the camera in his hands has an inevitable integrity. Cardullo construes this sequence as a visual conceit for the entire film and its place in Leigh's canon:

> It is a corporal metaphor for the beautiful but scarred soul of Maurice's sister, Cynthia Rose Purley, in addition to being a grotesque commingling of two faces or facets of film: the fantastic Hollywood cinema of beautiful people and its opposite number, the naturalistic, in this case British, picture of the down-and-dirty, the nitty-gritty, or the lean-and-mean. (115)

The eventual pivotal meeting between Hortense and Cynthia begins with a phone call from an unknown daughter to her birth mother in which Cynthia's past literally comes calling. Incidentally, Alison Chitty's simple but stylish modern design for Hortense's apartment with its blacks and whites and an orange or two for color belies the description of Mike Leigh's interiors as dispirited and unfashionable. Cynthia has just emerged from a bitter argument about birth control with Roxanne, who has stormed out of the house into the bed of Paul (Lee Ross), her construction worker boyfriend, a "scaffolder" as he is called in the film. A close-up of Brenda Blethyn with secretions dripping from her nose after an intense episode of crying, recalls her scene of Gloria's hysteria in *Grown-Ups*. It also connects biographically with Leigh's story to Prairie Miller included in Movshovitz about his desire to film reality at age twelve. As he stood in his parents' home in Manchester, he recalled: "My grandfather was carried downstairs in a coffin by four old men with drips at the ends of their noses. And my response to this tragi-comic occasion was the thought that it would be great to make a film about this" (82). Leigh has repeated this vignette from his youth in numerous published interviews.

Although Cynthia hangs up suddenly after this first exchange, she does take down Hortense's phone number. Shortly thereafter she calls Hortense, who comes to the phone from her bath wrapped in a white towel and with white cosmetic cream on her face, which makes a striking visual effect in light of their biological connection. The two women arrange to meet at the Holborn Underground Station, but Cynthia hangs up before Hortense is able to ask her how she can identify her. As Hortense says to herself as she holds the now-dead phone, "I don't even know what you look like." Prior to her meeting with Hortense, Cynthia returns home with food and beer for Roxanne, who comes downstairs after her bath with her head wrapped in a towel as her mother enters the house. This echo of Cynthia's two daughters fresh from respective baths often slips by without notice on initial viewing but provokes thought once realized.

Consequently as London life passes in front of them at Holborn Underground Station in the open form Leigh favors for such scenes, neither Cynthia nor Hortense can see each other as potential candidates for the relationship they are about to renew as mother and daughter. On the street they ignore each other and look for others. Cynthia looks off in the distance, and Hortense paces in front of her, scanning the field. It is Hortense who makes the first move and asks the woman smoking beside her if she is Cynthia, and the latter, of course, assumes there has been a mistake. In his review of *Secrets & Lies*, Richard Corliss of *Time* reports Brenda Blethyn's claim that she had never previously met Marianne Jean-Baptiste. When Blethyn was addressed with "Are you Cynthia?" she assumed her questioner was a member of the film crew: "So when Cynthia says there has been a mistake, that was my honest reaction. It wasn't acting" (66). It is a fine and in some ways plausible story, since Leigh is notorious for withholding salient information about his film narratives from his actors when he thinks it is necessary to secure authentic reactions, but this instance invites a degree of incredulity.

Despite Cynthia's immediate denial of any connection between them, Hortense persuades Cynthia to join her for tea at a deserted restaurant near the station to review the papers she has brought with her. Once Leigh focuses in medium close-up, head-on two-shot, on the two women seated side by side at a table for easy passing of documents, he devotes a nearly eight-minute long uninterrupted take of the two in conversation and in nonverbal, shared discovery. Cynthia, flanked by Hortense, who is dressed in an understated black suit, sits rather symbolically nearer the wall. She smokes, and her eyes dart about as though looking for an exit. At first Cynthia denies that she has ever been with a black man. Then Blethyn, completely into the heart and mind of Cynthia, stares as if she were witnessing an event from her own past that has long been repressed.

After a series of extremely revealing and subtly achieved facial responses, Cynthia absorbs the full impact of the moment and blurts out "Oh, bloody hell," "Oh, Jesus Christ," and "I'm so ashamed." Hortense with great composure remonstrates that she should not feel ashamed. "Who was he?" the daughter asks. However, Cynthia, who says she wants to be honest, informs Hortense she cannot tell her that. Jean-Baptiste registers her frustration and disappointment expressively by first looking straight ahead and then away from Cynthia. The large and bold emotions are left to Blethyn. Suddenly, Cynthia articulates what viewers have been noticing about the many superficial differences between the two women in dress, voice, speech, and behavior: "Look at ya. I'm a bit of a disappointment to you, ain't I?" Hortense replies "No," to which Cynthia says, "You didn't have to say that." "I know," concedes Hortense. The birth mother insists her daughter was better off without her: "I done you a good turn."

Hortense asks Cynthia whether she has a boyfriend and receives an answer in the negative with the additional aside that they had got her into enough trouble already. Blethyn in a bravura performance begins with extreme laughter, and slowly her face turns from comic to tragic mask as she realizes the import of what she has been saying and how she said it. Cynthia identifies with Hortense's adoptive mother when she has confirmed that the adoptive mother was quite proud of her professional daughter and says she would be too. Her instinctive maternal feelings for Hortense emerge along with the recognition that she did not raise her or could have raised her to become the professional young woman beside her. Hortense asks Cynthia why she did not want to see her. "Because nobody knows about you, sweetheart," is Cynthia's reply. Moreoever, Cynthia explains that at sixteen when she gave birth although she wanted to hold her baby following the delivery, she simply could not bring herself to do so. "If I had seen you, I would have wanted to keep you. You do believe me, don't you, sweetheart?" Cynthia implores her daughter.

Hortense tells Cynthia that she has known she was adopted since age seven when her mother told her of her birth while returning to England on a flight from Barbados. Cynthia asks if she had been upset. Hortense replies that she simply looked out the plane's windows at the clouds. Leigh records a look on Blethyn's face, as she casts her eyes in the same direction as Hortense's distant glance to her right to suggest that she, too, is seeing those clouds through the eyes of her rediscovered daughter. He, then, makes the cut and places the two women together in the reality of Hortense's car rather than in the imaginative, empathic fantasy space of that Britain-bound plane long ago from Barbados.

Andrew Dickson's evocative score with cello and harp underscores the quiet of this brief car sequence returning Cynthia to her East End house. It is the kind of haunting, almost minimalist music composed by Dickson and others that has been used effectively in earlier Leigh films. After the intimacy of the long take in the restaurant, Leigh's director of photography, Dick Pope, distances the action as well as the emotion by keeping the camera in a long shot as Cynthia exits the car and rounds a corner to her house.

The presentation returns to shots and counter-shots with a short scene supposedly a day later of shared connection between Cynthia and Roxanne that contrasts markedly with the restaurant scene between Cynthia and Hortense. Both women are smoking at the end of a shared meal; Leigh emphasizes their physical and behavioral resemblance. Roxanne notices something different about her mother and inquires whether she is all right. Obviously Cynthia is silently thinking about her recent encounter with Hortense. Roxanne notes that she found a frozen chicken. When her mother asks if it was found in the road, Roxanne disgustedly explains, "in a bin." Cynthia rationalizes that there are surely worse jobs. Somewhat puzzled by her mother's behavior and remarks about laughter and tears, Roxanne leaves the house, whereupon Cynthia phones Hortense to say how much she enjoyed meeting her the day before. They arrange to meet again for Italian food.

Meanwhile Leigh includes an intriguing but not wholly successful digressive sequence back at the photographic studio with the sudden return of the nearly derelict Stuart Christian (Ron Cook), from whom Maurice had purchased the photography business. Christian is first seen from a distance encountering the maimed beauty consultant as she gets into her car after her photo session with Maurice. The content here parallels and sometimes challenges the themes of loss and return, disillusionment and restored happiness of the film's principal narrative. The old photographer asserts that he still has a professional eye. Stuart, now a scruffy, embittered drunk, has left an Australia he found too large and too hot. His wife never joined him, and he no longer has any ties to her. His mother has since died while he was abroad. He says about all this loss, "It's my dad I miss."

Stuart criticizes what Maurice has done with the old establishment, saying of the interior décor and furniture, "It looks like a dentist's waiting room." Additionally, he rebukes Maurice for the limited number of weddings he does per year. Maurice does 40 weddings by himself; Stuart did 140 but farmed them out to others. "Nobody does weddings personally," he observes to Maurice who replies, appropriately, "I do." Stuart offers his services should Maurice ever need them. As Stuart leaves, Jane, Maurice's assistant, expresses relief, saying she thought he would never leave. Maurice, the present successful owner of the business who has given his signature to the enterprise, can only utter, "there but for the grace of God...." This scene, like some others that have been criticized in Leigh's later *Topsy-Turvy,* while entertaining in itself, seems somewhat superfluous in advancing the plot.

In a series of short vignettes, Leigh shows the developing relationship toward attachment between Cynthia and Hortense in small details like Cynthia's new softer, more becoming hairstyle as they become better acquainted over meals, at the movies, and primarily in conversation. The love and joy between mother and newly found birth daughter are clear, complicated, and presumably different from what has occurred between Cynthia and Roxanne in their shared history. Hortense and Cynthia are creating their history now. At their first meeting, Hortense and Cynthia are back at a restaurant where Leigh again films them in a two-shot but now occasionally in profile and less tightly in close-up. Cynthia inquires where the food is, and, to Hortense's amused delight, then adds, "I'm ravishing." Happily together, both women experience the state of absorption sometimes termed "flow," the total engagement that produces a sense of contentment.

Invited by Maurice and Monica to celebrate Roxanne's twenty-first birthday at their home, the first time Cynthia will have visited her brother's and sister-in-law's new suburban house, she requests that the invitation be extended to her new friend, Hortense, whom she claims is a co-worker at the box factory. Hortense reluctantly agrees to join her new family for the festivities in the confidence that only Cynthia knows of her biological connection to any of them. John Lahr reports that "the character of Hortense literally didn't meet the characters in her birth mother's family until the day before the final barbecue scene was shot—a nine-hour improvisation—because that's when she would have met them in real life" (54).

Figure 3. The benign, smiling Cynthia Purley (Brenda Blethyn) enjoying dinner in the company of her (unpictured) birth daughter, Hortense, from *Secrets & Lies*. (Courtesy Simon Mein, photographer, and Mike Leigh)

As so often in Mike Leigh films, a social occasion with food and drink, in the hope that entertainment and conviviality will overcome past hurts, brings the principal characters together at the end of *Secrets & Lies* to celebrate Roxanne's birthday. Once again in a Leigh film, relatives make the journey from at most modest residences to upscale estates. House-proud Monica displays her well-appointed home, taking particular care to close the lids of the toilets in the multiple bathrooms. These bathrooms contrast with the loo outside the kitchen in Cynthia's house that Maurice visited earlier and the same type of facilities shown in *Hard Labour* and *The Kiss of Death.* Tauke's observations on Monica's house as correlative to the character are astute:

> She suffers from horror vacui, the fear of emptiness. Her house has six bedrooms, places for the absent children, despite the fact that there are just two people living in the house. In the master bedroom, Monica has recreated a fairy tale complete with featherbeds, layers of filmy netting, and a four-poster bed; this room, with its dreamy disguises, is where her imperfections are most hidden. (191)

Maurice acts as the hospitable host and generous chef at the barbecue with grilled chicken, steaks, "burgers and bangers." Hortense arrives after the other celebrants, but the festivities proceed affably following her arrival. This family barbecue sequence is another of Leigh's incredibly deft long takes, over six minutes, only slightly shorter than the earlier Holborn sequence of the initial meeting of Cynthia and Hortense. Seven people around the circular patio table receive equitable treatment that would impress King Arthur, and through deep focus Maurice at the grill gets included. Afterward, the party moves indoors for birthday cake and champagne within sight of Maurice's picture of the child Roxanne on the mantle. The ensuing action features, as Coveney quotes Philip French in the *Observer*, "truth-telling and blood-letting, and here Leigh cuts between big close-ups and shots in which a foreground figure is in focus and a second person behind them slightly out of focus. This is masterly movie-making that never draws attention to itself" (xx).

Maurice and Monica present their birthday card to Roxanne with a generous cash gift contained therein. Hortense excuses herself to visit the powder room to gain some temporary composure for the remainder of the afternoon. While she is gone, Cynthia reveals to the gathering that Hortense is her daughter. This revelation throws the party into chaos because Roxanne is taken completely by surprise and reacts with considerable hostility toward her mother as she bolts from the house. Maurice and her boyfriend Paul persuade Roxanne to return; Maurice explains to his niece that her mother "never had enough love" bestowed upon her. The sudden appearance of Hortense and Cynthia's revelations about her represent more dramatic events than what usually takes place in many of Leigh's films, which by their very nature force all the characters to question their relationships and deeply held assumptions. Leigh's characters generally change little or not at all unless some major event prompts self-examination.

Cynthia continues to accuse Monica of not being a proper wife to her baby brother: "Why don't you give him no kids?" she asks her sister-in-law. Possibly given new courage from the truth-telling of his older sister, Maurice reveals his own the truth about his and Monica's infertility and to his wife confesses that "I love you to bits, but it's almost destroyed our relationship." He thus exposes yet another family secret: "There, I told it; where are the thunderbolts?" Maurice, the ever-patient and long-suffering husband, brother, and uncle, cites the title of the film and addresses the group: "We're all in pain. Why can't we share our pain? I've spent my entire life trying to make people happy, and the three people I love the most in the world hate each other's guts. I'm in the middle. I can't take it anymore."

While this sort of emotional outburst is not uncommon in Leigh's films, it is unusual to have it enacted by a male character as Timothy Spall in short-lived tears does in this scene. Maurice, quickly recovering, apologizes to Hortense and calls her a "very brave person." He also, without too much irony, says, "welcome to the family." She demurs on his favorable assessment of her personhood and calls herself merely "a stupid one." "No," he counters, "you wanted to find the truth, and you were prepared for the consequences." Cynthia, chastened by knowledge of Monica's secrets, goes to her and embraces her weeping sister-in-law, who tells her, "You're so lucky, Cynthia." At which point Leigh includes a telling eye-match of an exchanged gaze between mother and Roxanne. Maurice's shop assistant Jane, now in tears herself simply as an observer, tells Maurice she wishes she had a dad like him.

Suddenly, Cynthia reveals the identity of her biological father to Roxanne. His name was Bingham; he was an American medical student she met on holiday. One morning he was gone, but she describes him as "a nice man." Ruefully, Hortense, without tears, inquires whether her father was also a nice man. Cynthia asks her not to break her heart, but she offers no further information about her father to this other daughter, who rises from her chair to comfort Cynthia. So some secrets persist, leaving Hortense unsatisfied but still generous in her caring response to her birth mother. Despite her own state of being moved to tears and notwithstanding her mother's plea of "Please, Roxanne, please, sweetheart," Roxanne does not join this grouping. She keeps her distance across the room as seems appropriate and consistent for her character, but her tearful face in close-up with the sounds of her mother's tears across the room ends the scene. Anything more fully demonstrative on Roxanne's part might ring false. Although Leigh fills this sequence with justifiable tears, it is neither excessive nor sentimental as expertly played by his fine ensemble cast. Bert Cardullo writes of the numerous tearful scenes with Cynthia: "But her tears are earned, and they are varied depending on the situation or the cause. So much so that, for once in a movie, crying becomes a device for plumbing character, not for tugging at audience members' heartstrings and making *them* cry" (117). This sequence fulfills the pattern of family-systems theorists by displaying the insight that families respond to life and react to changes and milestones as a unit. Somewhat of an anomoly in Leigh's canon, Cynthia does change rather more strikingly than usual during the course of the narrative by becoming recognizably a stronger woman through her liberation from secrets and lies, newfound flexibility, and ability to adapt.

Leigh gives us as pendant to this extended ensemble scene a brief, quiet interlude of Maurice and Monica in bed that is the soul of simplicity, leavened with sympathy. Maurice expresses his fear that his wife doesn't love him the way she used to. Monica, now more tender than ever before, assures him she truly and deeply does love him. They rejoice in having and loving each other. Even with its brevity, this scene is deeply touching; it is reminiscent of comparable sequences between Cyril and Shirley near the end of *High Hopes* as well as the marital bed of Wendy and Andy in *Life Is Sweet*. It contrasts sharply with a comparable scene with W. S. Gilbert and his wife at the end of the later *Topsy-Turvy* but anticipates, as we can now see in retrospect, the denouement of *All or Nothing*.

The last scene of *Secrets & Lies* returns the action to Cynthia's house where the half-sisters, Hortense and Roxanne, talk in their mother's tiny backyard. Leigh frames them in the structural skeleton of a broken greenhouse. As they look at an old high chair stored in this shed, Hortense confesses that she always wanted a little sister because her brothers were so much older. The two women discuss their emerging and not unpleasant feelings about being related now as half-sisters. Roxanne asks Hortense whether she would like to go out with her some night, and the latter accepts the proposal with cheerful readiness. She wonders how Roxanne would introduce her; Hortense first thinks that to be identified as Roxanne's half-sister would require too long an explanation. Significantly, her sister sees no particular problem in simply stating the truth. In light of the preceding secrets and lies, this assertion represents a moral breakthrough, as Hortense concurs, "Better to tell the truth, isn't it?" The tone and atmosphere of this scene evokes memories of other sisters in Leigh, most notably Natalie and Nicola at the end of *Life Is Sweet* but also perhaps those male siblings, Mark and Colin, in *Meantime*.

Leigh cuts to and retains during the action that follows a God's-eye shot on the backyard scene of this benign family reunion as Cynthia enters, bearing a tray of tea things. "Sweetheart, tea's up," she cheerily proclaims. She takes her seat on a chaise longue and looks with pleasure at her two daughters sitting opposite her, whom she describes as "like a couple of garden gnomes." Cynthia, simply but in her own way also ebulliently, describes her awareness and sense of gratitude for the life within, around, and beyond her at this moment, "This is the life, ain't it?" And her two daughters share and affirm her sense of well-being with "Yeah" in unison.

Secrets & Lies began at a funeral for an adoptive mother and ends resolute in its acceptance of life and the suddenly awakened emotional currents of restored family relationships with a birth mother. This happy ending does not wipe out the reality of Cynthia's and the other characters' loneliness and need for love that border on desperation. On the other hand, Leigh yields to more of a contrived ending than is usual in his work although he casts nothing in ready-made mold of thought or of expression. Cardullo speculates that "the singularity of Leigh the director's uneasy or unstable aerial camera here causes us, if not to doubt Cynthia's certainty, then at least to question the tidiness of Leigh the writer's feel-good ending" (119). Such an interpretation supports Leigh's usual ambiguity even at the close of this film that has approached the condition of mainstream cinema more than most examples from his canon.

CHAPTER FOUR
Failings and Flourishings in Season of Youth: *Naked* and *Career Girls*

Naked

From what for Leigh was an almost upbeat ending of *Life Is Sweet,* the apogee to 1993 of his studies of family life, the director plunged into his darkest and most discomforting film. In his interview with Jay Carr, "*Naked*: English Director Mike Leigh Turns His Uncompromising Vision on the Way Things Are," from *The Boston Globe* included in Movshovitz, the filmmaker says of this film budgeted at $2.5 million:

> ...it takes more of an anarchist view. I despair that society really will be able to organize itself, ever. In the last couple of years, look what has happened in the world. So in that sense the film is about something fundamental rather than just local. In the end, what it is about is this guy, like a kind of lost communication satellite, floating around the atmosphere, wasted. It's about the waste and the unpredictable nature of things, as I see it." (56)

As Leigh suggests, David Thewlis as Johnny in *Naked* (1993) is the embodiment of the alienated male despite his display of egotistic and animalistic energy. It is a character study in a raw form. Johnny is not predictable, nor does he have a righteous cause to fight for. The camera observes but does not judge his behavior. The world Johnny lives in is often uncaring and distant, and Dick Pope's camera frequently keeps its distance as well. Johnny is a multidimensional character with his own private torments and pleasures that Leigh exposes without explaining. Leigh maintains the audience's ambivalence toward Johnny by showing him in an environment of relatively unpleasing people where he shines a little brighter than he would have alone. Because he talks so much, Johnny eventually has something to say that we agree with. His life on the fly embodies a willingness to be someone most of us do not have the courage to be.

Thewlis won the Best Actor Award and Leigh the Best Director Award for *Naked* at Cannes. The decade since its release has not appreciably diminished the controversy over *Naked*, although in the interim the film has achieved prestige that transcends the notoriety it initially garnered. Stanley Kauffmann, in his lukewarm review in the *New Republic* upon the film's United States release, commented that "if Godard were Leigh's age and British, he might well have made this picture" (28). Similarly, according to Graham Fuller in his "Mike Leigh's Original Feature": "Stylistically and thematically, *Naked* seems closer to the intellectually driven European art cinema of directors like Wenders, Kieslowski, Resnais, and even Bergman than to the school of telly-bred English social realist drama where Leigh started out" (ix). The existential strain is surely not without precedent in Leigh, but no other character apart from Johnny seems so desperately in need of being wrested out of an abyss.

At the same time, no other character in Leigh's works assumes the adversarial relation to society and his own historical time period that this apocalyptic character does. As Leigh describes him in his Fuller interview, he is "extremely complex and multi-faceted and driven by compassion, angst, hatred, and self-loathing" (xxxvi). Johnny interrogates his own soul less unrelentingly than he grills other people, much of his self-awareness being eclipsed by demonstrations of his clear intellectual superiority to them. Leigh credits David Thewlis in the same interview with whatever intellectual depth Johnny attains (xxx). The actor read widely in the books he thought a character like Johnny would read as part of his preparation for the role.

The Dostoyevskian role-playing of the character becomes consequently just that, a Nietzschean performance with less substance than Johnny's glib talk derived from a melange of literature, history, philosophy, and science might superficially suggest. He appears more a product of his reading from books like James Gleick's *Chaos* than of his own volition. He announces the death of his mother with horribly misogynistic disparagement of the female sex. There may be less to Johnny the philosopher than first meets the eye and mind, notwithstanding how much the ear might be enchanted by his verbal facility. Despite European antecedents that might come to viewers' minds, John Lahr traces a distinct British lineage for Johnny whom he terms "a terrific literary creation" in that "a select line of hectoring wit leads from John Osborne's Jimmy Porter to Joe Orton's Sloane down to Leigh's Johnny" (53). At first, one might suppose that the title of the film describes Johnny, who at the start seems completely open and honest. Before long it is apparent that with all his talking, badgering, and questioning of other characters he seldom allows himself to be emotionally "naked" except perhaps in the transparency of his desires. Coveney argues for Hamlet analogies with Johnny who "doesn't use his intellect to engage with other people." Rather, according to Coveney, Johnny "uses it as a buffer to his own near-psychotic condition and as a weapon of subordination, just as Hamlet uses his own wit as a stalking horse under whose cover he shoots at others (that's everyone) less witty than himself" (28).

Andy Beckett in a review of Dave Haslam's *Manchester, England: The Story of the Pop Cult City* notes that Haslam attempts "to chronicle and explain a collective sensibility: Manchester's famed cheekiness and hedonism and aptitude for cultural invention" (32). That description seems remarkably apt as a characterization of Leigh's and Thewlis's Johnny, who manifests the Mancunian sensibility during the forty-eight hours of this film's narrative time despite being down and out in London. Leonard Quart, who wrote the chapter on *Naked* in Ray Carney's *The Films of Mike Leigh,* describes this anti-heroic protagonist as "a man who is always outside, with infinite places to go but nowhere he can feel emotionally at home enough to stay" (228). Johnny becomes a picaresque seeker, and his consorts in this film are fellow pilgrims on a journey through life without a reliable compass of traditional belief systems.

The film opens even before the front title has appeared with a rapid tracking shot of Johnny fully clothed brutalizing a woman (Angela Curran) with whom he is having a rough sexual encounter in a Manchester alley under a streetlamp. She proclaims: "I'm gonna tell my Bernard of you! You're fuckin' dead!" This explosive scene is followed by quick handheld sequences of him hurriedly leaving a house clutching a shoulder bag and subsequently stealing a car that contains a baby carriage (a motif from *Four Days in July* and *Meantime*) extending from the trunk. The credits roll over the car on rather deserted highways as Johnny progresses toward London.

Leigh, in his dialogue with Graham Fuller, says of this opening: "*Naked* begins by showing Johnny in the most negative light possible, so that you have to make a journey from there and confront yourself with the fact that you may actually find him charismatic, as well as loathing him" (xxxii). A more favorable response to Johnny might begin for some viewers as early as his amiable questioning exchange with Sophie (Katrin Cartlidge), who sports a tattoo of a swallow, by tradition an emblem of a prostitute, when Johnny meets her as the housemate of Louise (Lesley Sharp), his old girlfriend from Manchester who is out at work as he arrives at her flat in London. The published screenplay of *Naked* contains Johnny's query to Sophie: "Have you ever thought, right…I mean, you don't know, but you might already 'ave had the happiest moment in your whole fuckin' life, and all you've got to look forward to is sickness and purgatory?" (9). When Louise does show up, surprised to find Johnny, she asks,

"What are you doin' ere? You look like shit." Johnny counters, "Just tryin' to blend in with the surroundings" (11). As John Lahr remarks of Johnny, he "wears his self-loathing like a badge of honor" (53). Louise leans over and kisses him as Johnny sings "Halitosis! Halitosis! Halitosis!" to the tune of Handel's "Hallelujah Chorus." Coveney describes this aspect of Thewlis's character, "Johnny isn't nice, but he is appealing" (19); he is both a narcissist and satirist turned against all power, including the power of his own, if not necessarily other people's, vulnerability. But it is his vulnerability that contributes to making him, to an extent, sympathetic and hints at his potential to morph his invented self into something better at some future point, though not unless he survives, which seems unlikely given his circumstances in this film.

As a way to elevate Johnny by the kind of equation Leigh sometimes employs, he provides a doppelganger of sorts in the character of the wealthy, hedonistic, and openly sadistic businessman Jeremy/Sebastian (Greg Cruttwell), possibly representing Leigh's judgment on Thatcherism re-emerging from earlier films. Leonard Quart sees this character as "a caricature of an upper-class, drawling, decadent psychopath. Jeremy is a man who feels he can't be touched, seeing himself as guarded by money and class privilege; he is often shot from a low angle, evoking his power over the women he tramples" (233). This device was not always well received by some critics. Claire Monk, for example, in her *Sight and Sound* review calls this character "a preposterous cardboard yuppie so little recognisable from real life as to be virtually abstract" (49/11). Likewise, as Andy Medhurst characterizes him, Jeremy/Sebastian "adds economic abuse to the sexual kind, presumably making him 'worse' than Johnny who, as a Cardboard City philosopher is indulged by the film to a rather frightening degree—he might be a rapist but at least he's not posh" (10/11).

The Mike Leigh of *High Hopes* similarly applies to Jeremy/Sebastian the coolly intricate amorality of money. More obviously than Johnny, Jeremy/Sebastian is an exploiter of the world's resources, including human ones; people are to him simply tools to be used to gratify his own desires, although he does pay for what he takes unlike the often-thieving Johnny. The protocols of commercial transactions may be the only rules Jeremy follows. On the other hand, people come to Johnny willingly without being necessarily in his employment, as is often not the case with Jeremy/Sebastian.

That Sophie lets Johnny use her does not make her unlikable. More reprehensible is the way Johnny reels people in only to push them away if they get

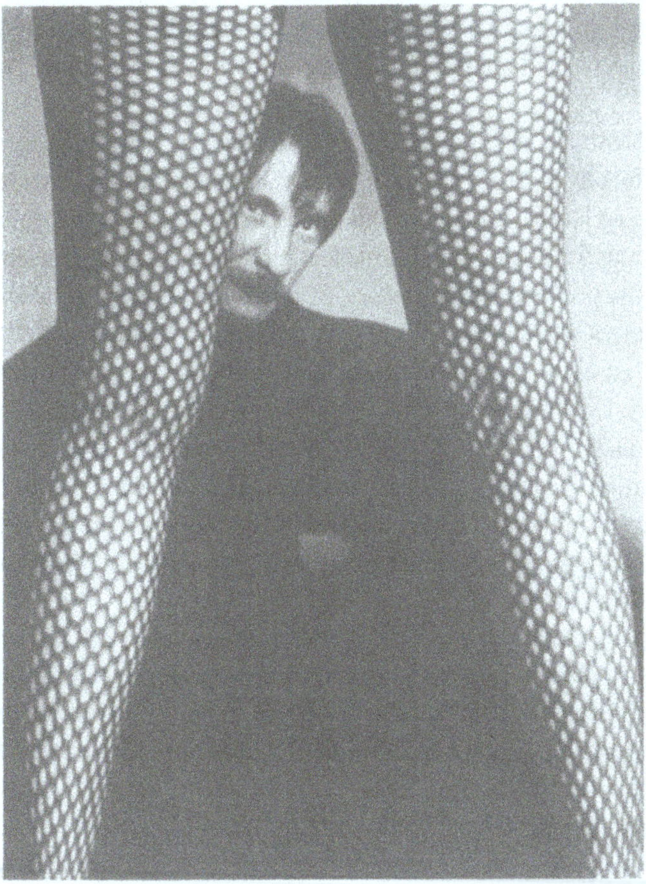

Figure 4. Johnny (David Thewlis) framed by the stocking-covered legs of Sophie (Katrin Cartlidge) from *Naked.* (Courtesy Jerry Ohlinger Archives)

too close, which is what he does with Sophie. She falls in love with him only to have him become more abusive, verbally and even physically, as he bangs her head against the arms of the sofa during sexual intercourse. Desson Howe in his *Washington Post* essay, "It's the Movie of the Decade, No, No, It's Just a Decadent Movie" in Movshovitz, cites David Thewlis's "take" on Johnny from a telephone interview he conducted with the actor: "He [Johnny] has grown up with a distaste for sex. So he blames women for his own sexual arousal" (46). When Johnny with his belongings takes his leave of her, Sophie asks "Are you coming back?" From below at the bottom of the stairs, he answers with his own question, "What the fuck for?" (27). Leigh shows himself open to the variety of ways of being human without closing his eyes to the great human propensity to inhumanity. In Johnny's London adventures we experience his profound loneliness and how his lack of a promising future and the futility of his present existence affect a brilliant mind without destroying his indomitable will to go on living.

On a Soho street, where he reveals "wherever you are in London . . . you're only thirty feet away from a rat," Johnny encounters Archie (Ewen Bremner), whose name he learns only later. This man is a drugged-out, obscenity-shouting, illiterate young Scot searching for his lost girlfriend, Maggie (Susan Vidler), to quote from the published screenplay: "Stupid fuckin' cunt's gone and got lost." Johnny inquires whether the young man dreams "in Scotch" i.e., "Like, dream about sporran-clad, caber-tossin' haggis, gallopin' over porridge-covered glens?" (28). Like many punsters, Johnny has a talent for aphoristic concentration, and such imaginative and verbally brilliant asides enliven his characterization throughout *Naked*. Johnny learns that Archie is in London because he put his father in the hospital after he hit him with a poker, a little latter-day Celtic Oedipal activity reminiscent of J. M. Synge's *The Playboy of the Western World* (1907).

This sequence offers the sort of paradox that Leigh relishes. Having betrayed Louise with Sophie and walked out of the house owned by Sandra from whom the two women rent rooms, Johnny succeeds in reuniting Archie and Maggie who come together, circling and calling each other profane names. Apart from idiom, the return of the two young Scots is not all that far removed from the less than satisfactory reunion of Johnny and Louise seen earlier. The episode, however, allows us to see that Johnny is capable of looking beyond his own needs and helping someone to find another lost soul even though he is a most unlikely Cupid and practices cruel strategies against the couple. For example, he asks Archie what it is like being himself, knowing that Archie has never thought so introspectively, and queries Maggie on why she wears a good-luck charm if, as she claims, she is not superstitious. She retaliates effectively by guessing that the twenty-seven-year-old Johnny looks about forty.

Dick Pope's cinematography for these night scenes on the street looks appropriately noirish and conveys a desolate, decaying urban place with evocations of homelessness, bag ladies, and pervasive loneliness. Urban anomie seems pervasive; the environment mirrors the characters' disarray and isolation. The mood, as Coveney declares, "is quite theatrical...the two young Scottish vagrants circling each other and literally wheeling out of Johnny's life, and our sights, leaving Thewlis in the foreground, head bowed in the grip of a nocturnal isolation that became the most familiar image of the film in the posters and publicity" (25). Leigh explained to Graham Fuller that "*Naked* was shot using the bleach bypass process; it's mostly been used for period films in the past. You miss out the bleaching in the lab and it gives you a saturated quality" (xxxix). This film is far more sophisticated in its use of light and shadow than in Leigh's earlier television work.

Taking respite by huddling down in an entrance to a locked office block, Johnny finds himself invited for shelter into the building by a middle-aged security guard, Brian (Peter Wight), whose wife abandoned him thirteen years ago and now lives in Bangkok. This biographical fact may help to explain Brian's frequent references to "harlots and whores." In response to Brian's question of whether he has anyplace to go, Johnny replies: "Yeah. . . I've got an infinite number of fuckin' places to go. The problem is, where you stay" (38). Once inside the building with Johnny, Brian explains that his guest must be invisible even as he, the guard, must be seen. Brian, a solitary but well-read autodidact like Johnny himself, quite different from Mr. Thornley in *Hard Labour*, actually encourages Johnny's philosophizing in a wide-ranging existential dialogue about the unreality of the present seen against past and future. Both men reflect the lonely path autodidacticism often proved for the British working class. Hitherto in the film, Johnny has dominated other people intellectually, forever asking rhetorical philosophical questions for which he expects no answers, but he has met their bafflement with a grin. The more equal match of the shared erudition and exploratory sensibility of Brian and Johnny makes a statement for Leigh on what formerly comprised the standard qualification for membership in the British professional or political elite. That qualification was conditional, of course, upon its having been certified by the Oxbridge establishment and the right public school, but Johnny and Brian attest that reading has opened their minds and made them question their world. Johnny, the existentialist, denies the possibility of the future, unlike Brian, who comforts himself with thoughts of retirement to his cottage in Ireland. The sterile empty space of what Johnny terms architecturally a "post-modernist gas chamber" is what Brian guards. On his tour inside the building, Johnny concludes, as the screenplay puts it, that Brian has "succeeded in convincin' me that you do 'ave the most tedious fuckin' job in England" (42).

Never before in Leigh's films or in Dick Pope's cinematography has an attraction toward abstract and formal elements in photography via lighting and silhouettes achieved so spectacular an effect in visually complementing dialogue and performances as in this sequence. In a happy marriage of formalism and the human element in telling the story, the camera records Johnny and Brian on their chiaroscuro walk through the building into its elevators and lavatories. Johnny delivers his diatribe on the forthcoming apocalypse, and Brian carefully records his time and place through the various security checks. Johnny had previously described Brian's plastic black-and-white electronic device as looking like a "Dadaist nun." With lunatic ingenuity, Johnny connects bar codes with the beast from the Bible's Revelation of John whose number is 666. Mike Leigh shared the source of that symbol with Lee Ellickson and Richard Porton in their *Cineaste* interview in Movshovitz: "The discovery that the European bar code adds up to 666 was key. We picked that up from a pamphlet. We were walking through Soho, and some nut case offered us this pamphlet....That is definitely a reality" (72). Moreover, Johnny continues with the provocative (if erroneous) fact that "wormwood" in Russian is translated as "Chernobyl." In Johnny's view, "the end of the world is nigh, Bri. The game is up" (45). A notable sequence renders dual silhouettes of the men in discussion dramatically presented within another of Leigh's longer takes, almost literalizing the darkness of their talk. It also boasts an equally impressive sound design in the insistent harp accompaniment of Andrew Dickson's musical score.

As if to instruct Brian on the limitations of inhibition, Johnny crosses the street from the office building to enter the building of a woman (Deborah Maclaren) they have been spying on. A number of women in the film let Johnny into their homes due in part to his charm but also because these women feel some of the same isolation and loneliness that he manifests. From a distance this particular woman appears a fading beauty as she drunkenly dances by herself in an attic room without curtains. Michael Coveney interprets this scene in some respects as "equivalent to the closet scene where Hamlet begs his mother not sleep again with his murderous stepfather" (26). Face to face, she is older than Johnny thought and curiously masochistic, "Fuckin' bite me! Come on!"—a circumstance that inspires abuse from Johnny but no actual sex because, as he informs her, she looks like his mother. Viewers learned earlier from his conversation with Louise that Johnny's mother, a barmaid, had died. He has also been put off by the tattoo of the skull and crossbones the woman wears.

Surprisingly, this woman tells him that her favorite book is Jane Austen's *Emma.* Johnny steals this novel along with three other paperbacks while she is sleeping. Once more in Leigh the potential for a symbolic trope between a classic nineteenth-century British novel and a twentieth-century character is left hanging in the balance for whatever association viewers might like to pursue. Perhaps analogical application of Emma to Johnny rather than the woman reader would prove promising because like Emma he also demonstrates excessive pride and cannot resist imposing himself on the lives of others. *Emma* does seem an unusual choice for this woman. Likewise the presence of a map on Ireland on her wall is an artifact that Johnny notices, but the woman herself apparently hasn't until he brings it to her attention. It may hint, as Leigh suggested in his interview with Graham Fuller, that her flat "perhaps has belonged to somebody who was operating for the IRA" (xxxviii). This kind of provocative but unexplored detail is omnipresent in Leigh.

Johnny returns to the street to find Brian on his way to breakfast after his shift. He denies that he "shagged" the dancing woman of Brian's voyeuristic fantasies. Johnny ignores some advice from Brian, but, according to the published text of the screenplay "*looks at* Brian, *perhaps a touch nonplussed* " by his former benefactor's admonition, "Don't...waste...your life" (57).

Leigh cuts back to the house occupied by Louise and Sophie. Jeremy has taken up a beachhead on the couch when Sophie comes home. He introduces himself to her as the landlord, Sebastian Hawkes, and friend of Sandra, their other roommate away in Zimbabwe. What ensues is a series of sexual scenes between the two of them. In one of these Jeremy/Sebastian lies on his back attired in only his near-thong bikini underpants while Sophie, wearing only panties, kneels over him and lashes his chest with her long hair. He then requests that Sophie dress in one of Sandra's nurse uniforms; she announces, "Oh, what? We're gonna play doctors and nurses now, are we?" While Sophie demurs that she really cannot go through with whatever scenario Jeremy/Sebastian has in mind, he violently seizes her, and Leigh visualizes for the audience what is described in the directions of the screenplay: "*She is wearing the uniform. He is naked. He is taking her from behind, aggressively, violently, horribly. He is grunting.* Sophie *is screaming desperately*" and shouting at him, "Fuck off! Leave me alone! No! You fuckin' bastard!!" (61).

This sequence of rape contrasts with Johnny's continuing urban odyssey where whatever violence shown is directed against him rather than initiated by him. Leigh has him become a man more sinned against than sinning when compared to Jeremy/Sebastian. He accompanies a café waitress (Gina McKee) back to the sublet she is renting from two gay men about to return from the United States. They seem to be kitsch classicists of some sort, judging from the décor and artifacts in their apartment. Johnny asks the girl whether Zeus lives there. As he inspects their library, Johnny does not want to sound, as he puts it, "Homer-phobic," with a pun that the girl does not understand—and the published screenplay fails to acknowledge accurately, printing the less evocative and unambiguous "homophobic" (63). He openly expresses his admiration for

The Iliad and *The Odyssey* among the texts found in the flat. Coveney reports on the back-story designer Alison Chitty concocted for the two men in this flat: "They were an upper-working-class, slightly pretentious gay couple called Dave and David, who liked going to opera, traveling (especially to Morocco) and cooking with woks. One worked in the Vehicle Licensing office at Stratford in the East End, the other in the Keith Prowse ticket agency" (217). Admitting to a form of madness in creating an environment before knowing precisely what Mike Leigh wanted, she went so far as to send letters to the supposed occupants at the address to be used for location. Also very evident in their apartment on the bookshelf is a large photograph of Rock Hudson.

At first the waitress acts very hospitably toward Johnny. She permits him to take a much-needed bath, gives him booze, and feeds him beans. He evokes Alfred Hitchcock to the cardigan-dressed young woman as he prepares to enter the bathroom for his shower: "You're not gonna creep up on me with a big knife dressed as your mother, are you?" and then adds, "Although it looks like you already are dressed up as your mother" (62).

Figure 5. Johnny (David Thewlis) celebrating the western canon of literature in a densely detailed *mise-en-scène* from *Naked.* (Courtesy Simon Mein, photographer, and Mike Leigh)

Then as they amiably continue their conversation by the fire, she begins to cry and tells Johnny to "fuck off." She follows up this declaration by gathering his clothes and throwing them down the stairs. He comes aggressively toward her but kneels and buries his head in her stomach. She goes to touch his hair but stops herself without Johnny's being aware of this gestural conflict. He delivers a stunning, almost Lear-like imprecation to her, beginning with "it just goes to show you that no matter 'ow many books you read, there's some things in this world that you never, ever, ever, ever, *ever* fuckin' understand" and ending on the following curse as found in the screenplay:

> …I hope that when you're tucked up tonight, all snug and warm underneath your tear-sodden fuckin' duvet in your ankle-length Emily Brontë windin'-sheet, that you spare a thought for me, with me head in a puddle of cold dog's piss. An' I hope that you dream about me. An' I hope that you wake up screamin'. (*He opens the door and goes into the lobby.)* An' I hope that all your fuckin' children are born blind, bow-legged, hare-lipped, homeless hunchbacks! (70)

In succession after he leaves the café waitress, Johnny is brutally beaten up by a "bill-sticker," or poster man (Darren Tunstall), who glues up advertising posters on walls. This man first befriends him and gives the vagrant Johnny a lift in his truck. Johnny keeps up a steady patter, which presumably exasperates the man: "I've 'ad a lot of bad experience with walls, you know, what with, er, talkin' to them and climbin' 'em. And me dad's driven me up a good few in 'is time, you know what I mean?" (73). He additionally rhapsodizes on famous walls of the world like the Great Wall of China, the Wall of Jericho, the Berlin Wall, and the Wailin' Wall. Johnny tries unsuccessfully to place posters himself and berates the bill-sticker: "What are you doin'? Cancel everythin'. In the beginnin' was the Word, and the word was 'CANCELLED'. D'you get like satisfaction out of this? D'you think you're makin' a contribution? You're like sort of publicly promulgatin' vacuities? Are you with me?" (73). Finally, without warning, the man savagely attacks him and drives away with Johnny's bag in the truck. As John Lahr describes the Johnny who receives blows here: "Johnny's only sure cover is compelling language: words—comical, hysterical, apocalyptic—spill out of him, provoking extreme responses from the world. His character—an extraordinary act of imagination by Thewlis" (53).

Alone, Johnny stumbles into the middle of the road, screams, drops down on his knees, and crawls to the sidewalk. Later we see him walking slowly down an empty, narrow passage in the deep focus Leigh often uses for street scenes like those in *Bleak Moments*. Out-of-focus shadows cloud the foreground, as a gang of youths appears and walks down the passageway toward Johnny; they reach him and quickly beat him up, the camera staying removed to middle distance but recording the event as the youths run away deeper into space. One youth with long hair and seen from the back, which is the only vantage viewers have, like a female form, returns after the group assault to deliver a final blow or two upon the fallen Johnny, a retributive playback to Johnny's opening violence back in Manchester.

Meanwhile, Louise has returned to the flat where she finds Jeremy/Sebastian still in his underpants and the ravished Sophie on the floor. He becomes flirtatious with Louise, complimenting her on her shorts. She rebuffs him, "Would you take your 'ands off, please?" (65). Apologizing, he does so. These floral shorts that Louise wears in *Naked* represent an inspired choice of costume by Lindy Hemming. They are at once both homely and attractive, therefore, wholly appropriate to the character Lesley Sharp plays. In a later moment of intimacy between Johnny and Louise, he recalls "I remember when you bought those shorts. I warned you about 'em then" and she retorts, "Yeah…well…I only got 'em to piss you off" (86). Obviously Johnny sees her partly as a mother-substitute but also as a girlfriend. The sexual attraction smarmy Jeremy/Sebastian manifests toward her reinforces this latter role for her.

Because Louise observes Sophie's bruises, she infers that what has transpired during the afternoon deserves more serious concern than she first thought. Her roommate discourages Louise from calling the police to get Jeremy/Sebastian out of their flat since he refuses to leave on his own: "Look, you may be the landlord from hell," Louise tells him, "but that doesn't give you the right to lie on our couch" (66). Sophie, acknowledging sexual politics, makes Louise aware of how incredible her story would seem to police: "They're gonna take one look at 'im in 'is suit and one look at us, an' 'oo d'you think they're gonna believe? There's fuckin' dope all over the place" (66). In the meantime, Jeremy/Sebastian lies smugly on the sofa.

Following this scene with their landlord and at the supposed moment Johnny is delivering his retort to the café waitress, Leigh offers a brief pub sequence with the two women who have vacated their premises in the hopes that Jeremy/Sebastian will eventually leave them alone. Louise and Sophie discuss abortion and "proper relationships" between men and women, i.e., as Louise defines the terms, "livin' with someone 'oo talks to you after they've bonked you" (71). Although she wanted to keep her child, Sophie reveals that she had an abortion in Paris at age fifteen after an affair with a philosopher whom she insists she really loved. This antecedent philosopher in her life may suggest why

Sophie was initially attracted to Johnny. Sophie expresses her quandary about men: "I don't know what they want from you 'alf the time. What they start off likin' you for they end up hatin' you for. Don't like you if you're strong, don't like you if you're weak; hate you if you're clever, hate you if you're stupid. They don't know what they want" (71). Louise, who appeared cynical and somber at the beginning of the film, has become someone who is able to care for and about someone.

The emerging female solidarity between Louise and Sophie in the later part of *Naked* prefigures much of the content and texture of the later *Career Girls*, in which Katrin Cartlidge plays a very different type of confident career woman. Both Cartlidge and Sharp, neither actress conventionally beautiful, increase in physical attractiveness as the film progresses, a phenomenon noted earlier about other female protagonists in Leigh films. "One of Leigh's anti-conventions," Stanley Kauffmann remarked in his review of *Naked,* "is to use women who are not pretty. This ploy succeeds in a wry way: the more we know these woman, the prettier they become" (29).

Bloodied and beaten, Johnny in the middle of the night returns to Louise's residence. Johnny is delirious and delusionally brings up fragmented but traumatic remembrances from his boyhood. Jeremy/Sebastian, still in a state of undress in the apartment, joins the women and Johnny on the landing to observe scornfully of the abused and incoherent Johnny: "Aren't people pathetic? Right. I'm going to beddy-byes.... If anyone wishes to join me, I'll be under the duvet" (77). With Johnny's body now damaged, this assertion of Jeremy/Sebastian's bodily comfort seems especially soulless.

Now in bed, Johnny begins to sing about returning to rainy Manchester; Louise joins in with him in a quietly touching scene as she touches his face with the back of her hand. "In *Naked,*" John Hill submits in his *British Cinema in the 1980's*, "a return to the north appears to hold out the possibility of a certain form of identity and inter-connection which is absent from the film's portrait of London as a city of lonely and alienated people" (173). Coveney reports that "Leigh used to sing this song with his friends in Habonim (The Builders), the international socialist Jewish youth movement he joined as a schoolboy" (29). Like Sophie, Louise wants Johnny, but, unlike Sophie and others, she does not want him at any price. Louise joins the other characters seen at work, the night security guard, the waitress, and the poster man. While none of these people appears overjoyed with their respective occupations, each exhibits a modicum of integrity and purpose not demonstrated by the vagrant characters like Johnny, who can do little more than rationalize his aimlessness. Leigh in his interview with Graham Fuller describes Johnny as "a man of ideas and passions and frustrations, and positives and negatives, therefore he *has* to be a character who constantly confuses and surprises us" (xxxix). If he were stronger he would use his intelligence and verbal facility for worthwhile causes. Louise offers Johnny a promise of the only viable relationship possible for him, but, in his self-destructive fashion, he rejects it to go on the road in solitude with no destination in sight.

This moment of tenderness between Louise and Johnny contrasts with a subsequent one between Louise and Jeremy/Sebastian, where she threatens with genuine menace to cut off his male member. Finally the landlord departs, having left a considerable amount of money for Sophie's services rendered. Leigh supplies an overhead shot of Jeremy/Sebastian's departing, black luxury sedan.

Louise and Johnny have a final poignant scene in the bathroom, but even here Leigh avoids the all-too-easy compassion that is a function of a sentimental view of life. When Louise tells him she is going back to Manchester, perhaps to stay, and asks him to accompany her, which he appears almost to assent to do, Johnny gives her a "cuddle" as she requested. In deciding to return to Manchester, with or without Johnny, Louise shows her independence. Johnny may want women to love him, but he always backs off when they do. He remains the incorrigible metaphysician and raises the theological question as quoted in the screenplay: "What if God just put us 'ere for his own entertainment? That's all we are. Just somethin' for 'im to 'ave a bit of a laugh at" (88). Johnny, who has been sick in the bathroom, decorously closes the toilet lid as he converses with Louise, thereby demonstrating a bit of bathroom etiquette often exhibited by female characters in Leigh's films although unexpected from someone of the male gender, especially Johnny. As Sophie came into the bathroom to join him and Louise early in this sequence, Johnny had quipped: "What is this, a spectator sport or something? The 100-metre vomit" (87). Sophie exits the bathroom, and Johnny lets down his guard behind a closed door for an honest conversation with Louise. One of my students described the bathroom as having a special importance for Johnny, who may often live on the streets, because it represents "the ultimate expression of civilization—a well-lit, warm place where you come in out of the cold and get cleaned up, where you can have a few comfortable moments all to yourself."

Amid Louise's succor of the battered Johnny, Sandra (Claire Skinner), the nurse, returns from her Zimbabwe visit with her now ex-boyfriend. She is perhaps the most solid citizen shown in the film, but Leigh presents her, somewhat inexplicably, as a comic foil for Johnny. This is not the first time in Leigh's films that he has turned the moral world upside down so that respectability itself becomes a kind of jest, with a nod perhaps to W. S. Gilbert's penchant for the topsy-turvy. Johnny does not exert physical domination over Sandra. Despite his battered state, Johnny once more seems to be enjoying himself and his own persona, and his enthusiasm is contagious. He competes with her in raillery and by completing her fragmented sentences, but, in contrast to his bathroom scene with Louise, there is no meeting of word with word between these two people. In accent far more middle crust than either Louise's or Sophie's, Sandra expresses her dismay at the disorder in her house in continual fragments of incomplete sentences. The actress who played Natalie, the slightly butch plumber of *Life Is Sweet*, appears much more conventionally feminine here. Sandra shows herself the thorough professional like Angela in *Abigail's Party* and patches up Johnny's wounds, but she also finds herself overwhelmed by the needy inhabitants of her once efficiently run house. Sophie, sobbing uncontrollably, has become unglued by her realization that Johnny and Louise have a history together and may have a future relationship that will leave her out. Sophie vacates the premises, bearing a large chromium-plated "S" that may have fallen off a store sign as well as her bag. Her departure underscores how in this urban environment people come together and disconnect in what appears to be a seemingly random manner.

Leigh treats Johnny's final sequence alone with Sandra, the last of the housemates, in comic fashion. Predictably he comes on to her, telling her "I find you attractive. Very attractive." All Sandra seeks are traditional British comforts and coziness: "My bath! Hot toast...hot milk...hot-water bottle...bed, sleep" (94), which Leigh quickly cuts to as described in his screenplay, *"soaking up to her neck in a bathful of suds. Her eyes are closed. She sighs contentedly"* (95). Such bathtub moments are found in a number of Leigh's films, from Mark looking happier in the tub than elsewhere in *Meantime* to Valerie's champagne-accompanying soak in *High Hopes*. John Hill evaluates Claire Skinner's "clever, but highly mannered performance." He judges Sandra's response to Johnny as "simply silly and suggests a reluctance on the part of the film to make use of the women characters to interrogate more fully the behaviour of its central male character" (173).

Leigh's own explanation of this role and why he cast Claire Skinner for it is characteristically humorous and a matter of practicality. He noted (in his *Cineaste* interview with Lee Ellickson and Richard Porton in Movshovitz) his assessment of this duet between Johnny and Sandra: "I don't know if it's my favorite scene, but the scene with Sandra gives me such a tickle. Claire Skinner was so successful as Natalie the plumber in *Life Is Sweet*, and I was keen to get her to do something different" (73). Because Skinner was doing a television series at the same time, Leigh assured her she could do something at the end of his film; the result of his strategy was the character of Sandra: "It was a bonus because we built up a whole thing about this character. You expect this formidable Florence Nightingale and you get this complete screwball, as nutty as anyone else" (73). As Sandra is soaking in her tub, Johnny in the living room puts on his shoes and pockets the three hundred and eight pounds that remains from Jeremy/Sebastian's payment to Sophie for her sexual services.

In the final sequence, Johnny still has not resolved his problems and continues to run, though, in his crippled state, not very rapidly. His solitary independence denotes for him an existential freedom that often not only hurts himself but also certainly others like Louise. He is, as Stanley Kauffmann described him, "an inquirer who lives on the hope that he won't find answers, scrounging along in several ways, shrugging himself free of emotion and commitment" (29). Johnny comes out of the Victorian gothic-style house, hobbling on one leg because of his injuries, clinging to a post at one point to get his balance, and then he painfully moves slowly down the middle of the road along the yellow line of the highway. Johnny's position here may stand for the line between love and hate, good and evil that are at war inside of him. The camera moves steadily ahead of him almost in syncopation with Andrew Dixon's score of nervous progression doubling back upon itself played by harp, viola, and double bass. The sudden changes of pace and instrumental color suggest quick and pungent strokes of an isolated character. Johnny becomes increasingly distant from the house where he formerly had received comfort as the camera tracks ever farther ahead of him until a sudden cut to black where the film ends.

The camera, reflecting as much as determining the audience's response, backs away from Johnny at the end. Yet throughout *Naked's* long running time of 131 minutes that precedes this typically open-ended Leigh conclusion, the filmmaker and his able cast have put the audience off less than they have pulled us in, even though the balance between the two may sometimes seem a toss-up. "I think if the film works," Leigh observed in his Fuller interview:

> You go away locked in debate. There are no easy answers, really. People ask if there was ever a temptation for Johnny to go back to Manchester with Louise. We investigated the possibility, but it seemed to me that what had to happen is what does happen, which is that the film finally has to be left, and Johnny with it, suspended in mid-air. The journey that this guy is on continues, to nowhere—on to somewhere. (xxxix)

With his paranoid millennial angst and without any rendezvous with responsibility, Johnny is too disconnected, alienated, and intellectually muddled to redo and remake the world. But at least at the end of the film, unlike Vladimir and Estragon, whom he somewhat resembles, at the end of Samuel Beckett's *Waiting for Godot*, he is on the move as an act of daring even though we have no clue as to where he is going or why. Throughout *Naked*, Johnny has confirmed our suspicion that the happy, adjusted life many people seek may not be the brightest, most ennobling, or, even, ultimately, the most human one. He remains a mandarin in his knowledge of texts but not with respect to traditional British academic credentials and social class. Johnny begins and ends *Naked* as a thief, of a car at the beginning and money at the film's close. Nowhere does he attain the harmonious equilibrium required of the tragic hero or of the man we are to take as a spokesman for ourselves, but Johnny is true to his own existential self. As Leigh's viewers, we feel we have contemplated in Johnny's struggle an aesthetic representation of a confrontation with Necessity, less classically Greek than diminished in the postmodern way popular culture recycles ancient archetypes.

Career Girls

Sandwiched between major films of the stature and heft of *Secrets & Lies* and *Topsy-Turvy*, Mike Leigh offered the appealingly modest and small-scaled *Career Girls* (1997). At one point in *Naked* Johnny disparagingly refers to Louise as a "career girl." Leigh's *Career Girls* restores a more positive sense to that identity as part of a major societal shift that celebrates single women and the intensity with which they create surrogate families out of friends. These young women want men to value them as Mike Leigh does with his characters here. But they have not been ready to compromise their own values and identity simply to be among the married. The film's brevity (only 87 minutes) plus its mixed comic and bittersweet tone hark back to the television films of the seventies and early eighties. Now, though, Leigh shows a new focus on women who have careers in the marketplace but remain open about their emotions and their vulnerabilities. While vulnerability can connote negative qualities like weakness, its positive side is an open heart, as illustrated in Leigh's portrayal of these career women.

Leigh's innovation of showing the past as well as the present as an unpacking of his own method of filmmaking hints at an increasing self-reflexivity that will surface in *Topsy-Turvy*. Thematically, in *Career Girls* Leigh is able to examine the journey that occurs in each young person's life from 20 to 30, evocative of Cyril's observation in *High Hopes* that from 25 to 35 are the best years of your life. At the same time, Leigh contributes to what has become the new phenomenon at the start of the twenty-first century: the so-called quarterlife crisis as these women wrestle with some of the kinds of issues long associated with middle age. Apparently all the stages of life are increasingly becoming telescoped. While neither young woman's mother appears in the film, mothers are discussed. Annie still lives with hers, and recently, when her mother picked up a boyfriend at her advanced age, her daughter has been experiencing a small amount of envy as she confesses to Hannah. Throughout her life, Hannah has been required to assume almost a parental role for her inattentive mother, and that burden continues now even in adulthood. Both women seem anxious about their independence and guard it carefully.

For the first time in his career, Leigh employs a flashback structure, and in doing so, he exposes a crucial element of his own method. In *Career Girls* he foregrounds action of the past or what usually in his extensive workshop sessions with the actors is left as simply the unseen back-story outside the dramatic frame while he concentrates on the immediacy of character and action in the here and now. In the long preparation phase for Leigh's films, he asks his actors to live through years of a character's development. "The past is simply part of the present, and therefore doesn't have to be dwelled on, or, as in a conventional drama, withheld for a 'powerful' climactic revelation" (84) as Terrence Rafferty in *The New Yorker* succinctly explains Leigh's usual method. In *Career Girls*, Leigh arrests those moments in the past and uses them to motivate the action with double articulation of time, past and present. The form of the film, though it may seem overly portentous for something so slight, embodies or at least tweaks the tension between determinism and chance in its handling of plot and character.

Two former college roommates meet for a reunion in London where they attended college six years before, shared a flat initially with Claire (Kate Byers), and lived finally in a flat on their own. Psychology major Annie (Lynda Steadman), now residing in the North of England with her mother and working in a personnel management job, comes to visit Hannah Mills (Katrin Cartlidge), who graduated with a first in English literature. Hannah currently works for an upscale stationery company that gives her a company car. Nothing especially dramatic occurs during their weekend beyond reaffirmation of their emotional bond that has endured since college and will doubtless continue even without subsequent return visits. As Hannah tells Annie in a stylish Chinese restaurant quite different from the "take-away" one they lived over during their student years, "You're the only person who ever really appreciated me."

The film's action cuts between the present and flashbacks of their undergraduate lives at North London Polytechnic. Dick Pope, Leigh's skillful cinematographer, filmed sequences from the past with a handheld camera and blue filter stock to suggest the long-ago and grungier eighties. Leigh's more than usually experimental visual effects offer an additional stylistic parallel between *Career Girls* and *Naked.* The look Leigh and Pope come up with, appropriate for the fragmentary memories of student years and accompanied by songs from The Cure, contrasts with the bright, crisp contemporary appearance of London in the nineties. Both women in their collegiate personae are presented as stereotypical outsiders, and Leigh, as he has done in the past, inscribes upon the bodies and behavior of these characters attributes that distance them from others. To that extent *Career Girls* descends from earlier examinations of quirky, spastic, and otherwise impaired characters from *Bleak Moments* through the cruelty of *Naked* to the portrayals in this film. The quantity of quirkiness, mental and physical, exhibited by characters as if mannerisms constitute personality seems here more contrived and smothering than in Leigh's other films. Leigh's excellent casts usually build character gesture by gesture; here construction appears to be more tic by tic.

Thus Annie suffers from a virulent case of facial dermatitis, the cause of much fingering and dithering on her part, as well as asthma. She always has her eyes downcast; indeed her willingness to look people in the eye is a mark of her maturity as Hannah comments during their subsequent reunion. Even as an undergraduate Hannah presents herself as witty, abrasive, and sharp-tongued but also unsure of herself at the core of her being. Leigh's conception of her is almost that of a decent and responsible female version of Johnny from *Naked.* He even invests her with her male antecedent's penchant for puns, e.g., "living in the pasta." Hannah observes shortly after meeting Annie in a flashback, "You look like you've done the tango with a cheese-grater." She, then, suffers guilt when her remark sends Annie tearfully into the bathroom. That night Hannah apologizes to Annie, "I was only pissin about." Part of the cause of Hannah's manner is traceable to living with an alcoholic mother, never seen in the film but often referred to. When the two women meet again as adults, Hannah observes that Annie and her mum are like sisters, but that she, Hannah, had "independence shoved down her throat" because of the maturity required of her from her earliest years. The relationships between mothers and daughters that

Leigh has illuminated so fully in *Life Is Sweet* and *Secrets & Lies* surface in this film only in occasional allusion.

Besides the relationship of Annie and Hannah to each other, Leigh emphasizes their respective interactions with three other characters. These include Claire, their erstwhile roommate; "Ricky" Burton (Mark Benton), a fellow, somewhat mentally impaired, psychology major with Annie, who subsequently drops out of college after she rejects his declaration of love; and Adrian Spinks (Joe Tucker) with whom both girls had brief affairs but whom Annie thought she loved. Annie explains her former feelings for this insensitive man: "When you're in love with a bastard, you can't help yourself." Leigh shows these several relationships and their crucial characters in the two separate time frames of the narrative. The fact that Annie and Hannah encounter these three people in the present as well as in the past occasions comment from them about synchronicity, repetition, and coincidence. Leigh deliberately calls attention to the artifice of his film's plot contrivance, "not unlike the way Annie can't resist calling attention to her angry skin," as Amy Taubin parenthetically noticed in her *Village Voice* review, "with a bit of dialogue about the odds against such coincidences" (67). Such chances begin to look like necessity.

Figure 6. Hannah (Katrin Cartlidge) (l), and Annie (Lynda Steadman) (r) as college student roommates in *Career Girls*. (Courtesy Jerry Ohlinger Archives)

Significantly, these people from the past do not recognize Annie and Hannah in the present with the exception of Ricky, whose confusion obscures memory and reality at best. For example, they become reacquainted with Spinks as a real estate salesman who shows Hannah, in the company of Annie, a spacious flat she has arranged to see. He has no recollection at all of Annie who did love him, but he asserts that he does find Hannah vaguely familiar.

The stoned Spinks of their undergraduate days had evaded commitment in sexual relationships: "Vagina, nice place, I wouldn't want to live there." Now he is a married man with a young daughter. Both Spinks and the man they met earlier whose Docklands flat is up for sale assume a lesbian relationship between the two women, who are presumably shopping for a future residence together. Likewise, Ricky, who "fancied" Annie at one point out of frustration, calls Annie and Hannah "lesbos." When the "swinging," bathrobe-attired, divorced future tenant (Andy Serkis) of the handsome Docklands apartment overlooking the Thames discovers that Annie and Hannah are straight, he begins seductive behavior involving offers of champagne, among other inducements, to entice them. On his balcony Annie experienced what Hannah terms "a touch of Hitchcock," but without vertigo, and Hannah can quip, perhaps self-reflexively for Leigh, about the view, "I suppose on a clear day you can see the class struggle from here." Leigh shows that the free mobility of meritocracy has replaced the ideas of Marxist leveling argued by Cyril in *High Hopes.* Hannah and Annie recognize their old roommate, Claire, as she is running in the park, but she does not acknowledge them; indeed she seems not to recognize them in her self-absorption in exercise.

Benton's "Ricky" Burton, occasionally brilliant, always unstable, and curiously lovable in his declared "fancy" for Annie, is another of the over-the-top characterizations that remain controversial in Leigh's work. Stella Bruzzi in her *Sight and Sound* review of *Career Girls* describes the former roommates' ineluctable encounter with Ricky: "Given the meetings with other characters, we know by a simple process of elimination that this meeting is coming, but this shields us not a jot from the torture of witnessing (along with the two women) Ricky's tumble into half-lucid schizophrenia" (38).

That such predictability is so patently telegraphed in *Career Girls* indicates an alteration from Leigh's usual practice of foiling this sort of predictable expectation. Ricky has returned to London and the corner where Hannah and Annie had lived. The take-away restaurant is closed, and Ricky holds a wrapped oversized plush elephant, a gift for a child, Harry, whose photograph he shows the two women but whom he confesses he seldom sees. He does recognize Annie and asks her, "Where are the scabs?" He adds by way of self-disclosure to his old friends: "I'm not an idiot. I'm like an *idiot savant*, I just haven't found my *savant* yet."

This meeting in the nineties provokes the final flashback of *Career Girls*. Years before the two girls had tracked Ricky down to his seaside hometown after he had left London following Annie's rejection of his amorous attentions. At that time he became abusive and obscene toward them and accused them of being "nosy parkers." Stella Bruzzi finds the juxtaposition of these two scenes emblematic of the film as a whole: "Like Annie and Hannah, we are left bereft in the knowledge that we feel for Ricky, but are ultimately powerless to help him.... Rather than let us feel comforted and replenished by our cathartic experiences, it confronts us with the futility of film's love of emotional identification. We the audience are *idiots savants* too" (38). Her observation is a wise one as to the way Leigh practices both identification and alienation in his narratives. Amy Taubin makes a more sanguine inference, if not for the audience at least for Hannah and Annie: "Ricky's regression is the measure of the career girls' success" (67).

Once again in Leigh's films, Emily Brontë's *Wuthering Heights* emerges as a reference point as it does in *Bleak Moments*. Here the novel provides an envelope for the relationship between Hannah and Annie, who sometimes see themselves as analogous to the Brontë sisters. "We always get the bronte of everything," the incorrigible punster Hannah claims. Hannah introduces her new roommate Annie to the occult use she makes of the novel. She evokes the presence of "Ms Brontë, Ms Brontë," and it must be "Ms," as Annie explains once she has been initiated into Hannah's practice, "like Multiple Sclerosis." Unlike her English major roommate, Annie can boast she has visited the Yorkshire parsonage in Haworth where Emily Brontë was inspired to write her novel. Hannah poses a question for the future, usually about potential amatory relationships ("Ms Brontë, who will I have sex with next?"), perhaps a relevant question arising from the desire for oneness that looms so large in the novel. She, then, opens *Wuthering Heights* at random for the answer with a well-chosen word usually parsed for its sexual connotations by this late-twentieth-century college girl. When Hannah bids farewell to Annie on the platform beside the train that will take her friend back up North, she gives her a copy of the Penguin edition of *Wuthering Heights*.

Brontë's novel is both a relic from the women's nostalgic past and a talisman of their having successfully completed the rite of passage into mature adulthood. Emily Brontë's hero and heroine may love and torture each other in a world of their own, remote from the real world, both social and psychological,

CHAPTER FIVE
Homage to and Deconstruction of the Heritage Film: *Topsy-Turvy*

Mike Leigh's audacity in creating *Topsy-Turvy* (1999), his seventh theatrical feature, continues to astonish. Of all the late-twentieth-century directors to revive an essentially defunct genre, the movie musical, with an historical costume picture set in the late nineteenth century about actual Victorian personages, W. S. Gilbert and Arthur Sullivan, Leigh might seem among the more improbable. In his biography of the director, Michael Coveney did reveal long before production work began on *Topsy-Turvy* that "Leigh sheepishly describes himself today as a 'closet Gilbert and Sullivan freak'" (49). Much of the story is a backstage look at how a stage show is put together, one of the oldest movie commonplaces. However, Leigh surely had earned the right to take up these matters since he had by this time in his stage and film career written and directed twenty-two plays for the theater. Was part of his impulse for this film a tribute to the pleasure and education the theater had bestowed upon him? What is audacious and gratifying is how well and with what characteristic sureness Leigh succeeds in creating a biopic that unmistakably bears his distinctive signature. Given his collaborative approach to filmmaking, Leigh appears ideally suited to celebrate one of the greatest collaborations in English cultural history. While the pairing of Gilbert and Sullivan ran from 1871 to 1896, Leigh dramatizes only the events around their legendary production, the premiere of *The Mikado* on March 14, 1885. The film is one of the greatest movies ever made about mounting a stage production with an exemplary cinematic assimilation of theater. Leigh's presentation of the action is completely consistent with his earlier films in its intimate approach to characters and interpretation of the period through historical details, for example, running the gamut from fashion to the conditions of dental treatment as well as closely observed behavior and evocative dialogue.

Gayden Wren in a recent study of the art of Gilbert and Sullivan, *A Most Ingenious Paradox,* argues that these operas are at bottom "a series of powerful, very human stories whose themes are as universal as their parody and satire are dated, and it is this fact that I think accounts for the operas' longevity" (4). Therein may lie a significant parallel between Leigh and the subject matter of this film. Leigh's cast of characters in *Topsy-Turvy* has never been so large, but he manages the same kind of ensemble intimacy with individuals that he has successfully presented in all his preceding films. Wren further ascribes a distinctive "'riff' feeling, a jazz-like sense of almost improvisatory looseness to its [*The Mikado*'s] dialogue and songs," where "many of its scenes are not built on what happens as much as how it happens—'character riffs' on a simple premise" (172). Without much strain, a certain common denominator may be invoked on this point to bring Leigh and the Victorian collaborators together.

Before Leigh and his extensive collaborators began working on *Topsy-Turvy*, rumors were afloat in London that the director's next project would be a parody of Merchant-Ivory films. In typical Leigh fashion, his portrayal of Gilbert and Sullivan may well instead suggest a form of homage to as much as a subversion of Merchant-Ivory and the so-called heritage film made with solid, realistic details and memorable Leigh touches. The director does not disclose in advance what he will be working on in a film project, since, of course, he really does not know himself. However, *Topsy-Turvy* proved an exception, since there was a "leak," as he called it, about Gilbert and Sullivan as his future subjects with a budget projected at about four times that for *Secrets & Lies*, which would get him past the $10 million mark for the first time in his career. The actual cost of *Topsy-Turvy* came in nearer to $20 million. Notwithstanding this considerable budget increase, I commented to him that I assumed Arnold Schwartzenegger would not be playing W. S. Gilbert. Leigh rejoined in the same jocose spirit that "actually I would like to have him play both roles, but it would create havoc with the budget as you imply." Leigh reported to Ryan Gilbey in *The Express*: "But it was important to me to make something that was more detailed than the kind of costume dramas we see. People don't make films that examine the various social, economic, political, sartorial, medical factors that make people who they are—but we have done just that!" (43).

Rather than creating a period movie in the conventional sense, Leigh has presented what Henry Fitzherbert termed in the *Sunday Express* "an intimate 'epic' in which the period is interpreted through behaviour and fashion. The camera never sits back to soak up immaculate vistas of recreated Victoriana, but probes and magnifies the telling details of everyday life" (54). He is true to a recreation of late Victorian England seen on its own terms, at its own pace, with no attempt at playing for easy laughs or surely with no bout of nostalgia for the class system. Leigh observed to Ryan Gilbey about the conventional theater experience of seeing Gilbert and Sullivan, as he did as a child, "Obviously I'm retrospectively critical of all the bourgeoise associations about theatre" (43). *Topsy-Turvy* also becomes by analogy a mirror of our own time and of Leigh's aesthetic value as a contemporary filmmaker whose passionate precision reconstructs the past. Indeed, through this film, Mike Leigh merits a chorus or two of Gilbert and Sullivan's "He Is an Englishman," to borrow from *H.M.S. Pinafore*. David Denby in his *New Yorker* review of Leigh's film ably summarized this aspect: *Topsy-Turvy* "is one of the greatest tributes ever paid to British civilization at its meridian hour" (132).

One might interject an additional tribute to the continuity of British civilization, this time around circumstances of late-twentieth-century England, implied in the making of this film: the fact that its production was partly financed by funds from the National Lottery through the Arts Council of England merits gratitude. The content of the film with its focus on creative processes in the performing arts is completely appropriate to Leigh's interest, considering his own distinctive method and preoccupation with such matters. Then, too, thematically, the series of burlesques on human nature in general and on English nature and institutions in particular from Gilbert and Sullivan prefigure Mike Leigh's works to some degree. But the color, scope, and content here is properly theatrical, beginning with the opening credits. The silent chorus of white-gloved ushers lower the curiously beautiful deep-blue seats at the Savoy, and Leigh suddenly cuts to Arthur Sullivan popping up and being made ready to conduct the orchestra for *Princess Ida* about to open at the Savoy.

The film is not always totally accurate in its narrative. Gilbert had already begun the libretto for *The Mikado* before he attended the Japanese Exhibition that provides the context for the epiphany leading to a new kind of Savoy opera in *Topsy-Turvy*. Mike Leigh as interviewed by Michael Billington comments on this deliberate departure from historical fact in the film:

> ...Gilbert thought of the Mikado—which solved the problem of their impasse—before the Japanese exhibition came to London. But when it came he was immediately attracted by it and indeed did, as we have in the film, have Japanese folk from the exhibition come to the Savoy theatre to show the actors how to be Japanese. But the order is different. I just thought dramatically it was more interesting for him to get the inspiration by going to it in the first place and have to be persauded by his wife.

As Anthony Tommasini in a *New York Times* essay, "Sullivan Without Gilbert? Don't Ask" explains Gilbert's inspiration, "the notion of using stiff Japanese protocol and exotic Oriental imagery to parody British rectitude, law and society takes hold of him" (Section 2, 34).

In the specific moment of revelation in the film, when a Japanese sword Gilbert has purchased as a souvenir of the exhibition falls from his study wall almost upon his head, Leigh registers a parody of such moments in past biopics. Leigh himself, in his discussion with Billington, suggests how *Topsy-Turvy* operates in contrast to the received understanding of so-called costume pictures because it is "really about creating a world in a distilled cinematic way that goes beyond the surface, naturalistic thing of simply recording... [it] challenges your assumptions, that subverts your assumptions about what the surface presents." As Joe Morgenstern describes Leigh veteran Jim Broadbent's performance as Gilbert in this sequence from *The Wall Street Journal* review, the specificity of detail and response is wholly consistent with Leigh's usual approach:

> ...he [Broadbent] stares at the exotic object, and the camera stares at him in close-up for 20 seconds. That's an extraordinarily long stretch of screen time, but not a second too long for what Jim Broadbent packs into it—bemused curiosity, then growing interest, then amusement, then delight, then slow-burning excitement that ignites visible commitment. (Wl, 2)

Brenda Blethyn demonstrated a similar gamut in her recognition scene at the café with her biological daughter in *Secrets & Lies*. Here Leigh uses a subtle dolly shot to a close-up of Gilbert as he wields the sword in Kabuki fashion as he has witnessed at the Japanese Exhibition. Then a sudden cut to the Lord High Executioner in *The Mikado* confirms the artistic use Gilbert will make of the implement. Throughout the film Leigh bridges process and product to perhaps the best effect he has ever demonstrated.

Interestingly enough, Leigh is most authentic historically with personal and material details, often almost casually introduced and swiftly played out but responsible for the layered and persuasive texture of the whole. Gilbert's father (Charles Simon), an irascible novelist and former naval surgeon, is deeply suspicious of the electric doorbell, for example, and the rate of technological change in late Victorian Britain serves as a recurrent parallel to the late twentieth century in Leigh's film. If, as Timothy Garton Ash has observed, "one of the great British arts is to conceal the reality of change behind the appearance of continuity" (WK 15), Leigh challenges that notion in this film. Dr. Gilbert quickly dismisses the telephone through which Gilbert and D'Oyly Carte discuss in code the previous evening's receipts at the Savoy: "Sheer waste of time; it can only result in further erosion of the written word." Gilbert's father experiences day terrors in the presence of his son as he remembers nightmares induced by forces he ascribes to his estranged wife. The scene of his father's potential dementia may remind seasoned Leigh viewers of senile Mrs. Bender in *High Hopes* and the misogynistic theorizing of something Johnny in *Naked* does not utter but surely has the potential to do so.

More darkly, instances of addiction, both to alcohol and drugs, sexual frustrations of the meek and love-deprived Lucy, "Kitty," Gilbert, and matter-of-fact arrangements for Sullivan's American mistress to obtain an abortion figure in the action of *Topsy-Turvy*. Lesley Manville gives another fine and subtle performance in a Leigh film as Kitty Gilbert. She shines especially at the conclusion when she manages to convey both convincing Victorian demeanor and a lively, intelligent spirit longing to be set free. Leigh does not hesitate to show sometimes the sour lives behind the sweet music and witty lyrics; he gets behind the public surface of the theatrical world to private moments of pain that reveal genuine emotion. As always Leigh remains sensitive to human frailty even when celebrating success. Steve Vineberg has astutely commented on Leigh's treatment of the foibles of the D'Oyly Carte performers: "He's intimate yet tactful; he knows just how much he can expose without cheapening them....He's interested in the ways in which these women and men handle the very human frailties that this time and place (and profession) officially deny that they have" (B11).

Leigh once more illuminates the particular difficulties faced by women in a male-dominated society. A widowed actress with a little boy cannot hope to establish a relationship with a new man despite the quantity of her admirers. Another actress, performing on a painful leg which requires bandaging before the curtain rises, tells her colleague in their shared dressing room: "Well, you shouldn't reveal your little secret [her young son] until he's fallen hopelessly in love with you, and has asked you to marry him." The look of the film with its lavish production values and huge cast compares to the best of Merchant-Ivory or John Madden's *Shakespeare in Love* (1998), but, in addition, Leigh makes his usual nod to problematic subtexts in his treatment of what other directors might consider recalcitrant material.

Leigh chooses to examine a period of stress, after they had been collaborating for over thirteen years, in the relationship of librettist/lyricist Gilbert and composer Sullivan in the hideously hot summer of 1884 when the box office of their latest collaboration, *Princess Ida*, was languishing. Sullivan is suffering from a painful kidney ailment and a longing to compose some serious music. Given Leigh's wry wit and abiding interest in gastronomy, he has Kitty Gilbert tell her husband as she chases after him down a long corridor at breakfast time before a cut to a scene with Sullivan, "Willie! Your kidneys are getting cold."

Sullivan desired to be the English Mendelssohn (at age 14 he became the youngest recipient of the Mendelssohn Scholarship), but his comic operas with Gilbert permitted him to maintain the luxurious lifestyle the film shows he so much enjoyed. Many musical authorities over the years have seen in Sullivan's scores a typically Mendelsohnian polish, dexterity, and melodic appeal. Nevertheless, because of a convergence of factors, Sullivan (Allan Corduner) at this point feels unable to become engaged sufficiently to compose a score for more of his partner's lightweight, magical-themed libretti. As a supposedly anonymous London reviewer's grudgingly favorable response to *Princess Ida* (this Gilbert reads with a sense of disgust) expresses it: "W.S. Gilbert abundantly proves he is still the legitimate monarch of the Realm of Topsy-Turvydom." And then, adding insult to injury in Gilbert's estimation, this reviewer goes on to call the story itself a dull one. What Leigh's film does not mention is that Gilbert had written a play in 1874 titled *Topysyturvydom* "on the notion," as Dennis Denisoff observes, "of a gender-inverted society where women are men and men are women" (59). Edmund Wilson wrote years ago in "Gilbert Without Sullivan," which was anthologized in *Classics and Commercials,* that "Gilbert had been trying to foist upon his partner what he considered a magnificent theme: a magic charm which would convert human beings into the realities of what they pretended to be" (363). Sullivan can no longer cope with a libretto where everything has been turned upside down by sorcerers, magic potions, enchanted coins, or similar arbitrary devices. In a scene in D'Oyly Carte's office where he is attempting to reconcile the partners, Leigh begins by showing fragments: hands, cigars, disembodied aspects before the two men sit down and become whole. It is a device that was effectively used at the close of the dinner party sequence in *Who's Who* to suggest disarray between people.

Leigh's opening sequence of Sullivan waking late from a nap and being readied to conduct the opening of *Princess Ida* uses the same kind of lurching tracking shot seen before in Leigh's work. It resembles the beginning of *Naked*, but the crucial difference in content and tone does not alter the director's desire in the contexts of both films to involve viewers in a visceral and essentially kinetic experience. Henry Fitzherbert found this sequence on the nature of celebrity as the servants scramble to meet Sullivan's demands for brandy and cigarettes, "reminiscent of the opening tracking shot of *The Bonfire of the Vanities* in which Bruce Willis's bestselling author prepares to meet the press" (54). The bon vivant, even libertine, Sullivan, despite ill health, appears somewhat more Gallic and cosmopolitan than conventionally British. He has a mistress, Mrs. Fanny Ronalds (Eleanor David), frequently uses French, and visits a Parisian brothel, where he encounters Leigh alumna, Katrin Cartlidge, as Madame. The film's music director, Gary Yershon, appears as the brothel pianist.

Richard D'Oyly Carte is played with gentlemanly aplomb by Ron Cook, who was the down-and-out former photographer in *Secrets & Lies*. The extraordinarily successful producer of these D'Oyly Carte operettas has recently built the Savoy Theatre for these productions and now must try to reconcile his two contracted collaborators when Sullivan rejects Gilbert's new piece of "topsy-turvydom." Under their contract with D'Oyly Carte, the duo was obliged to provide a new opera upon six-month notice or else indemnify their producer for any losses incurred from their default. Gilbert, the workaholic, despairs of finding a solution to this impasse, and the stabilizing influence of D'Oyly Carte and his wife Helen Lenoir (Wendy Nottingham) seems on this occasion insufficient.

Ray Carney, while not writing specifically about *Topsy-Turvy*, makes an observation about Leigh that seems quite germane to why the filmmaker might find this disagreement between Gilbert and Sullivan particularly relevant for his own purposes: "Leigh celebrates uniqueness. He creates partnerships in which the partners don't blend and merge, but each brings something different to the table. The result is the most stimulating sort of relationship: one in which the individuals are both dependent and independent" (216). Twentieth-century American playwright and famous collaborator George S. Kaufman wrote in a letter to Howard Teichmann, his last collaborator, which the latter quotes in his biography of Kaufman, that the total result of collaboration is frequently "far more than the combined abilities of two people might give you.... The two people often fly far above their talents, and if I don't know about collaboration who the hell does?" (270–71). As the film would have it, Japanese art and culture suddenly ignite Gilbert's imagination and, in turn, stimulate Sullivan into renewed energy to work with his collaborator. Among the numerous historically accurate pleasures in *Topsy-Turvy* is Wendy Nottingham's portrayal of Helen Lenoir, a remarkable Victorian businesswoman who was an accomplished diplomat. Leigh demonstrates how much of the whole foundation of the Savoy operation rested on her. She supplied all the detail; her husband produced and promoted. Their right-hand man in the business is Richard Barker in another choice role for a Leigh regular, Sam Kelly.

Through the introduction of the actual collaborative process, *Topsy-Turvy* becomes a reflection of concerns in Leigh's own career, which makes this film curiously more autobiographical in some ways than any other in his substantial body of work. Leigh creates an epic film about process, something akin to his method as a filmmaker. To be sure, Leigh may try the patience and endurance of his viewers during the first hour or so of this film with appearing and disappearing characters and oblique, sometimes opaque, principles of narrative sequencing. However attenuated his leisurely storytelling or lack thereof first appears, Leigh delivers finally a stunning product from these disparate resources. He takes full advantage of the generous time permitted him in a grandiose feature-length film that runs for two hours and forty minutes. In the Ryan Gilbey article in *The Express*, Leigh discusses the special challenge and pleasure of the larger canvas required for *Topsy-Turvy*: "I'm very at home with domestic subjects, people in houses and so on, just as Vermeer was at home with women standing in rooms. But as a film-maker I never got the chance to work on a bigger canvas, and there was this unfulfilled area in me...." (43). The long middle portion of Leigh's film is given over to the extensive rehearsal process preceding the opening of *The Mikado* in 1885, from running lines to designing costumes. Rehearsal sequences are presented back and forth with scenes of the finished product from the staged *The Mikado* to suggest how process and product happened in the late-nineteenth-century London theater. The thorough theatrical professional Gilbert serves as painstaking director for the production, harnessing talent, tempering emotions, and successfully integrating numerous elaborate production elements. His prescriptive practice would seem quite opposite to Mike Leigh's own procedure although doubtless both men were equally hard driving. Gilbert demonstrates, as Leigh has written for the CD recording of the film's soundtrack, "the serious purpose...about all of us who strain and struggle to make other people laugh" (6).

Scenes are devoted to such technical matters as how to sing triplets with the proper rhythm, as Sullivan presides over a voice rehearsal or colorful details of how corsetless Japanese women should advance across the stage. The abandonment of foundation garments proves an especially profound loss to Victorian Britons of both sexes, so it seems. The romantic male lead in the company, Lely (Kevin McKidd), for example, remonstrates with Gilbert, claiming that he cannot produce the required vocal vigor without the necessary diaphragmatical support that the corset provides. Gilbert cajoles him into compliance: "Come, come, Lely. This is not grand opera in Milan. It is merely low burlesque in a small theatre on the banks of the River Thames. You have a fine, strong voice which will be more than adequate for our purposes, with or without the corset. Kindly remove it this instant." Alison Steadman has one excellent scene as Madame Leon, costumer for *The Mikado*, during which she tries to change established British habits and behavior relative to dress, as the performers demur over costumes that expose their ankles among other hitherto concealed body parts.

Certainly *The Mikado* as originally presented by D'Oyly Carte's company could scarcely be considered a model of realist theater in the twentieth century. Still Gilbert dedicates considerable effort with his invited trio of young Japanese women from the Exhibition to instructing his three little wholly English maids from school in authentic movement, fan handling, and the like in order to achieve an authentic Japanese quality in their performance. Jack Purdy writes in his Baltimore *City Paper* review that "Leigh is showing us the birth of the modern theatrical sensibility, being midwifed by a man who previously couldn't care a fig about realism" (30). Amusingly, this emphasis on realistic details connects Gilbert and Leigh as blood brothers, especially with respect to the honesty, relevance, and accuracy that Leigh cherishes in his films. "Of course," as Steve Vineberg correctly concludes, "*The Mikado* is as thoroughly British as *H.M.S. Pinafore.* The made-up Japanese names and Eastern-flavored trills in the chorus numbers, the fans and the pigtails, have the effect of emphasizing that fact, just as the fantasy costumes and makeup in *The Wizard of Oz* are flourishes around the unmistakable vaudevillian antics of its stars" (B11). Additionally, as Gayden Wren has observed, the score for *The Mikado* may be Sullivan's "most English score, with glees, madrigals, and other characteristic English song formats turning up repeatedly" (167).

Leigh shows in these scenes the provenance of a modern theatrical sensibility being advanced not by Ibsen but by W. S. Gilbert, a practitioner who, in his previous topsy-turvydom, presumably cared not at all about verisimilitude. Gilbert bears witness to the notion that comedy is serious. The actors in *The Mikado* must play their roles reasonably straight if they are to be funny. At a point when the breach between Gilbert and Sullivan appears irreparable, the librettist dares his collaborator with the challenge that if he wishes to write a grand opera about a prostitute dying of consumption in a garret, "I suggest you contact Mr. Ibsen in Oslo. I am sure he will be able to furnish you with something suitably dull."

Perhaps what Gilbert represents is the application to the stage of John Ruskin's gospel of patient particularity and respect for a sense of fact. In this regard he is a Victorian progenitor of Mike Leigh as well. Of course, to viewers at the beginning of the twenty-first century, *The Mikado* may be unconvincing as anything but a highly patronizing portrayal of stereotyped Japanese; therefore, the film's rehearsal scenes become, in part, metaphoric for cultural colonialism. Similarly in the film, British racism suddenly is given voice upon news of General Gordon's defeat by the Mahdi's troops at Khartoum. Grossmith opines about this national tragedy: "The Hottentot in the desert doesn't play cricket. His natural habitation being the jungly-bungly tree. He is as yet hardly able to walk upright, don't you know." Leigh's inclusion of these elements gives something of his usual late-twentieth-century ironic bite to this historical material. Nevertheless, on balance, it is better to consider much of what Leigh documents at least onstage with *The Mikado* as embodying Gilbert's most individual gift for extravaganza and satirical nonsense. Leigh shows his fascination with the amount of labor exhibited by Gilbert to produce theater of essential triviality, laborious souffles, as it were. After all, no less an authority or contemporary than G. K. Chesterton wrote in *The Victorian Age in Literature*: "Of the Victorian Age as whole, it is true to say that it did discover a new thing; a thing called Nonsense" (152), of which W. S. Gilbert is the supreme public avatar.

The omission in *Topsy-Turvy* of any specific look at Gilbert working on his lyrics seems odd. After all, Gilbert was the first lyricist in England to make his lyrics an integral part of the characterization and plot, and Leigh's own interest in literature might predispose him to address this creative aspect of Sullivan's collaborator. Leigh does include one scene where Gilbert is shown reading his new libretto to Sullivan, who exhibits laughter and much pleasure in the lines his collaborator shares with him. This scene is followed with another where Gilbert continues his reading aloud but this time to his wife. She observes, presumably somewhat ironically, that "It certainly is rich in human emotion and probability," and Gilbert replies, oblivious to her irony, "Hardly."

Indirectly, the director illuminates the contribution of Gilbert to Sullivan's posterity by the inclusion of a scene showing Sullivan accompanying his American mistress while she sings his most famous sentimental drawing-room song, "The Lost Chord." Written after the death of Sullivan's younger brother, it is a setting of an undistinguished Victorian text by the British poet Adelaide A. Proctor. Leigh precedes this performance at the salon with a pianist playing a chromatic and crypto-impressionistic piece by Gabriel Fauré. The qualitative difference between the Fauré and the Sullivan is all too apparent. As Colin Wilson observes in his *Chords and Discords*: "It was a happy accident that threw Gilbert and Sullivan into collaboration, even though one gets tired of Gilbert's wit far sooner than of Sullivan's music. He might have continued as a composer of sentimental drawing-room songs and boring oratorios, and been totally forgotten today as Stainer or Parry" (136).

Leigh does not shy away from revealing serious defects in Gilbert's personality. His choice of Jim Broadbent for the role is especially fortunate, because this actor convincingly portrays the troubling ambivalence of the character. The height of jest for Gilbert is that he was himself a pillar of Victorian dignity, in his conservative, choleric, straitlaced attitude and behavior representative of much in England that he was satirizing. He is the repressed Englishman who takes his vocation seriously and expresses himself best through his craft. If he embodied much of what he seems to rebel against, to that extent Gilbert was rebelling against himself as Broadbent effectively portrays him. Gilbert's humor often puts self-importance in its place, notwithstanding his own propensity toward pomposity, and properly ridicules ignorance.

Gilbert may also be seen as another emotionally stunted Leigh character who evokes memories of Peter's dread of displaying open emotion in *Bleak Moments*. Andy Medhurst in his *Sight and Sound* review of *Topsy-Turvy,* amusingly titled "The Mike-ado," astutely addresses this dimension of Gilbert as portrayed by Broadbent: "The son of two clearly deranged parents and the husband in a stilted marriage, Gilbert clings to his formulaic writing because formulas offer certainty, a certainty unattainable in the destablishing realm of emotions" (37). Herein lies the crux of this historical figure as a scion of a dysfunctional family that immediately allies him with numerous others in Leigh. Who would doubt that by this point in Leigh's career he would not offer convincing historical personages as Mike Leigh characters and get away with it?

On one occasion when a member of the orchestra refers to Sullivan as "Dr. Sullivan," Cellier (Stefan Bednarczyk), Sullivan's musical director, corrects him by recalling that Dr. Sullivan, Sir Arthur's father, who was also a conductor, is deceased. Sullivan thanks Cellier for the correction. This is the only allusion to Sullivan's family in the film, but its inclusion offers a contrast for the collaborators with respect to families. One might speculate on how galling it was for Gilbert that Sullivan was knighted in 1883. Gilbert had to wait until 1907, after the demise of both Queen Victoria and Sullivan.

Topsy-Turvy includes significant glimpses of Swenck, as his estranged mother calls her son, in his troubled family relationships with wife, father, mother, and sisters. His mother (Eve Pearce) tells her daughter, Maude (Theresa Watson), who had encountered her brother at the Japanese Exhibition, "Never bear a humorous baby." Maude assures her mother she will endeavor not to. One biographical detail of Gilbert's life Leigh's film regrettably does not include—that at the age of two, taken on a tour with his parents, he was kidnapped by brigands in Naples. W. S. Gilbert was returned to his mother and father for a mere twenty-five pounds! The analogy with O. Henry's "The Ransom of Red Chief" is all too easy to imagine. This species of detail could be familiar coin in the world of Mike Leigh. "I can assure you, Papa," Leigh's Gilbert explains to his father at one point, "that the very last person with whom I wish to have any communication at all is your estranged wife…the vicious woman who bore me into this ridiculous world." Later, declining his wife's suggestion that he should visit a dentist to relieve his painful toothache, Gilbert replies, "Madam, I had rather spend an afternoon in a Turkish bath with my mother than visit the dratted dentist." Leigh follows up this exchange with Gilbert's horrific dental visit for a tooth extraction to underscore further the physical reality of life in Victorian Britain. While these moments devoted to Gilbert's parents may add nothing to the plot, as some reviewers noted, they do, in the subliminal way Leigh prefers, suggest the sources of Gilbert's bizarre inspiration.

As in earlier films, Leigh negotiates a remarkably delicate nonjudgmental course in his portrayal of a complex character. He seems to come down on the view that the basis of Gilbert's success lies in his power of sustained irony and paradox shown in his gentlemanly good humor that mocks affectation without alienating his audience. Gilbert as man and theater director in the film issues pleasantly dry remarks and pungent understatements. Maybe Leigh neglects the lyricist in the act of writing perhaps because he shares something of the conclusion reached years ago about W. S. Gilbert by Louis Kronenberger in *The Thread of Laughter: Chapters on English Stage Comedy from Jonson to Maugham*:

> Gilbert's librettos suffer from something unattractive and even repellent in his own personality. They have the really bad taste that comes from a lack of heart; they suggest the kind of man who was not simply cruel in order to be funny, but who was almost funny in order to be cruel. Writing so unhuman, so inhuman, as Gilbert's *should* be artificial, but his seems not merely that, it seems—to use a word that Shaw even ventured to apply to Gilbert's lyrics—arid. It is as unwatered by charm as it is unwarmed by feeling. (207)

Leigh's approach to Gilbert in contrast to Kronenberger's appears somewhat more moderate and magnanimous; nevertheless, the inclusion in *Topsy-Turvy* of "If You Give Me Your Attention" from *Princess Ida* with its lament "I love my fellow creatures—I do all the good I can—/Yet everybody says I'm such a disagreeable man!/ And I can't think why!" might well apply to Gilbert himself, and it is tempting to speculate on any possible inferences Mike Leigh might make along the same lines when critics labeled his approach "patronizing" or otherwise opprobrious. But it must be said that Sullivan was prompted to compose his best music by Gilbert's lines. And, as is true of "The Lost Chord," Sullivan without Gilbert is rather dull; Gilbert without Sullivan can still be very funny as with "The Bishop of Rum-ti-Foo."

To both men equally goes the credit for writing English operettas that can be understood. English is a tricky language to set to music. Sullivan succeeded where precious few other composers did, thanks in large measure to Gilbert. This feature of their collaboration comes across especially well in the vocal numbers of Leigh's film. Leigh does not pursue Sullivan's musical ambition in the second half of the film even though it is addressed strongly at the beginning. Exactly why Sullivan found *The Mikado* so much more rewarding than earlier Gilbert plots is likewise left unexamined.

Few composers before or since Arthur Sullivan have employed with equal dramatic power the different forms of the human voice, but he lacked originality. Anthony Tommasini has addressed this matter of Sullivan's derivative music as an advantage for his collaboration with Gilbert where Purcell odes, Handel choruses, Italian opera recitatives, and Rossini patter arias could all be appropriate. "Imitation is the essence of comedy however," Tommasini writes, "and Sullivan had keen instincts about the kinds of music to put with Gilbert's dry, witty words. When a verse suggested a jaunty dance tune, an Italianate aria, a pastoral ditty or an agitated recitative, he provided it, exaggerated slightly for comic effect with an odd turn of phrase, a mawkish harmonic progression or some inflated dramatic intensity: whatever it took. The results were hilarious" (Section 2, 34). To Gilbert's credit as a collaborator in musical theater, his scenes are conceived so that they may be readily molded into formal musical structures.

Sullivan's solo songs often effectively suggest a popular continuation of the old Italian *bel canto*, with its lyric grace, its elegant refinement of detail, its noble pathos, and frequent brilliant coloratura. His telling and direct solos can go straight to the heart as well as provoke, when needed, laughter. Leigh's recreation of selected sequences from the works of Gilbert and Sullivan do justice to this dimension of their collaboration. Andy Medhurst was not the lone reviewer who submitted that "Leigh's appetite for the music is evidently immense, resulting in too many indulgent performances of their songs" (36).

But the great glory and distinguishing feature of the Savoy operas is the chorus. Sullivan's talent, like that of so many other composers in the English tradition of the oratorio, rests indisputably upon his skill in writing for bodies of voices. Leigh respects the chorus as fully as he can within the time limitations of his already quite long film. He commemorates its special importance with a dramatic sequence where the prescient ladies and gentlemen of the chorus respectfully request and prevail upon Gilbert to restore the Mikado's "Song" from Act Two with "its object all sublime to let the punishment fit the crime." Gilbert eliminated it from the production following a dress rehearsal. This action may also hint at increased democratic assertion at the end of the nineteenth century in Victorian England. Andy Medhurst picks up other elements backstage that anticipate later events and changes of attitude with the following: "…there are enough hints of queer undercurrents in the backstage milieu to remind us that the Oscar Wilde trial was only a few years away" (37).

Leigh's accomplished actor-singers in *Topsy-Turvy* perform their own vocals to surprisingly good effect. One can only imagine what dubbing would have been implemented had the film been a major Hollywood movie in the sixties. That Rob Marshall's Academy Award–winning *Chicago* (2002) did not dub an actor like Richard Gere perhaps suggests the salutary influence on American movies of Mike Leigh's example of *Topsy-Turvy*, but that probably is wishful thinking. In his *Guardian* Interview at the National Theatre with Michael Billington, Leigh commented that in the 1880s "the Savoy also worked with actors, not opera singers for the most part." Leigh veteran Timothy Spall, for example, playing leading Savoy performer Richard Temple, delivers the Mikado's numbers with refinement and gusto. Andy Medhurst describes Spall's performance of the aging star Temple as "a perfectly judged study of juxtaposed fragility and bomabast" (37). Likewise, Martin Savage's Grossmith, who performs a variety of patter songs from the repertory, seems an exemplary Savoyard in every respect. His portrayal brings back memories of beloved earlier twentieth-century D'Oyly Carte performers like Martyn Green and John Reed. Mike Leigh and his musical director, Gary Yershon, honor D'Oyly Carte by selecting performers who are as completely worthy of Gilbert and Sullivan as his nineteenth-century company was. The orchestra in the film performs on period instruments, and Carl Davis slows the tempos more than is customary in twentieth-century performances of the comic operas so that Gilbert's text remains clear. In sum, Leigh and his collaborators trust the original material as contemporary conceptual stage directors may not.

In *Topsy-Turvy* the high and practiced technical skills associated with D'Oyly Carte seem part of a long unbroken history. Francesca Jaynes, Leigh's choreographer, together with the musical director worked from original prompt copies of the productions, which Gilbert, as the film shows, directed. He recorded the bits of stage business with sketches and diagrams in his thick

"Business Book," the guide for all D'Oyly directors who succeeded him. Sullivan, who conducted the original performances, did not publish his orchestrations. Carl Davis, the Brooklyn-born composer who had previously worked with Leigh, assembled the pieces from Sullivan's large output for the film's magnificently full musical score. It is especially notable for Davis's appropriation of melodies from Sullivan that he uses with shimmering grace to support and enhance a nonmusical sequence such as the final moving bedroom scene between Gilbert and Kitty. Davis underscores their sad lack of physical connection with the "Women's Trio" from the Act Two Finale of *The Yeomen of the Guard*, "'Tis Said That Joy in Full Perfection" heard earlier in the film as Gilbert declared it humiliating to be called "The King of Topsy-Turvydom." Since this operetta will be a part of the future collaboration of Gilbert and Sullivan after *The Mikado*, it is interesting how much of it is used in Davis's score for the film. Because Kitty Gilbert projects her own scenario for a future operetta in this bedroom scene with her husband, music from *The Yeomen of the Guard* is strangely appropriate.

This intimate scene of failed conjugality begins with Gilbert observing to his wife after the triumphal premiere of *The Mikado* that "there's something inherently disappointing about success." Perhaps that admission accounts for his failed familial relationship, unwilling as he is to be disappointed off stage. Kitty observes as a rhetorical question: "Wouldn't it be wondrous if perfectly commonplace people gave each other a round of applause at the end of the day?" She demonstrates by clapping enthusiastically herself to which Gilbert adds his own applause of "Well done, Kitty! Bravo Encore!" She expresses gratitude to him, since this prompted endorsement is the most demonstrative one he has given her anywhere in the film, but he insists, despite her reluctance to accept his conclusion, that she must be tired as he prepares to take his leave of her bedroom. Elegant two-shots of him full face and her in profile and then sometimes reversed in position alternate with leisurely shot-counter-shots of the husband and wife speaking together but neither quite sharing their deepest thoughts. She detains him long enough to propose a scenario for his new work, which turns out to be rather crypto-Freudian.

Framed together by the drapery of the four-poster bed, they sit as though on stage, Kitty in the "wings" and Gilbert stage right. Here, the bedclothes are heavy, a barrier to any physical intimacy. In her narrative for a new musical, Kitty creates a heroine who grows old and plain while the ladies' chorus becomes younger and younger, a mirror image of Kitty's own predicament. While she laughs and Gilbert immediately perceives a situation once more topsy-turvy, the moment is agonizingly self-reflexive on her part. The music cue begins as Kitty becomes more animated, describing the plot of her proposed opera. Here a husband whom she describes as not the hero refuses to give his desiring wife the key to open a door, but she ascends the stairs anyway to find the door unlocked, where "on the sands, are hundreds of nannies, all pushing perambulators about." This oblique expression of Kitty's longing for children concludes with her tearfully noting that "every time she tries to be born...he [the husband] strangles her with her umbilical cord." Close-ups of the two reveal their struggle and failure to communicate beyond metaphor. Like Peter in *Bleak Moments*, Gilbert is unable to provide the comfort required; he merely replies after a long delay, "Mm...I shouldn't imagine Sullivan'd much care for that." As complement to this scene, a quotation about Gilbert by J. B. Priestley seems relevant: "There is about Gilbert an aggressive clubman masculinity, together with a lack of that feminine element which brings fertility to the creative artist" (92).

The music changes ironically to "He Loves" from Act Two of *Iolanthe* that continues into the next sequence, a cut to Sullivan's bedroom, now daytime. Here he lies snuggled with his longtime mistress in a curvacious bed, wherein she explains to her composer-lover that she has made her "own arrangements," presumably for an abortion. In what apparently was an earlier incident, he had made arrangements for her. As she explains to him, "After all, it is 1885, Arthur" and then goes on to tell him how much she loved *The Mikado* as she thinks he has put everything he is into it. In contrast to the preceding sequence with the Gilberts and Dick Pope's skillful use of separating shot-counter-shots, this sequence consists entirely of two shots of both Sullivan and Fanny until the very end. After she has kissed him, she tells him she must fly in a lone close-up followed by a comparable close-up of him pondering what has occurred. For neither Gilbert nor Sullivan will there be a next generation such as Leigh has previously provided with his studies of families.

Leigh imprints his distinctive signature on these two respective scenes, so similar and yet contrasting, of Gilbert and Sullivan and the women in their lives as coda to the earlier triumphant ensemble re-creation of the finale at the premiere of *The Mikado.* Lest we perceive the triumphant duo as larger than life, Leigh, ever the realist filmmaker, brings Gilbert and Sullivan back to their all-too-human condition. Kitty Gilbert approaches the kind of breakdown that other Leigh female characters have succumbed to in earlier films. That she does not succumb as they did is appropriately and decorously Victorian, yet it also is as expressive as the more overwrought climaxes seen elsewhere in his work. Kitty herself speaks of "climax and anticlimax" in her scene with Gilbert.

From these interiors of bedchambers for Gilbert and Sullivan, Leigh returns to the theater itself where the film began with shots of seats being lowered to spotlight a single performer, the vulnerable Leonora Braham (Shirley Henderson) as Yum-Yum. She is first seen in her dressing room, somewhat drunk, fortifying herself with sherry prior to her performance. She already has a child whom she adores but, like the other two women, lacks a necessary element to create a family. In her case, she needs a husband. This melancholy widowed mother and leading soprano has struggled with drink throughout the film, having been cautioned on occasion about it by D'Oyly Carte himself. Once on stage, she delivers a stunningly pure and lilting rendition of "The Sun Whose Rays Are All Ablaze," which is sung early in the second act of *The Mikado*. Dick Pope's camera cranes back over the orchestra and audience to conclude *Topsy-Turvy* with a long shot, beautiful and elegantly loving, but tinged with a certain sadness, that encompasses both the audience and the actors on stage to become the essence of theater through the medium of film. "We're very wide awake/The moon and I!" sings the soprano to suggest the fusion of lucidity and lunacy that is life and art. There is a slight hint of a fade to black that Leigh makes more conspicuous use of at the end of *All or Nothing*. A caption appears on the screen, informing us that "Gilbert and Sullivan wrote five more operas, including *The Yeomen of the Guard* and *The Gondoliers.*" This declaration is followed by a final caption with the additional information that Sullivan wrote only one grand opera, *Ivanhoe.* "Although moderately successful at the time, it is now mostly forgotten, and isn't as much fun as *The Mikado*," and the list of the large cast immediately begins to scroll.

Topsy-Turvy is a synthesis of Leigh's understanding of performance and tribute to the performer in recognition of his or her full collaboration in the artistic process and its product. But the eloquence is realized cinematically, and Dick Pope merits everyone's gratitude for how he conveyed it. Several key setups throughout the film have shown actors before their dressing-room mirrors. Timothy Spall has been presented most effectively this way almost to the point of implied doubleness between the man and his roles caught in the round, so to speak, because of the filming. Likewise at the end of the film before her final song, Leonora gazes into her dressing-room mirror and recites Yum-Yum's soliloquy on her own loveliness from Act Two of *The Mikado,* which she proclaims is not vanity but only nature.

Unlike many of his films, which open and end with exterior shots, Leigh keeps almost all the action of *Topsy-Turvy* within interior settings; any enlightenment pursued in this film is of an interior, not an exterior, nature. However, during the premiere performance of *The Mikado*, Gilbert leaves the theater and prowls the London streets in a brief expressionist Dickensian or Hogarthian sequence. He is accosted by a mad old woman, anticipating the moonstruck song of the solo that ends the film. Meanwhile, this scene is accompanied by sounds of bottles breaking, chains clinking, dogs barking, a man shouting, and a baby crying. Additionally, Leigh uses for background original dramatic music composed by Carl Davis with hints of the "More Humane Mikado" theme, which, back at the Savoy, Temple was singing on stage in the preceding scene. Utterly repulsed by her claim that she is good and that he is "lovely big boy," Gilbert calls the old woman "a stinking bitch" and rushes off amid ominous city sounds and chaos of men rushing pursued by a four-wheeled carriage.

Gilbert's traditional want of feeling for unattractive women has its precedents in the comic operas, for example, his portrayal of Katisha whom Leigh commemorates in illustrative segments from *The Mikado.* Louis Kronenberger even claimed that this aspect of Gilbert's satire approached sadism with respect to women like Katisha, Ruth in *The Pirates of Penzance,* Lady Jane, and others (208–209). Such a perspective speculatively links Gilbert with Johnny from *Naked.* In both instances, the filmmmaker displays the limitations of his male protagonists, be they Victorian or contemporary.

Leigh cuts again to the Savoy where Grossmith sings "The Criminal Cried as He Dropp'd Him Down," which connects the exterior sequence just viewed with the ongoing production of *The Mikado*. As usual, Leigh implicates from the particular. Like Dickens, Mike Leigh's realism may be stirred by a feverish force of near-hallucination as in the street sequence, but that capacity lies beyond Gilbert's theatrical carpentry, which serves as an envelope for his limited adventure in nighttown. W. S. Gilbert seems less than humane with the old woman on the street as his instinctive trust in life will later prove inadequate in his wife's bedroom. The collaboration of Leigh and Jim Broadbent creates a W. S. Gilbert who subtly and sadly reveals the flat-footedness often ascribed to this historical personage. More recently Jim Broadbent turned in a quite different, overstated performance as club owner Zidler in Baz Luhrmann's *Moulin Rouge* (2001). Lurhmann's postmodernist musical film seems almost a surreal MTV abstract or abridgment of certain elements in Leigh's *Topsy-Turvy*, yet only Luhrmann would dare his audience to savor Broadbent's rendition of "Like a Virgin," so long associated with Madonna.

As with his early films, Leigh and his collaborators shape the dramatic material in nuance. The difference in *Topsy-Turvy* is that the customary layers and subtext are found below a surface that is more glittering than usual. As in the past, Leigh forces the moviegoer to look at things in the world, this time the Victorian world of Gilbert and Sullivan, think about them, relate them, question them, be frustrated by them. It is just about impossible to see this film and not reach Joe Morgenstern's conclusion that *Topsy-Turvy* "is as smart as it is beautiful" (W2).

Like Leigh's earlier *Secrets & Lies* with its long list of Academy Award nominations, *Topsy-Turvy* received nominations in most categories, including Best Picture, but curiously Mike Leigh was not nominated for Best Director as he was with the earlier film. Like *Secrets & Lies*, the story of Gilbert and Sullivan garnered few awards at the ceremony itself. Lindy Hemming's superb costumes were duly recognized with the award for that category, and Christine Blundell's makeup won the Oscar for makeup design. At least twenty-three film critics in the United States and Britain had selected Leigh's film as one of their top 10 films for 1999, and *Topsy-Turvy* was judged best film at the Venice Film Festival along with Jim Broadbent receiving the Best Actor award. The late Tom King in a "Hollywood Journal" piece in *The Wall Street Journal* queried Barry Diller, the chair of USA Films that released *Topsy-Turvy*, which, as he put it, "won a slew of critics' awards. But it was a box-office failure. What happened?" (W4). Diller responded in a way to reaffirm that filmmaking remains an industry:

> Mike Leigh is a very interesting director and we thought the subject matter was more appealing that it was, but we were wrong. The film is a wonderful movie. But I would consider us a total failure if all we did is get on Top 10 lists and nobody came to see these movies. Like anything, it's either an artful dodge or an artful balance. (W4)

Quite apart from any well-deserved awards, *Topsy-Turvy*'s paean to collaboration in the creative process while taking account of historical influences on arts and culture serves as a testament of faith in the kind of cinema practiced by Mike Leigh. This time he realized his goal with a larger cast and on a grander scale than usual. The filmmaker was not being hyperbolic when in a number of interviews he referred to this particular film in his body of work as "epic." The film was welcomed enthusiastically worldwide by what John Milton, no mean creator of an epic himself, might term, a fit audience found though few—if the quantity and quality of public approval must be judged by the economics of Hollywood blockbuster bottom lines, which are often more than slightly topsy-turvy.

Figure 7. Sir Arthur Sullivan (Allan Corduner) (l), and W. S. Gilbert (Jim Broadbent) (r) discuss details with the cast of *The Mikado* prior to opening night from *Topsy-Turvy*. Courtesy Jerry Ohlinger Archives)

CHAPTER SIX
Conclusion with a Leigh Epitome and Challenge: *All or Nothing*

A famous observation ascribed to Jean Renoir advanced the proposition that however many movies a director made, he or she was making just one film. Coveney quotes Mike Leigh's response to this hypothesis: "The point of it all is seeing how far away from that one film you can get" (151), and one might add just how good it is. With the surprising form and content of *Topsy-Turvy*, Leigh demonstrated versatility and daring in stretching the parameters of his own "one film." After his backstage look at Gilbert and Sullivan and his contribution to period drama and the heritage film, Leigh remained typically close-mouthed about what could be in the works or on the back burner, from which he occasionally restored earlier notions to finished films. What the press knew at the beginning of the twenty-first century was that Leigh's Thin Man Films had arranged French funding for his next three pictures as Ryan Gilbey had reported in *The Express* (43). The name of producer Alain Sarde in addition to that of his usual producer Simon Channing-Williams on the credits of *All or Nothing* (2002) testifies to Leigh's current enlarged European context.

In retrospect, Terrence Rafferty proved curiously prophetic in light of Leigh's recent *All or Nothing*. This critic observed at the beginning of the nineties in response to *Life Is Sweet* that Leigh is "interested not in demonstrating general, abstract truths, but in discovering small, particular ones, [and] he could go on making this sort of film forever without having to worry about repeating himself" (101). While *All or Nothing* may look as if Leigh has retrenched to his working-class domestic dramas of the seventies and eighties with people making do with unfulfilling lives, traditionally labeled "kitchen-sink" realism, such a description fails to do justice to Leigh's superb latest film as of 2003. It may be seen as a continuum of his novelistic approach to his utterly ordinary subjects. His nuanced seriocomic action and emotional depth displayed once again in the realistic domestic realm epitomize the filmmaker's talent. Ryan Gilbey in his *Sight and Sound* celebratory essay on "Reasons to Be Cheerful" about new films in English cinema during fall of 2002 surely is correct in suggesting that Leigh's "film title has the ring of a dare about it" (14).

To a degree most of Leigh's films present the challenge of an all-or-nothing proposition to viewers as to how to receive them with his often unfashionably, sometimes almost defiantly, slow and long takes that reward but also test an audience's capacity for empathy and endurance. Differences in the complexity of causality in this latest film invite inferences of alteration in Leigh's favored familial genre. Leigh in an interview with Leonard Quart titled "Going Beyond Despair" for *Cineaste* submits that in *All or Nothing* he has opted less for his usual method of cumulative detail than for a more causal arrangment of action and relationships. This narrative method makes Leigh's film more like a film-novel than some of his earlier ones. "This film is subtler," Leigh claims, "because everything that happens has got a dramatic impact. All these people are locked into each other's lives and crises.... There is an organic relation between the characters, and it all comes together. I'm not just going over old territory. That's wrong-headed analysis" (39). This quotation might be used as a qualification to *The London Times*' James Christopher's description of the film as "another sour meditation on the slippery ties that bind" (12).

The setting for *All or Nothing* is familiar Leigh territory, a drab high-rise council housing estate, which Americans call a public housing project, this time in South London, Greenwich, near the Millennium Dome that is shown at one point with the focus on a family of four. The parents in their duplex are played by two of Leigh's most distinguished, frequent, and versatile veterans—Timothy Spall and Lesley Manville. These performers never make false moves in their characterization. They anchor another of Leigh's remarkable acting ensembles.

Timothy Spall, playing with a jaggedly subdued, even aloof, rhythm quite different from his previous characterizations for Leigh, is Phil Bassett, a minicab driver who wears a permanent look of resignation for which his canine name seems somehow appropriate. He works for Gladiator Cars, a presumably black Jamaican-owned and -operated agency, with brother Neville (Gary McDonald) and sister Dinah (Diveen Henry) in charge of daily operations. At one point when Neville tells Dinah he will dock her wages if she leaves early, she retorts that she "will tell mummy," perhaps suggesting the source of agency ownership. This work setting returns Leigh to a similar taxi agency seen in the early television film *Hard Labour*.

Lesley Manville takes nagging to the point of unlikability in common-law wife, Penny, a Safeway cashier, with comparable fullness of being that she has brought to each of her portrayals for Leigh. The food motif used often in Leigh appropriately takes this character to work in a supermarket. Her thin and almost birdlike appearance provides a startling physical contrast to the other hefty, super-sized members of her family. Although Phil refers to Penny as his wife, she more candidly and ruefully explains to her mates during an evening out with the other women that he never proposed, and, consequently, there never was a marriage.

The couple live as a family with two nearly grown, overweight children. Rachel (Alison Garland) works glumly and without much affect as a housekeeper, mopping floors at a nursing home. Megan Turner writes of this character in her *New York Post* review of the film: "she is either a student or Zen or catatonic" (48). Rachel is shown to be a reader, and in typical Leigh fashion that pursuit as well as her often sensitive responses to the people around her confer a measure of quiet dignity upon her. Unlike most of the other young people shown in the film whose family relationships appear founded on insult and profanity, Rachel never tells anyone to "fuck off" as her contemporaries repeatedly do. The film opens with a long corridor shot of her washing the floors in the home when an aged inhabitant (Jean Ainslie) slowly makes her way down the long hall and Rachel cautions her not to slip: "Be careful, the floor's wet" and adds "Can I help you?" The old lady, for whatever reason, ignores Rachel and her mild attempt at interaction, and this kind of missed communication becomes a touchstone for much of the film's dialogue and action. Once again Leigh has used a bittersweet, unobtrusive musical score of simple, repetitive patterns composed by Andrew Dickson. His usual delicate combination of strings, with the strong and somber presence of the cello but this time round also guitar coupled with an occasional flute accompaniment, underscores the opening sequence and credits. Although Dickson's subtle score bears some surface similarity to Glass's minimalism, it contrasts markedly with Philip Glass's insistent and obtrusive score for Stephen Daldry's acclaimed *The Hours*, a prestige "literary" film if there ever was one, which was also released in 2002.

Rachel's brother Rory (James Corden) has progressed beyond the condition of mere overweight like his father and sister to morbid obesity. He is an unemployed, perpetually angry, and bullying late adolescent stuck in front of the telly, usually stretched out on his stomach as he lies on the sofa. In a notable sequence Rory's father temporarily dislodges his son's prone body in attempting to get loose change that might be trapped in the sofa. Phil follows up on this rather pathetic maneuver by requesting from Rachel and Penny any spare money they can give him. He needs to reach his minimum payment for the cab at the agency. Neville replies when Phil doles out this money, "I don't take shekels. Give me proper money, Mon."

One scene of a family dinner finds Rory with a plate on his lap voraciously consuming his meal, ignoring the table where the others are eating despite his mother's complaint to him about his manners. He hurls obscene expletives at her and fights with other young people on the housing estate when he ventures outdoors. It does not take unusual perception to judge that this father and mother are at an impasse in their own relationship that makes the dispute between Gilbert and Sullivan in *Topsy-Turvy* seem easily manageable in comparison. Penny turns to Phil, seemingly in hopes of obtaining his support in dealing with their son, but his profound resignation before life's difficulties prevails. In similar circumstances throughout the film, his typical response is "life is too short" or "take no notice."

Phil feels abiding love but fails to express it very adequately for his "wife" and children. He increasingly fears that his affection is unreciprocated as he reveals in the climactic scene with Penny. As a result of their apparent clinical depression, both Phil and Rory have trouble getting up in the morning. Phil refers to the fickle finger of fate as he tells Ron (Paul Jesson), his fellow driver, who has sustained a minor accident, that what happened might have forestalled a more serious mishap because "if you knew what was going to happen, you'd never get out of bed." Ron reports to his dispatcher that a Volvo rear-ended him instead of admitting his own imperfect driving in backing up into an obstacle. Later, while driving Penny to the hospital, Ron does indeed hit a Volvo, and Penny gets out to walk the remaining distance while Ron imprecates against the driver as a "fucking dickhead." With additional philosophizing Phil asserts his knowledge of life, i.e., of death: "the old clock ticks, world turns round, tide comes in, tide goes out. You're born, you die. That's it."

Phil, sleeping in, often misses out on lucrative early morning fares driving people to work or to London airports as Penny later berates him for this sin of omission. He does seem a somewhat hapless driver, receiving on one trip in lieu of a cash tip a bundle of extended-life hamburger buns from a passenger who hosted a would-be barbecue where no one showed. This material detail together with his scrounging for loose change offers an ironic comic statement on Phil's ability to be a satisfactory breadwinner.

More novelistically than in previous films with the possible exception of *Topsy-Turvy*, which may have inspired Leigh to continue the practice, *All or Nothing* features a large array of vivid characters with potential stories that could become feature films in their own right. Or as James Christopher formulates it: "The film is full of unfinished arguments and incomplete stories. In this respect he [Leigh] is his own slot machine: forever rearranging the oranges, apples and grapes but never quite hitting a feel good jackpot. God forbid" (13). Eric Allen Hatch in his Baltimore *City Paper* review of the film observes of these other potential narratives and incipient protagonists: "We can gauge how deeply the film's other characters have affected us by how much they're missed as they recede into the background" (26). This plenitude lends further credence to the comparison sometimes made between Leigh and Dickens beyond their shared mixture of realism, pathos, and comedy.

For Leigh devotees, as in some previous instances in his canon, there is much pleasure here in seeing the return of performers from earlier films in new roles. The excellent character actor, Sam Kelly, formerly from *Grown-Ups*, *Who's Who*, and *Topsy-Turvy*, appears as Sid, another cleaner at the nursing home where Rachel works. Despite the enormous age difference between them, Sid makes half-hearted amorous advances to his young female co-worker. He tells Rachel that he was married once for four months to a "bitch." Edna Doré, the senile Mrs. Bender from *High Hopes*, reappears in this Leigh film in the small role of Martha, and *Career Girls'* Mark Benton appears at a bar.

The most memorable example in *All or Nothing* of an encore performance for Leigh is Ruth Sheen, who was the young hippie wife desirous of a child in *High Hopes.* Here, cheerfully earning a meager living through ironing in addition to cashiering at Safeway with Penny, she plays Maureen, a competent, even-tempered, and surprisingly upbeat single mother with a good singing voice. She reveals this latter attribute during a karaoke evening: Sheen sings quite beautifully the Crystal Gayle song "Don't It Make My Brown Eyes Blue," which contains such a line as "Tell me no secrets, tell me no lies," offering useful intertextuality to the filmmaker. "For a few moments, the strength and joy that lurk hidden in the characters burst forth, testament to Leigh's belief in the transformative, restorative powers of performance itself, a belief thoroughly exemplified by the movie as a whole," John Patterson noted in his *L.A. Weekly* review.

It is in this setting that the drunken Carol asks of her women "mates"—Maureen and Penny—if they love her. This question addressed to Penny foreshadows her more profound questioning by Phil at the end of the film. Maureen's angry daughter, Donna (Helen Coker), despite being on the pill, becomes pregnant with Jason (Daniel Mays), an abusive boyfriend whom her mother calls "Scarface" because of an extended straight-line scar on his face, possibly emblematic of his bipolar personality. As an indication of his despicable attitude toward his girlfriend, when Donna requests that they talk, he counters with "I don't wanna talk. I wanna shag." When Donna assails her mother with the question about her own pregnancy, "How long did you know my dad, then?" Maureen, having previously rebuked her daughter for becoming pregnant after only two months' acquaintance with this most questionable and unreliable boyfriend, answers truthfully and with good humor, "I dunno. About five minutes." Jason will jilt Donna if she goes through with her pregnancy, and Leigh, in a moving scene of emotional connection, shows mother and daughter coming to their recognition of mutual love, implying that Maureen will assume care of Donna and the unborn baby.

The third family from the high-rise that Leigh views at some length without necessarily completing their story is the hard-drinking couple, Ron, another cab driver and his perpetually drunken wife Carol (Marion Bailey). Ms. Bailey was last seen drunk in Leigh's canon as the upwardly mobile Barbara in the television film *Meantime*. Their neglected and needy daughter, Samantha (Sally Hawkins), justifiably and contemptuously terms her parents "useless." Samantha, wearing at one point a mauve "Harvard" tank top, competes with her neighbor Donna for a fast screw with Jason. One brief scene, an example of some of the sexuality and "pervasive language" responsible for the R rating, reveals a bare-breasted Samantha making out in a car with Jason. Christopher's remark in *The* [London] *Times* about her as "a fiver away from her first trick" (13) strikes an apt note, but in the course of the action she rises to the occasion to aid the Bassetts. Leigh provides one brief scene in a lunchroom where Donna works that brings the three young women of the housing estate together in the same space. In the matter of food details, he shows Samantha with her Diet Coke and Rachel with a regular Coke.

The seductive Samantha ensnares and subsequently rejects Craig (Ben Crompton), a strange loner and stalker who carves her initial as his token of love on his chest—"Samantha on His Heart," as the DVD chapter title for this sequence puts it. Craig acts, as Leonard Quart observes in his *Cineaste* review of Leigh's film "like a symbol of the alienation and impotence of youth" (40). The hardened Samantha is moved by Craig's misplaced display of affection even as she is appalled by it. She tearfully embraces Craig. Then Leigh cuts to a very short vignette of her crying in her bed back in the family's duplex. As so often observed in Leigh films, no easy absolute judgment is possible for understanding his characters.

In the last third of *All or Nothing* Leigh generates an event, sometimes unjustly called melodramatic, a medical emergency that brings about a significant change in the lives of the Bassetts unlike a similar cardiac event in *Abigail's Party*. Rory suffers a heart attack in the courtyard "after an uncharacteristic bout of exercise" (13) as Christopher describes it. Samantha demonstrates clear-headed decisiveness, unlike her drunken mother, to summon an ambulance. Penny takes off for the hospital from her Safeway post in the kind of dynamic traveling shot Leigh and Dick Pope used so effectively in *Naked* and *Topsy-Turvy.* Phil, unbeknownst to anyone, has turned off his cell phone and two-way radio linking him with the taxi agency and has driven to the Kent coast where he cannot be contacted. Penny berates Phil unmercifully subsequently for being incommunicado during a time of family crisis. For those viewers familiar with *Topsy-Turvy*, Leigh's portrayal of the difficulties and anxieties with nineteenth-century communication technology in that film may here have its latter-day expression in *All or Nothing.* Those McLuhan extensions of human beings have become dominating and not merely extended. "What can I switch off?" Penny asks Phil in their later momentous emotional scene when she has had "enough," which was Phil's explanation for his action.

Throughout the film Leigh has shown Phil sullen and without a sense of connection with his passengers driving his cab as a cross section of London life temporarily occupies his backseat. These vignettes may renew memories of the subjects Maurice photographed in *Secrets & Lies* and a retrospective of Leigh's output. Early in the film one of these passengers, called only "Nutter" (Russell Mabey) in the final credits, explodes violently about a woman in his life and punches at the window of the cab, shouting vulgarities about the female sex that call forth memories of *Naked*. In contrast, Martin Savage, the singing Grossmith from *Topsy-Turvy,* becomes a silent taxi passenger in this film. Another passenger is an old man with flowers (Peter Stockbridge), whom we learn is going to visit a grave. Leigh follows through with a brief cemetery scene reminiscent of others from his past films. Spall's Phil, apparently waiting by the car for his passenger, looks over the graveyard; he subsequently articulates numerous reflections on the ephemerality of existence. Unlike Maurice, who, of necessity, faces the subjects he photographs in *Secrets & Lies*, Spall as a driver has his back to most of these passengers although a few sit next to him in the front seat of the taxi. He steals occasional glimpses in his rearview mirror of these customers who, for the most part, treat him as simply a functional extension of the cab they have hired.

An exception to his lack of interaction with his passengers takes place in an extended sequence presented with parallel cutting to the action attendant upon Rory's heart attack and its chaotic aftermath. Phil's client this time around is a loquacious, sophisticated Parisian woman who objects to tunnels. Cécile (Kathryn Hunter), whose name we learn at the end of the sequence, asks to be driven to the West End, where she plans to see *Don Giovanni.* She carries an unwieldy wrapped art object that she has purchased for a client in New York; Leonard Quart remarks in his review that "the woman at first seems to have wandered in from another film.…But unexpectedly, Leigh makes a seamless leap in tone, and despite their class and cultural differences, the two characters begin to bond genuinely over talk about their respective families" (40).

Phil diffidently shares with her his usually unstated loving feelings for Penny, as she expresses her frustration with her adult son whom she thinks treats her with insufficient love as she reminisces about an abortive twenty-fifth birthday celebration she had arranged for him. She is a divorced mother whose ex-husband lives in Algeria. They discuss their children, and the woman asks if the cab driver's son is fat like him. Phil describes love as like a dripping tap, adding "we're born alone and die alone," to which his passenger concurs that he's right: "it is fucking lonely." When they separate after the driver has helped the woman into her West End hotel with the large package, they exchange names upon the woman's request. Thematically this scene is key for what follows in the film's narrative, since from it Phil apparently derives the strength and courage to voice his fundamental question about love to Penny.

After his encounter with Cécile, Phil turns off his means of communication and drives to the seaside in Kent. Meanwhile back in the city hospital, Rory has asked his mother, who by now has reached his bedside, "Where's Dad?" Penny has rushed to her son, proclaiming "He's my little baby boy." At the end of this hospital sequence Leigh provides a handsome medium shot with hospital tray table and water glass in the foreground of Rory lying unresponsively in an intensive care unit bed with Maureen on one side of him and Penny on the other. Leigh intersperses these hospital scenes with a series of strangely beautiful long shots of the taxi in the Kent landscape, where the repressed Phil has temporarily escaped London. In one of these shots Phil walks out of the frame, and Leigh cuts to him by a waterside still at some distance. The progression is quite aesthetically attractive if somewhat vague as to specific narrative point beyond underscoring Phil's need for solitary reflection on his life and relationships. Finally Leigh supplies a close-up of Phil contemplating the ebb and flow of the waves. A brief symmetrical parallel sequence has shown the solitary Rachel walking by the water in Greenwich, the Millennium Dome briefly evident, to suggest again the parallels and quiet endurance of both father and daughter in contrast to the more volatile mother and son. Their respective retreat shows them both symbolically marooned in their island nation.

Back at the hospital Rachel and her mother learn of Rory's largely favorable prognosis from the attending doctor (Robert Wilfort). Rory's continued health will be conditional upon lifetime medication. The medical experts have concluded that Rory probably had congenital weakness in a heart muscle since childhood, exacerbated no doubt by his weight and diet. To the question of whether the boy smokes, which had been debated shortly after he was admitted, his mother denies this habit on the part of her son. Rachel ventures to voice the truth about her brother's smoking activity, "Yes, a bit," to which Rory, weakly flat on his back with oxygen, still predictably and consistently responds "Fuck off" to his helpful forthcoming sister.

Upon the entrance of her father, Rachel leaves the hospital room since only two visitors are permitted at the same time. When the parents finally reconnect at the hospital, Phil the "philosopher" talks about "fait accompli" and "kismet, innit," much to Penny's incomprehension. They discover that they must come to terms with themselves and honestly assess the basis of their own relationship before they can help their son. As Penny quizzes Phil about where he was all afternoon and shows dissatisfaction with his answer of "out and about," Rory wakes from his convalescent sleep and requests his argumentative mother, who denies any such intent, not to have a go at his father. This rebuke to his mother anticipates Rachel's later corroboration to Penny of how badly her mother seemed to treat Phil, which, again, her mother denies. Rory then turns his head and says, "Hi, Dad." After the shot-counter-shot sequence with the parents to end this family reunion, Leigh's camera pulls back to the middle-distanced shot like those of earlier bedside scenes such as the one with Rachel and her mother that Phil observed through venetian blinds when he arrived at the hospital. The ambulatory family, with Rachel walking slightly behind her parents, leaves the hospital via another long corridor shot paralleling the opening sequence in *All or Nothing* and reminiscent of similar setups both with interior and exterior settings in numerous Leigh films. Again the camera remains stationary as the characters proceed in deep focus away from it. Phil about halfway down the corridor puts his left arm around Penny, who submits to this connection for a while until distantly at the end of the corridor when she escapes his embrace with a shrug and steps away from him. The brief taxi scene, returning them home, recapitulates what we have become familiar with throughout the film. Rachel sits in the backseat. Phil, the driver, seems about to speak as Penny silently sits next to him in the front of the car.

What ensues is another of those scenes of epiphany in Leigh's films where his characters become stupendously alive. These scenes tend to divide critical response. Leonard Quart, for example, finds the sequence "emotionally cathartic but overly theatrical…[and] too explicit" (40), and similarly J. Hoberman has rather dismissively described the sequence as "more cathartic than redemptive, this sob-racked confession is the payoff for two hours of low-grade misery." Eric Allen Hatch, in contrast, evaluates it far more favorably: "The film builds toward these characters honestly assessing their relationship, and the penetrating scenes in which they do rank among the most emotionally naked in the work of a director who specializes in just that" (26). If it comes as something of a surprise, the scene is surely not unmotivated, and Leigh has given more than his usual number of causal coordinates by way of preparation for it.

Phil announces that he intends to work seven days a week, getting up early and working late. At the hospital he promised Rory a family holiday at Disney World. Penny, the grown-up who confronts the messy world in a way she assumes Phil does not, remains unimpressed. She tells him: "It ain't about holiday. It's about getting by day in and day out. It ain't a game" and mockingly asks him whether he wants praise for what everyday "normal people do."

With growing emotion, quite different from the submissive stoicism he has previously exhibited in his family relationships, Phil expostulates first matter-of-factly, then more tearfully to Penny: "You don't love me no more, do you?" She responds "What's that got to do with anything?" To Phil it has everything to do with their continuation as a family, and he insists that he must know if he is loved: "If you don't want me, we ain't got nothing. We ain't a family." Leigh gives Spall the opportunity to do the kind of extreme emotional scene for which Brenda Blethyn is famous in his body of work. In *Secrets & Lies*, Spall's Maurice presents only a hint of and then curtails the full thrust of such an outburst late in the film. Here Phil haltingly recapitulates his life with Penny after they first met when he felt like the bees' knees to have a "pretty girl like you with a fat bloke like me" to the present when he asserts that she has not loved him for years. "I ain't got no skills. I don't earn enough money. I get on your nerves," Phil laments. Leigh takes this exchange with slow, poignant beats and without music. Perhaps to that extent the sequence may be called "theatrical" inasmuch as film action rarely demonstrates the patience and devotes the amount of time Leigh gives to this kind of exchange, but the presentation makes for exquisite up-close cinema of essential human motion and emotion. Phil concludes: "You don't like me. You don't respect me. You talk to me like I'm a piece of shit," which she denies with increasing tears on her part. "You don't know you're doin it, but you do. It's like something's died," Phil observes. "I feel like an old tree that ain't got no water."

Penny goes to get tissues for Phil from her bag in the kitchen. He has been wiping his face on his sleeve. Leigh carefully records this movement, but before she returns, she notices Rachel sitting at the top of the stairs, having listened to her parents' scene together. Penny ascends the stairs to her daughter, who rapidly retreats to her bedroom. Leigh provides a chiaroscuro close-up of Rachel and her mother sitting on the daughter's bed. Rachel looks pretty as her mother embraces her, pulling her daughter's hair back from her face. Her daughter insists: "You do talk to him like that" to which her mother replies "I don't." "Sometimes," Rachel rejoins. Penny kisses Rachel on the forehead. Leigh cuts to legs of Penny who descends the stairs into the close-up of her tear-stained, anguished face divided into one half lighted and one half left in the dark until she slightly turns and her face takes on an aura of sudden prettiness in full illumination.

Another of Leigh's magnificent long takes finds Penny returning in their living room to Phil, who still sits in the large chair. He asks about Rachel, and Penny recounts that their daughter is "just a bit upset, that's all." She at last offers the pocket tissues she had placed from her bag into her jacket when she had walked past Phil to retrieve her bag at the end of the encounter that Rachel overheard; however, Phil now declines them. From her standing position, she takes Phil's hand. She then kneels. After expressing her own sense of loneliness to him, he tells her he loves her; she, slowly in full recognition of what that love means to her, in turn, kisses his hand. They embrace and kiss lovingly, holding each other's head face to face. The camera with great delicacy almost imperceptibly moves ever closer in on the couple to capture a quiet but lingering epiphany. Penny tells Phil that he used to make her laugh. He puffs out his cheeks, and she pushes them in again with laughter. He smilingly asks whether they could go to bed, and she affirms that they can. Leigh has taken something small and opened it out into something of great constancy. The two still caught in profile head to head, most uncharacteristically for him, Leigh fades to black at the end of this prolonged but never tedious take. Likewise, with further stylistic audacity, he maintains the black screen for multiple seconds following the fade.

The final sequence, titled "Getting Better" on the DVD, returns the family to the hospital in daylight to greet Rory, who has been moved out of an intensive care cardiac unit into a semiprivate room. They come bearing gifts: his father brings him bananas, and his mother, as is revealed in the course of the scene, has brought her son a dressing gown and slippers about which he appears pleased, especially the moccasin slippers he apostrophizes with "Cheers." Penny remarks that her son has renewed color in his cheeks, and, indeed, the whole family looks considerably improved and better turned out. Penny wears an attractive black top and a small silver cross around her neck. Phil's hair looks a little less stringy and greasy, and he has shaved. At one point in this scene Phil removes "a bit of fluff" from Penny's top, for which she expresses thanks.

Rory's recovery has engendered general renewal through familial give and take and possible second chances. All members of this family throughout the film have craved appreciation from one another, and now they appear to have at least a modicum of it shared mutually. Even brother and sister demonstrate a sense of affection for each other. Rory wonders why his sister is not at the nursing home. Rachel has not been sleeping well, as Penny explains to her son because of worry about him, but Rachel plans to return to work the next day. Rory tells the group what he had for dinner. They are all surprised that he enjoyed eating fish with a sauce and not even batter fried. And he ate what he describes as little green cauliflower bits, which his mother, ever the alert Safeway cashier, interprets as "oh, yes, broccoli." This culinary declaration on Rory's part contradicts James Christopher's assertion that "no one here [on Leigh's Greenwich sink estate] has ever heard of greens, let alone eaten any" (12).

Phil has indeed turned over a new leaf as far as his work habits are concerned. He has taken a Greek family headed for Cyprus to Gatwick for an early morning flight. He narrates an incident that occurred in the car when one of the young sons traveling with his father, brother, and grandmother complained to his father that the old lady had farted. This tale greatly amuses Rory who laughs heartily, winning appreciative smiles from his father and a sense of communion among all members of the family.

In a nicely executed eye-line match, father and mother exchange affectionate glances, and the camera pulls back on the hospital bedside scene. Inaudible dialogue about "Nanny's" get-well card for Rory that he displays continues with the suggestion that these characters go on living after the film stops in the tragicomic recognition of hope for better things to come in their lives. Andrew Dickson's musical score modestly returns with his pleasing guitar theme. Instead of his usual cut, Leigh again gives a hint of a fade, and the end credits scroll upon the screen.

Once more Leigh has remained faithful to his abiding dedication to showing, as Rafferty has phrased it, "the possibility of seeing the world through someone else's eyes—someone specific, whose life can be shared only through patient observation of its random and idiosyncratic details" (104). Viewers of *All or Nothing* willingly follow Leigh's evolving progression of mood and tone regarding the fragility of love. What Leigh achieves in this film and in nearly all those that precede it comes to seem a persuasive necessity but not an emotional didacticism. He does not tell us what we should feel in the way he presents the not-so-sudden shifts of attitude, unstudied awkwardness, and emotional modulations of the characters toward something approaching a stillness of balance.

The years since *Bleak Moments* and his current French funding have certainly proven that Leigh's work is not too "English" to travel well, for Mike Leigh has become one of England's most desired exports, with each new film seen as an event to be anticipated and savored afterward. *All or Nothing* was an official entry to the Cannes Film Festival in 2002, but its theatrical release by United Artists/MGM in the United States during the fall movie season was inexplicably erratic and minimal almost to the point of nothingness. Unlike *Secrets & Lies* and *Topsy-Turvy*, Leigh's *All or Nothing* did not end up on potential Oscar lists, where many thought it belonged.

The transfer and release of *All or Nothing* on DVD was accomplished by February of 2003. In October of 2002 the film opened in New York City and then disappeared without being given sufficient time to find its audience or being widely distributed in neighborhood theaters. Despite the almost unanimously favorable, even enthusiastic, reviews in both England and the United States, in the stateside release *All or Nothing* subsequently received limited distribution to other major American cities. The DVD transfer looks quite good, but apart from the theatrical trailer none of the interviews with Mike Leigh and his collaborators that enhanced the DVD of *Topsy-Turvy* has been included for *All or Nothing*. Because Leigh's films not only withstand but benefit from repeated viewings, DVD versions of his work are treasured, yet experiencing these feature films in a theater setting with a diverse audience is always satisfying and often deeply enriching.

What astonishes us in Leigh's humane studies of unlikely protagonists and the quotidian experience of their everyday lives is the universality he has achieved because of, and not despite of, their personal and local provenance. Never puerile, Leigh makes his films by and for complex adults without reliance on the formulaic; he does not replace living people with stereotypes or mouthpieces of identity politics. *All or Nothing* cleary demonstrates the intimacy and vulnerability that embue Leigh's films with both their power and art. We must make our way carefully in interpreting what we see and understand as does the filmmaker himself whose whole oeuvre challenges postmodernist and antihumanist assumptions about characters' complexities and contradictions.

We may say of Leigh, as Maurice Valency wrote of Chekhov, that he "was certainly concerned with meaning, but not often with message. His works leave one with a sense of deeply felt and complex experience, part emotional, and in part intellectual, but never with the feeling of having digested an *exemplum*" (299–300). Leigh similarly disclaims that he is pointing out, let alone propagating morals: "I would say that my films are moral films, in that they are primarily motivated by a sense of how we should behave toward each other in terms of giving and sharing" (Fuller, xl). Thus, *All or Nothing* appears exemplary as a summing-up in Leigh's canon, but it may just as well serve as a prelude to a new phase in his career. He has always been and remains in his prime.

A MIKE LEIGH FILMOGRAPHY

(All films written and directed by Mike Leigh)

1971 *Bleak Moments.* Autumn Productions/Memorial Enterprises/BFI Production Board. Produced and edited by Les Bair, photography by Bahram Manoochehri, designed by Richard Rambaut, sound by Bob Withey, 111 minutes.
Cast: Anne Raitt (Sylvia), Sarah Stevenson (Hilda), Eric Allan (Peter), Joolia Capppleman (Pat), Mike Bradwell (Norman), Liz Smith (Pat's mother), Christopher Martin (Sylvia's boss), Ronald Eng (waiter), Reg Stewart (man in restaurant), Susan Glanville (importunate teacher).

1972 *Hard Labour.* BBC TV. Produced by Tony Garnett, photography by Tony Pierce-Roberts, sound by Dick Manton, edited by Christopher Rowlands, designed by Paul Munting, costumes by Sally Nieper, 75 minutes.
Cast: Liz Smith (Mrs. Thornley), Clifford Kershaw (Mr. Thornley), Polly Hemingway (Ann), Ben Kingsley (Naseem), Bernard Hill (Edward), Alison Steadman (Veronica), Vanessa Harris (Mrs. Stone), Cyril Varley (Mr. Stone), Linda Beckett (Julie), Louis Raynes (Mr. Philips), Rowena Parr (June), Alan Erasmus (Barry).

1976 *Nuts in May.* BBC TV. Produced by David Rose, photography by Michael Williams, sound by John Gilbert, edited by Oliver White, designed by David Corzier, costumes by Gini Hardy, 80 minutes.
Cast: Roger Sloman (Keith), Alison Steadman (Candice-Marie), Anthony O'Donnell (Ray), Shelia Kelley (Honky), Stephen Bill (Finger), Richenda Carey (Miss Beale), Eric Allan (quarryman), Matthew Guinness (farmer), Sally Watts (farm girl), Richard Ireson (policeman).

1977 *The Kiss of Death.* BBC TV. Produced by David Rose, photography by Michael Williams and John Kenway, edited by Oliver White, designed

by David Crozier, costumes by Al Barnett, music by Carl Davis, sound by John Gilbert, 80 minutes.
Cast: David Threlfall (Trevor), Clifford Kershaw (Mr. Garside), John Wheatley (Ronnie), Pamela Austin (Trevor's mother), Angela Curran (Sandra), Phillip Ryland (Froggy), Kay Adshead (Linda), Karen Petrie (policewoman), Elizabeth Ann Odgen (bridesmaid).

1977 *Abigail's Party*. BBC TV Play for Today. Produced by Margaret Mathwson, photography by Dave Mutton, edited by Ron Bowman, designed by Kenneth Sharp, costumes by Lindy Hemming, sound by Derek Miller-Timmins, 102 minutes.
Cast: Alison Steadman (Beverly), Tim Stern (Laurence), Janine Duvitski (Angela), John Salthouse (Tony), Harriet Reynolds (Susan).

1979 *Who's Who.* BBC TV. Produced by Margaret Matheson, photography by John Else, edited by Chris Lovett, designed by Austen Spriggs, costumes by Robin Stubbs, sound by John Pritchard, 80 minutes.
Cast: Simon Chandler (Nigel), Adam Norton (Giles), Richard Kane (Alan), Jeffey Wickham (Francis), Souad Faress (Samya), Philip Davis (Kevin), Graham Seed (Anthony), Joolia Cappelman (April), Lavinia Bertram (Nanny), Francesca Martin (Selina), David Neville (Lord Crouchurst), Catherine Hall (Samantha), Geraldine James (Miss Hunt), Sam Kelly (Mr. Chakespeare), Felicity Dean (Caroline), Angela Curran, Roger Hammond (couple in window).

1980 *Grown-Ups.* BBC TV. Produced by Louis Marks, photography by Remi Adefarasin, edited by Robin Sales, designed by Bryan Ellis, costumes by Christian Dyall, sound by John Pritchard, 90 minutes.
Cast: Philip Davis (Dick), Lesley Manville (Mandy), Brenda Blethyn (Gloria), Janine Duvitski (Sharon), Lindsay Duncan (Christine), Sam Kelly (Ralph).

1982 *Home Sweet Home.* Produced by Louis Marks, photography by Remi Adefarasin, edited by Robin Sales, designed by Bryan Ellis, costumes by Michael Burdle, music by Carl Davis, sound by John Pritchard, 90 minutes.
Cast: Timothy Spall (Gordon), Eric Richard (Stan), Tim Barker (Harold), Kay Stonham (Hazel), Su Elliott (June), Frances Barber (Melody),

Shelia Kelley (Janice), Lorraine Brunning (Tina), Heidi Laratta (Kelly), Lloyd Peters (Dave).

1983 *Meantime.* Central Television/Mostpoint Ltd. For Channel 4. Produced by Graham Benson, photography by Roger Pratt, edited by Lesley Walker, designed by Diana Charnley, costumes by Lindy Hemming, music by Andrew Dickson, sound by Malcolm Hirst, 90 minutes.
Cast: Phil Daniels (Mark), Tim Roth (Colin), Marion Bailey (Barbara), Pam Ferris (Mavis), Jeff Robert (Frank), Alfred Molina (John), Gary Oldman (Coxy), Tilly Vosburgh (Hayley), Paul Daly (Rusty), Peter Wight (estate-manager), Eileen Davies (clerk in unemployment office).

1985 *Four Days in July.* BBC TV. Produced by Kenith Trodd, photography by Remi Adefarasin, edited by Robin Sales, designed by Jim Clay, costumes by Maggie Donnelly, music by Rachel Portman, sound by John Pritchard, 96 minutes.
Cast: Brid Brennan (Collette), Des McAleer (Eugene), Paula Hamilton (Lorraine), Charles Lawson (Billy), Brian Hogg (Big Billy), Adrian Gordon (Little Billy), Shane Connaughton (Brendan), Eileen Pollock (Carmel), Stephen Rea (Dixie), David Coyle (Mickey), John Keegan (Mr. McCoy), John Hewitt (Mr. Roper), Ann Hasson (midwife).

1988 *High Hopes.* Film Four International/British Screen/Portman. Produced by Simon Channing-Williams and Victor Glyn, photography by Roger Pratt, edited by Jon Gregory, designed by Diana Charnley, costumes by Lindy Hemming, music by Andrew Dickson, sound by Billy McCarthy, 110 minutes.
Cast: Philip Davis (Cyril), Ruth Sheen (Shirley), Edna Doré (Mrs. Bender), Heather Tobias (Valerie), Philip Jackson (Martin), Lesley Manville (Laetitia), David Bamber (Rupert), Jason Watkins (Wayne), Judith Scott (Suzi), Cheryl Prime (Martin's girlfriend).

1990 *Life Is Sweet.* Thin Man/Film Four International/British Screen. Produced by Simon Channing-Williams, photography by Dick Pope, edited by Jon Gregory, designed by Alison Chitty, costumes by Lindy Hemming, music by Rachel Portman, sound by Malcolm Hirst, 102 minutes.
Cast: Alison Steadman (Wendy), Jim Broadbent (Andy), Claire Skinner (Natalie), Jane Horrocks (Nicola), Timothy Spall (Aubrey), Stephen

Rea (Patsy), David Thewlis (Nicola's boyfriend), Moya Brady (Paula), David Nelson (Steve), Harriet Thorpe (customer), Paul Trussell (chef), Jack Thorpe Baker (Nigel).

1993 *Naked.* Thin Man/Film Four International/British Screen. Produced by Simon Channing-Williams, photography by Dick Pope, edited by Jon Gregory, designed by Alison Chitty, costumes by Lindy Hemming, music by Andrew Dickson, sound by Ken Weston, 126 minutes.
Cast: David Thewlis (Johnny), Lesley Sharp (Louise), Katrin Cartlidge (Sophie), Greg Crutwell (Jeremy), Claire Skinner (Sandra), Peter Wight (Brian), Ewen Bremner (Archie), Susan Vidler (Maggie), Deborah Maclaren (woman in window), Gina McKee (waitress in café), Carolina Giammetta (masseuse), Elizabeth Berrington (Giselle), Darren Tunstall (poster man), Robert Putt (chauffeur), Angela Curran (car owner), Lynda Rooke (Johnny's victim), Peter Whitman (Mr. Halpern).

1996 *Secrets & Lies.* Thin Man/CiBY 2000/Channel Four Films. Produced by Simon Channing-Williams, photography by Dick Pope, edited by Jon Gregory, designed by Alison Chitty, costumes by Maria Price, music by Andrew Dickson, sound by George Richards, 140 minutes.
Cast: Timothy Spall (Maurice), Phyllis Logan (Monica), Brenda Blethyn (Cynthia), Marianne Jean-Baptiste (Hortense), Claire Rushbrook (Roxanne), Elizabeth Berrington (Jane), Lee Ross (Paul), Michelle Austin (Dionne), Lesley Manville (social worker), Ron Cook (Stuart), Emma Amos (scarred girl), Brian Bovell and Trevor Laird (Hortense's brothers), Clare Perkins (Hortense's Sister), Elias Perkins McCook (Hortense's nephew), June Mitchell (senior optometrist), Janice Acquah (junior optician), Hannah Davis (first bride), Terence Harvey (first bride's father), Kate O'Malley (second bride), Joe Tucker (groom), Richard Syms (vicar), Grant Masters (best man), Annie Hayes (mother in family portrait), Jean Ainslie (grandmother), Daniel Smith (teenage son), Lucy Sheen (nurse), Frances Ruffelle (young mother), Felix Manley (baby), Nitin Chandra Ganatra (potential husband), Metin Marlow (conjuror), Amanda Crossley, Su Elliott and Di Sherlock (sexy ladies), Alex Squires, Lauren Squires and Sade Squires (triplets), Dominic Curran (little boy), Stephen Churchett, David Neilson, Peter Stockbridge and Peter Waddington ("suits"), Rachel Lewis (graduate), Paul Trussell (grinning husband), Denise Orita (anxious woman),

Margery Withers (elderly woman), Theresa Watson (daughter), Gordon Winter (grinning man), Jonathan Coyne (fiancé), Peter Wight (father in family portrait), Gary McDonald (boxer), Alison Steadman (dog fancier), Liz Smith (cat fancier), Shelia Kelley (fertile mother), Angela Curran (little boy's mother), Linda Beckett (glamor portrait housewife), Philip Davis (man in suit), Wendy Nottingham (dour wife), Anthony O'Donnell (uneasy man), Ruth Sheen (laughing woman), Mia Soteriou (fiancée).

1997 *Career Girls.* Thin Man/Channel Four/Matrix Film Partnership. Produced by Simon Channing-Williams, photography by Dick Pope, edited by Robin Sales, designed by Eve Stewart, music by Marianne Jean-Baptiste and Tony Remy, songs by The Cure, sound by George Richards, 87 minutes.
Cast: Katrin Cartlidge (Hannah Mills), Lynda Steadman (Annie), Mark Benton ("Ricky" Burton), Kate Byers (Claire), Andy Serkis (Mr. Evans), Joe Tucker (Adrian Spinks), Marge Stanley (Ricky's grandmother), Michael Healy (lecturer).

1999 *Topsy-Turvy.* Thin Man Films/The Greenlight Fund/Newmarket Capital Group. Produced by Simon Channing-Williams, photography by Dick Pope, edited by Robin Sales. designed by Eve Stewart, music by Carl Davis, costumes by Lindy Hemming, makeup/hair design by Christine Blundell, musical direction by Gary Yershon, choreography by Francesca Jaynes, sound by Tim Fraser, 160 minutes.
Cast: Jim Broadbent (W. S. Gilbert), Allan Corduner (Arthur Sullivan), Timothy Spall (Richard Temple), Lesley Manville (Lucy "Kitty" Gilbert), Ron Cook (Richard D'Oyly Carte), Wendy Nottingham (Helen Lenoir), Kevin McKidd (Durward Lely), Shirley Henderson (Leonora Braham), Dorothy Atkinson (Jessie Bond), Martin Savage (George Grossmith), Eleanor David (Fanny Ronalds), Alison Steadman (Madame Leon), Dexter Fletcher (Louis), Sukie Smith (Clothilde), Stefan Bednarczyk (Frank Cellier), Katrin Cartlidge (madame), Gary Yershon (pianist in brothel), Julia Rayner (Mademoiselle Fromage), Jenny Pickering (second prostitute), Sam Kelly (Richard Barker), Charles Simon (Gilbert's father), Eve Pearce (Gilbert's mother), David Neville (dentist), Matthew Mills (Walter Simmonds), Nicholas Woodeson (Mr. Seymour), Amanda Crossley (Emily), Theresa Watson (Maude Gil-

bert), Lavinia Bertram (Florence Gilbert), Vincent Franklin (Rutland Barrington), Michael Simkins (Frederick Bovill), Cathy Sara (Sibyl Gray), Angela Curran (Miss Morton), Millie Gregory (Alice), Jonathan Aris (Wilhelm), Andy Serkis (John d'Auban), Mia Soteriou (Mrs. Russell), Louise Gold (Rosina Brandram), Shaun Glanville (Mr. Harris), Julian Bleach (Mr. Plank), Neil Salvage (Mr. Hurley), Matt Bardock (Mr. Tripp), Togo Igawa (first Kabuki actor), Eiji Kusuhara (second Kabuki actor), Naoko Mori (Miss "Sixpence Please"), Neil Humphries (boy actor), Brid Brennan (mad woman); Ladies and Gentlemen of the Chorus: Mark Benton (Mr. Price), Heather Craney (Miss Russell), Julie Jupp (Miss Meadows), John Warnaby (Mr. Sanders), Kacey Ainsworth (Miss Fitzherbert), Ashley Artus (Mr. Marchmont), Richard Attlee (Mr. Gordon), Paul Barnhill (Mr. Flagstone), Nicholas Boulton (Mr. Conynghm), Lorraine Brunning (Miss Jardine), Simon Butteriss (Mr. Lewis), Wayne Carter (Mr. Rhys), Rosie Cavaliero (Miss Moore), Michelle Chadwick (Miss Warren), Debbie Chazen (Miss Kingsley), Richard Coyle (Mr. Hammond), Monica Dolan (Miss Barnes), Sophie Duval (Miss Brown), Anna Francolini (Miss Biddles), Teresa Gallagher (Miss Coleford), Sarah Howe (Miss Woods), Ashley Jensen (Miss Tringham), Gemma Page (Miss Langton-James), Paul Rider (Mr. Bentley), Mary Roscoe (Miss Carlyle), Steven Spiers (Mr. Kent), Nicola Wainwright (Miss Betts), Angie Wallis (Miss Wilkinson), Kevin Walton (Mr. Evans).

2002 *All or Nothing*. Simon Channing-Williams Productions; Studio Canal; Thin Man Films. Produced by Alain Sarde, Simon Channing-Williams, photography by Dick Pope, edited by Lesley Walker, designed by Eve Stewart, costumes by Jacqueline Durran, makeup by Christine Blundell, music by Andrew Dickson, sound by Malcolm Hirst, 128 minutes. *Cast:* Timothy Spall (Phil), Lesley Manville (Penny), Alison Garland (Rachel), James Corden (Rory), Ruth Sheen (Maureen), Marion Bailey (Carol), Paul Jesson (Ron), Sam Kelly (Sid), Kathryn Hunter (Cécile), Sally Hawkins (Samantha), Helen Coker (Donna), Daniel Mays (Jason), Ben Crompton (Craig), Robert Wilfort (crash driver), Gary McDonald (Neville), Diveen Hnery (Dinah), Timothy Bateson (Harold), Edna Doré (Martha), Georgia Fitch (Ange), Tracy O'Flaherty (Michelle), Jean Ainslie (Old Lady).

REFERENCES

Ash, Timothy Garton. "Joining the Continent to the United Kingdom," in "The Week in Review," *New York Times*, June 17, 2001: WK:15.

Bank, Mirra. "Mike Leigh." *Films in Review* 48 (1997) Rpt. in *Mike Leigh: Interviews*. Ed. Howie Movshovitz. Jackson: University Press of Mississippi, 2000. 113–21.

Barker, David. "It's Been Real: Forms of Television Representation," *Critical Studies in Mass Communication* 5.1 (March, 1988): 42–56.

Beckett, Andy. "Bringing Down Chunks of the Ceiling," Review of *Manchester, England: The Story of the Pop Cult City* by David Haslam, *London Review of Books* 22.4 (Feb. 17, 2000): 32–33.

Berger, John. *About Looking*. New York: Pantheon, 1980.

Bergson, Henri. "Laughter," tr. Cloudesly Brereton and Fred Rithwell, in *Comedy*. New York: Doubleday, 1956.

The BFI TV 100 List. *Sight and Sound* 10.10 (Oct. 2000): 3.

Billington, Michael. "Mike Leigh Interviewed by Michael Billington." The Guardian Interview: 26 pp. 11 November 1999. http://www.filmunlimited.co.uk/GuardianNFT/interview/0,4479,110593,4,5.html.

Bloch, Judy. "A Conversation with Mike Leigh and Alison Steadman." *Film Quarterly* 45.3(1992). Rpt. in *Mike Leigh: Interviews*. Ed. Howie Movshovitz. Jackson: University Press of Mississippi, 2000: 16–25.

Brophy, Brigid. "The British Sense of Humour" in *Don't Never Forget: Collected Views and Reviews*. New York: Holt, Rinehart and Winston, 1966.

Brunette, Peter. "The Director's Improvised Reality," *Washington Post*, Dec. 27, 1991: C1, 2.

Brustein, Robert. *The Culture Watch: Essays on Theatre and Society, 1969–1974*. New York: Knopf, 1975.

Bruzzi, Stella. "Career Girls," *Sight and Sound* 7.9 (September 1997): 38.

Campbell, Peter. "At Tate Britain," *London Review of Books*, Aug. 9, 2001: 26.

Canby, Vincent. "Down from Hopeless, to Hilarious," *New York Times*, April 10, 1992: C1, 10.

Review of "Life Is Sweet," *New York Times*, Oct. 25, 1991: C 10.

Cardullo, Bert. "Secrets and Lies: *Angels and Insects* and *Secrets and Lies*" in *Practical Film Criticism—An Enlightened Approach to Moviegoing*. Vol.1. Lewiston, NY: Edwin Mellen Press, 1999.

Carney, Ray (with contributions by Leonard Quart). *The Films of Mike Leigh: Embracing the World*: Cambridge: Cambridge University Press, 2000.

Carr, Danny. "Bleak Moments" Edinburgh: Edinburgh University Film Society Programme, 1992–93.

Carr, Jay. "*Naked*: English Director Mike Leigh Turns His Uncompromising Vision on The Way Things Are," *Boston Globe*, Feb. 27, 1994. Rpt. in *Mike Leigh: Interviews*. Ed. Howie Movshovitz. Jackson: University Press of Mississippi, 2000: 55–58.

Chesterton, G. K. *The Victorian Age in Literature.* New York: Holt, 1913.

Christopher, James. "Film: That Kitchen Sink Feeling," *The* [London] *Times*, Oct. 17, 2000: T2, 12–13.

Clements, Paul. "*Four Days in July* (Mike Leigh)" in *British Television Drama in the 1980's*, ed. George W. Brandt. Cambridge: Cambridge University Press, 1993: 162–77.

The Improvised Play: The Work of Mike Leigh. London: Methuen, 1983.

Cook, Rita. "Mike Leigh: *All or Nothing* Filmmaking," *Screentalk* 3.1 (November/December 2002): 46–49.

Corliss, Richard. "Family Values," *Time.* Sept. 30, 1996: 66–68.

Coveney, Michael. "In a Class of His Own," *The Observer Magazine*, July 4, 1993. Rpt. in *Mike Leigh: Interviews*. Ed. Howie Movshovitz. Jackson: University Press of Mississippi, 2000: 35–41.

—*The World According to Mike Leigh.* London: HarperCollins, 1997.

Croy, Homer. *Star Maker.* New York: Duell, Sloan and Pearce, 1959.

Denby, David. "Under the Light," *New Yorker*. Dec. 27, 1999, and Jan. 3, 2000: 130–32.

Denisoff, Dennis. *Aestheticism and Sexual Parody 1840–1940.* Cambridge: Cambridge University Press, 2001.

Durgnat, Raymond. *Jean Renoir.* Berkeley and Los Angeles: University of California Press, 1974.

Eidsvik, Charles. *Cineliteracy: Film among the Arts.* New York: Random House, 1978.

Ellickson, Lee and Richard Porton. "I Find the Tragicomic Things in Life: An Interview with Mike Leigh," *Cineaste* 20.3 (1994). Rpt. in *Mike Leigh: Interviews*. Ed. Howie Movshovitz. Jackson: University Press of Mississippi, 2000: 59–78.

Felski, Rita. "Nothing to Declare: Identity, Shame, and the Lower Middle Class," *PMLA* 115.1 (Jan. 2000): 33–45.

Fitzherbert, Henry. "The Period Movie Is Turned Leigh's Portrait of Gilbert," *Sunday Express.* Feb. 20, 2000: 54.

Fowles, John. *Wormholes: Essays and Occasional Writings*, ed. Jan Relf. New York: Holt Owl Books, 1999.

Franks, Alan. "Different Class," *London Times Magazine.* Feb. 19, 2000: 28–29, 32.

Fuller, Graham. "A New Generation of Realists Scrap the Kitchen Sink," *New York Times*, July 23, 2000: AR 7,16.

—"Mike Leigh's Original Features, an Interview," in Mike Leigh, *Naked* and *Other Screenplays.* London: Faber and Faber, 1995: vii–xlii.

Gelatt, Roland. "Is Britain Dying?," *Saturday Review.* Feb. 8, 1975: 12–16.

Giannetti, Louis and Scott Eyman. *Flashback: A Brief History of Film.* Englewood Cliffs, NJ: Prentice-Hall, 1996.

Gilbey, Ryan. "From Abigail to Arias," *The Express*. Feb.19, 2000: 43.

—"Reasons to Be Cheerful," *Sight & Sound* 12.10 (October 2002): 14–17.

Gopnik, Adam. "The Culture of Blairism," *New Yorker*. July 7, 1997: 26–32.

"Sparkings: Joseph Cornell and the art of nostalgia," *New Yorker*. Feb. 17 and 24, 2003: 184–89.

Grawe, Paul H. *Comedy in Space, Time, & Imagination.* Chicago: Nelson-Hall, 1983.

Green, Martin. *A Mirror for Anglo-Saxons: An Appraisal of Life and Letters in America and England Today.* New York: Harper, 1960.

Hartley, L. P. *The Novelist's Responsibility: Lectures and Essays.* London: Hamish Hamilton, 1967.

Hatch, Eric Allen. "Life Is Bittersweet," [Baltimore] *City Paper*. Dec. 11, 2002: 26.

Hill, John. *British Cinema in the 1980's.* Oxford: Clarendon, 1999.

—*Sex, Class and Realism: British Cinema 1956–1963.* London: BFI, 1986.

Hinson, Hal. "Sweet Pungency," *Washington Post.* Dec. 27, 1991: C1, 2.

Hoberman, J. "Sweet Mysteries of Life," *Village Voice.* Oct. 1, 1996: 64.

—"Deconstructing Hairy: *Frida; Derrida; All or Nothing,*" *Village Voice* Oct. 23–29, 2002. http://villagevoice.com/issues/0243/hoberman.html.

Hohenadel, Kristin. "Not Your Everyday Everyman," *New York Times.* Oct. 20, 2002: AR 13, 24.

Howe, Desson. "It's the Movie of the Decade. No No, It's Just a Decadent Movie," *Washington Post.* Jan. 30, 1994. Rpt. in *Mike Leigh: Interviews*. Ed. Howie Movshovitz. Jackson: University Press of Mississippi, 2000: 45–54.

Jones, Edward T. Unpublished Interview with Mike Leigh, February 1997.

Kauffmann, Stanley. " Not So Merry England," *New Republic.* Jan. 3, 1994: 28–29.

Kennedy, Harlan. "Mike Leigh about His Stuff...," *Film Comment* 27.5 (Sept.–Oct. 1991): 18–24.

King, Tom. "Hollywood Journal: How Barry Diller Sees the Movies," *Wall Street Journal*. Feb. 16, 2001: W4.

Klawans, Stuart. "Life Is Sweet," *Nation.* Dec. 2, 1992: 717–18.

Kronenberger, Louis. *The Thread of Laughter: Chapters on English Stage Comedy from Jonson to Maugham.* New York: Knopf, 1952.

Lahr, John. "This Other England," *New Yorker*. Sept. 23, 1996: 50–57.

Lane, Anthony. "Faces in the Crowd," *New Yorker*. Feb. 10, 2003: 94–99.

Leigh, Mike. *Naked and Other Screenplays.* London: Faber and Faber, 1995.

—Liner Notes of Sony CD of the Original Motion Picture Soundtrack for *Topsy-Turvy,* 1999: 6–7.

Lewin, Alex. "IndieExposire: Smooth Operetta," *Premiere: The Movie Magazine.* January 2000: 60.

Lowenstein, Stephen, ed. *My First Movie: Twenty Celebrated Directors Talk about Their First Film*. New York: Pantheon, 2000.

Lyman, Rick. "Mike Leigh's Other Life as a Playwright," *New York Times*. Dec. 14, 1997: AR, 4.

Medhurst, Andy. "The Mike-Ado," *Sight and Sound* 10.3 (March 2000): 36–37.

—"Mike Leigh Beyond Embarrassment," *Sight and Sound* 3.11 (November 1993): 6–10.

Miller, Prairie. "An Interview with Mike Leigh," in *Mike Leigh: Interviews*. Ed. Howie Movshovitz. Jackson: University Press of Mississippi, 2000: 79–83.

Monk, Claire. "Naked," *Sight and Sound* 3.11 (November 1993): 48–49.

Morgenstern, Joe. "Charming 'Topsy-Turvy' Is the Very Model of a Modern Major Movie," *Wall Street Journal.* Jan. 14, 2000: Wl, 2.

Movshovitz, Howie, ed. *Mike Leigh: Interviews.* Jackson: University Press of Mississippi, 2000.

Nelson, Jenny. "Eyes Out of Your Head: On Televisual Experience," *Critical Studies in Mass Communication* 6.4 (December 1989): 387–403.

Panofsky, Erwin. "Style and Medium in the Motion Pictures" in *Film Theory and Criticism: Introductory Readings*, ed. Leo Braudy and Marshall Cohen. 5th ed. New York and Oxford: Oxford University Press: 1999: 279–292.

Parks, Tim. "On and Off the High Road: *Voltaire's Coconuts,*" *London Review of Books.* May 27, 1999: 28–31.

Patterson, John. "Shah-dap! Fah-koff! Dunno" Mike Leigh returns with *All or Nothing. L.A. Weekly.* Oct. 25–31, 2002 http://www. Laweekly.com/ink/02/49/filmpatterson. php.html.

Pride, Ray. "The Leigh Way," *New City* [Chicago]. Nov. 7, 1996. Rpt. in *Mike Leigh: Interviews.* Ed. Howie Movshovitz. Jackson: University Press of Mississippi, 2000: 108–12.

Priestley, J. B. *English Humour.* New York: Stein and Day, 1976.

Purdy, Jack. "Turning Japanese: Mike Leigh of All People, Explores the Birth of Modern Musical Comedy," [Baltimore] *City Paper.* Feb. 9, 2000: 30.

Quart, Barbara and Leonard. "Life Is Sweet," *Film Quarterly* 45.3 (Spring 1992): 49–51.

Quart, Leonard. "*All or Nothing* Review," *Cineaste,* 28.1 (Winter 2002): 38, 40.

"Going Beyond Despair: An Interview with Mike Leigh," *Cineaste,* 28.1 (Winter 2002): 39.

Rafferty, Terrence. "Marking Time," *New Yorker.* Aug. 11, 1997: 83–84.

—"Under One Roof," *New Yorker.* Nov. 4, 1991: 101–4.

Raymond, Gerard. "Secret Agent: Brenda Blethyn Fulfills Her High Hopes," *Village Voice.* Oct. 1, 1996: 64.

Reilly, John. "The Novel as Art Form" in *Literature and Culture in Modern Britain, Vol. 1: 1900–1929*, ed. Clive Bloom. London and New York: Longman, 1993.

Riding, Alan. "An Original Who Plumbs the Ordinary." *New York Times.* Sept. 22, 1996: Section 2, l, 22–23.

Rosenbaum, Jonathan. "England on the Inside: The Films of Mike Leigh" in *Movies as Politics.* Berkeley/Los Angeles/London: University of California Press, 1997.

Saul, John Ralston. *Voltaire's Bastards: The Dictatorship of Reason in the West.* New York: Vintage, 1993.

Scott, A. O. "When Noir Means More than Style," *New York Times*, July 22, 2001: AR 9.

Sontag, Susan. "Theatre and Film" in *Styles of Radical Will.* New York: Doubleday Anchor, 1991: 99–122.

Spiegel, Alan. "The Mud on Napoleon's Boots: The Adventitious Detail in Film and Fiction," *Virginia Quarterly Review* 52.2 (Spring 1976): 249–64.

Stam, Robert. *Film Theory: An Introduction.* Oxford: Blackwell, 2000.

Sterritt, David. "Mike Leigh Calls It as He Sees It," *Christian Science Monitor*. Sept. 7, 1993. Rpt. in *Mike Leigh: Interviews*. Ed. Howie Movshovitz. Jackson: University Press of Mississippi, 2000: 42–44.

Taubin, Amy. "Long Shots," *Village Voice*. Aug. 12, 1997: 67.

Tauke, Beth. "Filling Space: Utopian Conditions in *Secrets & Lies*," *Utopian Studies* 9.1 (1998): 189–92.

Thomson, David. "The Middle Age of British Television," *American Film* 1.6 (April 1977): 30–32, 49–50.

Thorburn, David. "Television Melodrama" in *Television: The Critical View*, ed. by Horace Newcomb. 3rd ed. New York and Oxford: Oxford University Press, 1982: 529–46.

Teichmann, Howard. *George S. Kaufman: An Intimate Portrait*. New York: Atheneum, 1972.

Tommasini, Anthony. "Sullivan Without Gilbert? Don't Ask," *New York Times*. Apr. 9, 2000: Section 2, 31, 34.

Turan, Kenneth. "The Case for Mike Leigh," *Los Angeles Times*. Sept. 22, 1966. Rpt. in *Mike Leigh: Interviews*. Ed. Howie Movshovitz. Jackson: University Press of Mississippi, 2000: 84–97.

Turner, Megan. "Brit Drama Full of Life" Review of *All or Nothing*. *New York Post*. Oct. 25, 2002: 48.

Valency, Maurice. *The Breaking String: The Plays of Anton Chekhov*. New York: Oxford University Press, 1966.

Vineberg, Steve. "The Art of Making Theater: 2 Views," *Chronicle of Higher Education*. March 3, 2000: B11.

—"British Filmmakers in the Training Ground of TV," *New York Times*. Nov. 11, 2001: AR 30.

Wilson, Colin. *Chords and Discords: Purely Personal Opinions on Music*. New York: Crown, 1966.

Wilson, Edmund. *Classics and Commercials: A Literary Chronicle of the Forties*. New York: Farrar, Straus, 1950.

Wren, Gayden. *A Most Ingenious Paradox: The Art of Gilbert and Sullivan*. Oxford: Oxford University Press, 2001.

INDEX

M

N

O

P

Q

R

S

T

FRAMING *film*

History & Art of Cinema

Frank Beaver, *General Editor*

Framing Film is committed to serious, high-quality film studies on topics of national and international interest. The series is open to a full range of scholarly methodologies and analytical approaches in the examination of cinema art and history, including topics on film theory, film and society, gender and race, politics. Cutting-edge studies and diverse points of view are particularly encouraged.

For additional information about the series or for the submission of manuscripts, please contact:

Peter Lang Publishing, Inc.
Acquisitions Department
275 Seventh Avenue, 28th floor
New York, NY 10001

To order other books in this series, please contact our Customer Service Department at:

(800) 770-LANG (within the U.S.)
(212) 647-7706 (outside the U.S.)
(212) 647-7707 FAX

Or browse online by series at:

WWW.PETERLANGUSA.COM

[illegible]

Frank Beaver, General Editor

Framing Film is committed to [illegible] high-quality film studies on topics of national and international interest. The series is open to a wide range of scholarly [illegible] and analytical approaches to the [illegible] of cinema art and history, including topics on [illegible] and society, gender and [illegible] politics. Cutting-edge studies and [illegible] points of view are particularly encouraged.

For additional information about the series or for the submission of manuscripts, please contact:

Peter Lang Publishing, Inc.
[illegible] Department
[illegible] Avenue, [illegible] floor
[illegible], NY 10001

To order other books in this series, please contact our Customer Service Department:

[illegible]

[illegible]

[illegible]

Or browse online by series:

[illegible]